The Angel Inside Went Sour

ESTHER P. ROTHMAN

The Angel

Inside

Went Sour

DAVID McKAY COMPANY, INC.
NEW YORK

THE ANGEL INSIDE WENT SOUR

TYPOGRAPHY BY FRANK KARPELES

LIBRARY OF CONGRESS CATALOG CARD NUMBER: 77-135584

MANUFACTURED IN THE UNITED STATES OF AMERICA

VAN REES PRESS • NEW YORK

Dedicated to my husband Arthur
and to my daughter Amy, who dedicates
her half of the dedication to
Trolle, her cat.

Contents

The Angel Inside Went Sour

chapter one

In the Beginning

RESOLUTION:

> ESTABLISHMENT OF PUBLIC SCHOOL 702 BROOKLYN
> From the Superintendent of Schools,
> March 24, 1958.

I have the honor to present the following resolution: RESOLVED that Public School 702 Brooklyn, be temporarily established on March 26, 1958, in rooms 302, 304, 306, 308, 310, and the glassed-in partition near the elevator on the third floor of the Board of Education Building, 110 Livingston Street, Brooklyn 1, New York.

Explanation: The proposed Public School 702, Brooklyn, is being established as a special emergency school for girls. It is planned to staff and equip this area to provide an educational program for girls recently suspended.

It is recommended that one supervisory position, one clerical position and seven teaching positions be provided for Public School 702, Brooklyn.

On motion, the resolution was adopted.

It must have gone like this:

A god, disguised as New York City's Superintendent of Schools, said, "What shall we do with all those awful girls who had to be suspended because they beat up teachers?"

And he thought and he thought and out of the void and the confusion he came up with The Plan.

"Let there be a school where teachers like to be beat up."

And in April 1958, on approximately the sixteen thousand and twentieth day of New York City's public school system, this god, still disguised as Superintendent of Schools, created a school for beaters of teachers and firesetters and cursers and otherwise thoroughly ineffable and incorrigible girls who needed to be made effable and corrigible.

But where to put them?

And he thought and he thought until insight. In Paradise.

So he vacated the third floor of the Board of Education building at 110 Livingston Street in Brooklyn, and, *lo!*, the Creation! Livingston School for Girls!

But the girls angered this god. Also a few archangels who were disguised as assorted associate superintendents. For the girls came to Paradise with curlers in their hair and kerchiefs on their heads, and everyone knows how a god feels about clothes in Paradise, much less curlers and kerchiefs.

The Expulsion was swift. In the Fall of the same year, the girls and the school were cast out.

How banished could one get in New York City? Not very. The god, no doubt, would have preferred a small village in the Alps, but because these were New York City children, he was forced to settle upon the small village in the midst of the city, the proverbial and philosophical habitat of the renegade, Greenwich Village. Unceremoniously, the Livingston Street

School came to King Street, 29 King Street, to be exact, to a soon-to-be-demolished building erected in 1875.

Diaspora. But not for me. I wasn't dispersed because I wasn't principal then. I was still a teacher at Bellevue Psychiatric Hospital, and I was out on maternity leave. As my physical state was conducive to regurgitation, I was perfectly attuned to heaving up and spitting out all the right educational clichés when I took the examination for principal offered by the New York City Board of Education. It was the first and last time the examination for principal of special schools was ever given. I passed, third on the list.

The list! Principal! Hallelujah! I had made it!

The question I neglected to ask was, "Of what? Where?"

When Amy, the daughter I bore, was one year old, I found out.

In August of 1959, one year and four months after the school was opened, I was summoned to the Board of Education by A Very Important Person in the Bureau for the Education of Socially Maladjusted Children of the Division of Child Welfare. The name of our bureau was enough to frighten me. It did. So did she. Very imperiously and definitely without enthusiasm, she informed me that I was going to be appointed principal of a special school. She asked me to consider two schools,—a school located in a men's prison, or the Livingston School, which by this time had moved to King Street. Frankly, I was not overjoyed at either prospect. Perhaps it was the way both were presented. I engaged in exquisite torture, trying to make the right decision. The decision was taken out of my hands, however, when the colleague ahead of me on the principal's list decided that he wanted the prison school. I was left with Livingston.

I toyed with refusing the appointment in the hope that this

might result in a later appointment to a school located in a psychiatric hospital. All my experience in teaching disturbed children had been in hospitals, and I was sure I would feel more at home in that familiar setting than in a public school containing some of the same problems and none of the resources. My interviewer, however, quickly informed me that if I were to decline an appointment now, I might not be offered another for several years.

I accepted.

"Who is principal of Livingston now?" I asked.

"Oh, her," my interviewer said sweetly. "She's only acting, you know."

Acting. In Board of Education language, it's equivalent to being called nonexistent. There's no status in being an acting anything, because acting supervisors have no tenure, and therefore no relevance.

Then she said, "She—Mrs. Z.—kisses those colored girls, you know." She paused and spat out, "Disgusting. She belongs to that Teacher's Guild."

From the startled look on the interviewer's face I knew that she was reacting to the startled look on my face.

She was obviously uncomfortable. I also knew she was suddenly remembering that while Mrs. Z. was a member of the Teacher's Guild, I was an active member of the original Teacher's Union, a group considered radical and infamous in the eyes of the Board.

"Don't worry about a thing, dear," she said after only the slightest hesitation, and I knew that it was the last time she would ever let me see her with her guard down. "The girls need you, Esther." She had never called me that before, either. "You'll be good for them. They need your calm and dignity."

What she didn't know was that it wasn't calm and dignity she saw, it was rigid fear.

I had taught children of all ages, sexes, and kinds. I had taught children in elementary school, junior high school, and high schools. I had taught intellectually retarded children, intellectually gifted children, and children who could not speak English. I had taught mentally ill children at Bellevue Psychiatric Hospital and children who were addicted to drugs at Riverside Hospital. I had taught remedial reading and journalism. I had in the meantime also studied psychology and passed my state boards—but I hadn't the foggiest notion of how to run a school for aggressive girls, although the Board of Education and my husband, Arthur, not in unison, of course, attested that I did.

I was determined to show my staff—my staff, what a beautiful possessive pronoun—that I was not frightened of them, of the girls, or of the title of my job.

Every time I said it—principal—I became six years old, entering *his* office with my mother.

"Your child is a truant, Mrs. Pomeranz," he said sternly. He wagged his finger at me. It was a long, fat, thick, supersized finger.

"If you don't come to school, you will be sent away."

And here I was, being sent away—to Livingston—a school for bad girls.

I decided to show everybody, the girls, the teachers, the school system, I was not afraid. On the very first day of my principalship I would come in late.

It was the most difficult lateness I have ever achieved. It wasn't easy to report to work at ten o'clock on a Wednesday morning when I had been coiffed, groomed, gloved, and poised for action since dawn.

When I finally arrived, Mrs. S., the assistant principal, and Mrs. A., the secretary, informed me somewhat ruefully that they had just called the Board to ask why I wasn't there. I quickly remembered about my calm and dignity and smiled. What else could I do with an open mouth? It just had not occurred to me that my assistant principal and my secretary would report me to the Board for lateness on my very first day. I decided never to forget that Mrs. S. was also only acting.

Mrs. S. took me on a tour of the 1875 building. My inchoate impression was of bigness and barrenness. As I walked up the seemingly hidden stairwells and through the winding corridors, my pervasive fear took definite shape—I would never find my way through the building. I would forever be lost.

I didn't feel any better back in the strangeness of my own office, especially after I had received my second phone call. The first phone call had been from my husband, Arthur. It was a welcome call. It was the second one that shook me. It was from Mr. Cohen, a patrolman from the Fourth Precinct, who told me that the school was in his precinct and that he had been stationed at the school all of last year. He asked me if I wanted him to return this year. His question came as a shock. I had never thought about having a policeman in school. In all the years that I had been teaching at Bellevue Hospital there had never been a policeman around my classrooms. Why here? Without knowing the answer, I told him we would continue in the same way as we had last year.

That is honestly what I hoped to do. Keep everything the way it had been the year before. Change nothing. Perhaps no changes would be necessary. My plan was clear and intelligent and reflective of every tenet of basic good human relationships I had learned at college. Observe. Make tentative judgments.

Reflect on those judgments. Discuss with teachers. Discuss with girls. Hypothesize, test, then act—perhaps. But as it turned out, I had no time for evolution.

"There's really nothing wrong with these hard-core children," Mrs. A., my secretary, counseled within an hour of our meeting, "it's their families who are so hard-core."

In all the years I had taken psychology and sociology and education courses, I had somehow had missed those words— hard core. They were chilling.

She didn't respond to my silence, or perhaps she was encouraged by it.

"Isn't it a shame," she chatted, "the way these girls behave? They really don't show any respect at all."

I couldn't help it. "I suppose if they came from soft-core families, they wouldn't be so hard-core?" I asked.

She looked surprised, but not entirely displeased. Maybe she thought that soft-core was a legitimate diagnosis!

"You know what I mean," she said comfortably. "They really aren't so different from other kids, it's just they're not taught respect. It's just their culture—"

I interrupted her. "Their parents wouldn't enjoy the privileges of respect or education or marriage or good health, is that it?"

There was no doubt about it now. Mrs. A. knew that there was a gulf in our thinking. On Thursday she told me she was giving notice. No secretary. As I really didn't know what a secretary in a school did besides make coffee for the principal and answer the phone, I wasn't too worried. I was notoriously bad at making coffee, but I could drink my own. Mrs. S. could answer the phone.

Mrs. S.'s desk was in my office, which meant I could never have a private phone conversation, much less hold private

professional meetings with teachers. I told her she needed an
office of her own. She accepted my nervous dictum with
equanimity, but in order to find an available room near mine,
we had to relocate a teacher and the guidance counselor. Mrs.
S. suggested calling them Thursday and telling them what we
were doing, so they wouldn't be too surprised when they came
in the next day for the faculty meeting and found they had been
moved.

I knew that no teacher should have her belongings moved
for her, particularly when the room had been assigned last year.
I also knew that I should wait to meet the teachers before I
acted, but I was afraid that if I waited to meet them face to
face, I wouldn't have the courage to tell them to move at all.

Mrs. S. made her phone calls. She later assured me that the
teachers had been most cordial to the idea. I knew she lied. I
knew teachers, particularly when I had so recently been one
myself. I would have been furious at having my room confis-
cated by someone else, including, or especially, the principal,
new or old. But it couldn't be helped. I needed privacy.

On Friday, the teachers all came in for conference and their
summer paychecks. There were now ten of them. The school
had apparently grown from seven teachers to ten. I gave them
an hour to greet each other and to introduce myself informally.
Then, I held my first faculty meeting. In monologue.

I started by telling the teachers how glad I was to be there,
how I had heard how wonderful the school was, how I was
counting on them to continue being wonderful, how difficult I
knew the girls were, but how they, the teachers, were still
wonderful. And they were—wonderfully silent.

I was used to faculty conferences, especially at Bellevue, that
were part involved discussions, part muted whisperings, part
personal jibes and jokes, part fun, part boredom. Mine was part

nothing. All boredom. The teachers did nothing but listen, not whisper, not pass notes, not ask a question, not comment, not doze. Just listen. It was frightening!

I felt myself catapulted into space, as if my body were floating off somewhere, while my voice carried on independently.

I told them of a phone call I had received from a student who had identified herself as Sarah. Sarah wanted to know when school was starting, she was so eager to return— wonderful, wasn't it wonderful? Wasn't Sarah a wonderful student to want to come to this wonderful school?

I found my voice imitating Sarah's slow, halting, slurring speech. I thought someone might smile with pleasure at my obvious empathy with Sarah. But no one did. I conjured up a mental image of Sarah, blonde, thin, waif-like. It suited her voice, a non-verbal, hesitant, frightened child, waiting for me to welcome her back. Evidently I had welcomed her sufficiently, because our conversation had ended on a note of warmth. Not so with the faculty. I left them cold. They still just listened.

I went on talking, something about curriculum and plan books and motivated lessons—all of it meaningless and incredibly stupid. Then I knew I had to say what I had to say, what they were waiting for. I explained that I had nothing to do with deposing the former principal, that I had been appointed from a list, and that she had not taken the examination. I explained, too, that I was sorry that she had been notified only two days before I came that she would not be principal. The teachers didn't believe me. I could feel their hostility, their disbelief, their criticisms. I had taken someone else's job away. They felt threatened, as if it could happen to any one of them next.

I ended lamely, on a note of apology, and I wasn't even

certain of what. As a matter of fact, Mrs. Z., the previous principal, didn't know it, but she had me to thank for being notified at all. I had called the Bureau of Appointments and asked where Mrs. Z. could be located in case I needed to ask her anything, and a voice of consternation had gasped at the other end of the phone, "My God, we forgot to transfer her anywhere!"

Great. On that first Wednesday, Livingston would have had two principals. No doubt about it, Mrs. Z. had been given the quickest transfer I had ever heard of.

I slunk into the alien office that was supposedly mine and reviewed my two days' principalship: on Wednesday, my secretary hated me; on Thursday, a sample representation of the faculty, and on Friday, all the teachers. What was going to happen on Monday, when the girls came to school? I dreaded the thought, but Monday did come.

Vivian was the first girl I met.

I heard her before I saw her. Her guttural bellows ho-hoed from the main stairway to the principal's office twenty feet away. And then, five and a half feet of skinniness was draped in my doorway—all of it loud and angry.

"Where's Mrs. Z.?" she demanded.

I answered her with a grammarian's regality, which I supposed was my puristic duty.

"Mrs. Z. has been transferred to another school. I am now principal. I am Dr. Rothman, and what is your name, may I ask?"

She burst into laughter. "Yeah, ask." And stalked down the hall ho-ho-hoing.

I followed her out of my office, trying hard to remain cool, detached, in charge, capable, competent, efficient, superior, and principal.

"What's that girl's name?" I asked another girl coming by.

"Why ask me? I ain't nothin' to her and you ain't nothin' to me." She kept staring at me long after she had finished insulting me.

Had my ex-secretary been right after all? Were these two hard-core?

Forbid the thought, God. There is no such thing as hard-core girls. There are only girls.

But the truth is, I had never seen girls like these, stomping, stampeding, screaming girls, slapping, fighting, running, cursing girls. The teachers seemed to be safe behind their closed classrooms, but the girls were everywhere, mostly on the second floor, outside my office.

"Where that bitch?" I heard Vivian ask.

"Now, Vivian, that's not nice," I heard Mr. F. answer. "You've got to give her a chance."

"She better know what's good for her," Vivian mumbled. "I like Mrs. Z. better."

"Of course you do," was Mr. F's reply, "because Mrs. Z. was so good to you."

I unashamedly drew closer to the door so I could hear better.

"Dr. Rothman is going to learn how things are," Mr. F. continued. "It's the first time she's been principal, you know, but she is a psychologist and she knows how girls like you think. So you better be careful."

Ouch!

Somehow, that was not my idea of being on my team.

The screaming and the cursing and the running through the halls didn't let up. I had never seen such perpetual turmoil.

But the greatest shock of all was that only two girls in the entire school were white. Weren't white girls disturbed in New York City? Bellevue had had its share when I taught there. Why not here?

Suddenly, I was clobbered by my own stupidity. Had the

faculty thought I was ridiculing Negro speech when I imitated Sarah? How could they know that I was unaware that Sarah was probably black—that in fact I had not thought of her at all racially. To me, she had just been a child. Would they believe that, especially when half of the faculty members were black?

I was immobilized by the sudden insight that some of the faculty might think I was a bigot. Mrs. S. didn't seem to notice my bewilderment.

"By the way, Dr. Rothman," she said, coming by, "perhaps you won't mind if I make a suggestion?"

I shook my head in agreement. I still couldn't speak.

"Well, then, never touch a girl, not even slightly."

"Why not?" I asked.

"Because they don't like it. In fact, they resent it and might hit you."

"But why would anyone want to hit me?" I asked. I was beginning to feel I didn't understand anything. It was like the first time I had actually seen my own baby. Incredible! The experience couldn't be absorbed. Emotions poured out in all directions, undifferentiated, overwhelming. Now it was the same.

Mrs. S. had no idea I was giving birth.

She looked at me as if I were totally incompetent. "It's not you as an individual," she said, "although, of course, they loved Mrs. Z. It's just that they're disturbed, and they don't like to be touched."

Disturbed. That was the magic word that brought me down to a reality I understood. I, not Mrs. Z., was Principal of Livingston. I was in control and would be. I had worked with so-called disturbed people for the past ten years, and I knew one thing—the word "disturbed" explained nothing.

I began to play games.

"Some girls might like to be touched," I offered. "They might think it's a sign of affection."

"Oh, no," she answered. "Never. Sometimes, they don't even like it when we call their names."

"Really?" I asked.

"Yes," she continued. "They see it almost as if it's an infringement on their rights." And then to prove she knew what she was talking about, she explained, "They have so little ego, they can't bear to have someone call their names. Their names belong to them, you see, no one else!"

"Well, I'm sure you don't call them by their names, then," I said. "What *do* you call them?"

She looked at me, obviously surprised by my naiveté.

"Of course I call them by their names," she answered. "How else would I call them?"

"By somebody else's name, of course," I said. "After all, if it's an infringement of their rights—like touching—and if you don't touch—why don't you just call them by somebody else's name?"

"Oh, no—"

"But why not? It's the same concept."

Mrs. S. looked at me, again in surprise, and for the first time, I could see, she felt really sorry for me.

"You don't understand," she said. "These girls are different."

Ah, but I did understand. Fully. From everything I had seen, from the few conversations I had had, it was obvious to me that the philosophy of the school was: weep and bemoan the fate of these poor unfortunate girls—but teach? And help them to change? Apparently not. And why not? Because disturbed people are incapable of learning. "Disturbed" seemed to be the key word, the slogan, upon which the school was based; could the teachers be substituting slogan for thought?

Slogan: Let the girls behave the way they do because they really can't help it. Let them continue on their way to self-destruction.

Only that never has been my idea of a school.

We must touch, we must reach out, we must relate to students in every way possible, for only through relating and using ourselves can we begin to make a dent in their lives.

I started denting the next day, when Cynthia and Georgia faced each other in combat just outside my office. Everything, it seemed, was just outside my office.

"Don't you put your hand in my face," Cynthia screamed at Georgia. "Who you think you be?"

Georgia merely snorted.

"Don't you spit at me," Cynthia continued. "You ain't my mother, and my mother don't spit at me."

This time Georgia grimaced.

"Even if my brother do it, I'll fuck him up, too." Cynthia came closer.

I decided it was time to intervene.

Deliberately I touched Georgia on the arm and made certain Mrs. S. saw me do it. I felt Georgia's body stiffen, but I kept my arm there. "Come into the office, Georgia. I want to talk to you."

"You too, Cynthia," I said, calling back to her over my shoulder. "You come, too, and we'll get this settled." I didn't dare touch Cynthia. She might explode, for after all, reaching out to a girl, like lighting a fuse safely, was a matter of timing.

"Sit down," I said.

They stood.

"Sit down," I insisted.

"I got my feet to stand on," Cynthia insisted.

"Me, too," Georgia said.

It was almost like a physical force emanating from me, a will, a determination, that pushed them down.

"Sit down." I was absolutely determined to have my way.

They sat, but at what cost. I was absolutely drained. And to what purpose? I wasn't certain why I had made an issue of it.

I faced both of them.

"Now, what happened?" I asked.

No one answered.

"Why are you angry at her?" I asked Cynthia.

"She stuck-up," Cynthia cried. "Who she think she is, acting like she's grown?"

Georgia was still silent.

"Is that true," I asked Georgia, "do you act stuck-up?"

"No, shit." Georgia spat the words out.

"Yes, you are," Cynthia cried again. "When I ask you to hold my coat, you don't answer."

Before Georgia could answer, I interrupted, "Perhaps Georgia didn't hear you, Cynthia, and besides, it sounds to me as if you really like Georgia, if you want her to hold your coat."

"She all right," Cynthia mumbled.

"See?" Oh, I was beginning to feel good. I felt like a teacher, and I began to lecture.

"Girls," I said, "let me explain something to you about human behavior. When people are shy and ill at ease, they often act stuck-up. When Georgia acts stuck-up, don't get mad at her, Cynthia—she's only shy."

"Understand?" I asked.

"Yeah," Cynthia answered.

I felt good. I felt great. I had done it, my first positive act, I had averted a fight. And what's more, I had taught. Two angry girls now understood a basic psychological truth.

Or so I thought—for one happy tenth of a second.

"I'm goin," said Cynthia, jumping up from her seat, brushing past Georgia.

"All right," I answered. The immediate job was done.

But Cynthia suddenly did a strange thing. She hesitated, turned, came back, and faced Georgia. Then she bowed low, swept out her arms in a pose of supplication and said, "Pardon me, Your Shyness."

She left the room in a hurry, laughing at the top of her voice.

"I'm goin." It was the first Georgia had spoken.

"No—" I yelled. The loudness of my voice surprised me, but I was furious, furious at Cynthia who had made a fool of me, at Mrs. S. who smugly knew everything, at my secretary, for perhaps being right, at the teachers for being incompetent, at Sarah for speaking slowly, at myself for being stupid, ignorant, unknowing, frustrated, powerless.

I dug into the desk looking for a pencil or a clip or a piece of paper that would give me something to do so that Georgia would not see my complete failure—the tears of rage that came to my eyes.

I found a ruler and tapped it on the desk.

"Well," I finally said. She looked at me with interest.

"Understand?" I didn't know what my question meant.

She looked straight at me, although I could not look straight at her.

"Yes, Your Shitness," she said loud and clear. And she fled.

I was stunned. No one had told me it would be like this, not any professor of any course I had ever taken.

And seeing the face of every professor of education I had ever had, I burst into laughter.

That was the moment at which I began to understand the phenomenon of laughter. Like the girls, I was through with tears and being mad at myself. I was going to fight the real enemies, the teachers. I was going to make a school out of this mess, and I promised myself I would never get angry at any girl again. Not ever again.

It was almost as if Ellen had read my mind. She came in fast to test my new resolve. Ellen, wiggling her hips, hopping from foot to foot, holding her stomach, and generally writhing, came gyrating into my office.

"Quick, gimme the key, I gotta go."

"Go where?" I asked. It was a superfluous question because I knew very well where she wanted to go.

"To the toilet, where you think?"

"Sorry," I said, although I wasn't sorry at all. That was before I learned to say to girls only what I really meant to say. Then I just used words.

"No key," I continued. "I let you go a half-hour ago."

I wasn't angry at Ellen. I was angry at the entire stupid situation that I had inherited. The bathroom was kept locked, and the only key was held by the Principal. Every time a girl wanted to go to the bathroom, she had to ask my permission, and the girls, of course, made a game out of annoying me.

"Can I help it if I got a weak bladder?" Ellen screamed. "Ask my mother if you don't believe me."

"I'm not asking your mother," I said, "and the answer is still no. You don't have to go."

"I got my ministration and I'm crampin," Ellen yelled. "You want me to bleed all over?"

"No," I answered, "I don't want you to bleed all over, and you're not going to bleed all over. And the word is menstruating, not ministration."

"I gotta pee," she screamed, "I gotta pee. You want me to pee on the floor?"

"We just went through that routine," I said, "and the answer

is still no. You're not going to get the key, and if you want to
force yourself to pee on the floor, go ahead and pee on the
floor, but you're not getting the key."

She was in shock. I could tell it. All the extraneous hip
movements stopped.

"You make me sick," she muttered under her breath.

"So?" I asked casually.

She changed tactics. Her scream became a whine.

"What do you know about havin to go to the bathroom?
Your ass is dead anyway."

I had to. I laughed. It was funny.

"Well, my ass may be dead," I answered in her tone, "but my
whole body will have to be dead before you get a key to the
bathroom."

Then she couldn't help it, she laughed.

I felt exhilarated. I had reached her. I knew I had reached
her, even though she left grumbling that I made her sick.

It was my first victory. Within a half-hour, however, I knew
it was only a partial one.

Miss L. came storming into the secretary's office where I was
talking to my new substitute secretary, who had already told
me she would work only a few days to help me out. Miss L. was
like one of the girls. She screamed.

"That girl," she cried, "she's a terrible liar. They are all such
liars, it's terrible the way they lie."

"What girl?" I asked.

"Ellen," she continued. "She said you told her to pee on the
floor, and of course I told her that a principal wouldn't say
such a thing."

"Oh, but I did," I assured her. "Ellen wasn't lying. Girls
generally don't lie." I repeated the story.

She sputtered and grimaced and, in general, did everything with her body to let me know she disapproved.

Finally, she said, "They do have to learn respect."

"Respect isn't taught," I answered. "Respect is earned. I'm sure you've heard that before."

She stopped sniffing long enough to get back at me.

"It is a cliché," she said.

"Right," I agreed, "but true."

"All I know," Miss L. went on, "is that the other principal wouldn't have talked that way."

"Oh?" I felt my anger rising. I had promised myself never to get angry at the girls. I hoped I would not get angry at myself again—it was too debilitating—but I had not promised myself not to want to smother a teacher, especially a hypocritical one.

"Miss L.," I asked, "were the girls always respectful to Mrs. Z.?"

"Well—yes."

"If what you say is true, then we have a new method of treating mental illness. Teach them respect and they're cured. Is that correct?"

"You're being facetious," she said.

"Yes," I answered, "I am. But what I said before is exactly true. I can't preach respect. I have to earn it, and so do the teachers." And although I tried not to, I began getting angry again, angry enough to talk like the girls. "And how can any girl respect any teacher who sends a girl to the office every time the girl wants to pee? Is that a valid reason to send a girl to see the principal, Miss L.?" I stopped for breath, drew myself up to my full height, which isn't very high, and tried to look down at her. I didn't succeed in becoming tall, but my words shrank her. "I am Principal, which means principal teacher, not principal overseer of the girls' bathroom."

It was that speech that persuaded my substitute secretary to stay permanently. Later, she told me that she could never leave an underdog, and the teachers were making bets openly on how long I would last.

But I meant what I said. I was not going to let teachers send every girl to the office who used the bathroom as an escape from the classroom. Neither was I going to let them send girls to me for cursing, chewing, refusing to open their books, or opening their books and refusing to work.

It was particularly amazing that teachers who labeled girls disturbed, deviant, or different became outraged each time a girl expressed her individuality.

But, of course, it was easier for teachers to blame a girl than to blame themselves. Mrs. N., for instance, was constantly critical of Harriet. In her weekly report which all teachers were required to write on each girl in her class, Mrs. N. wrote at the end of the first week of school:

> Harriet is sexy. There is no doubt of that. She pushes out her little breasts and her round little behind and swaggers around in a huge cloud of stinky odor all day, sliding in to whisper here, darting out the door to hurl a nasty comment there, giving off heat at the smallest, slightest, drop of anybody's interest. Oh, she's a prize to have in your classroom. She seems to want to be given away free to a first bidder. Any takers?

I couldn't believe it. Mrs. N., a teacher like Miss L., who constantly talked of respect, had none to give. So perhaps it was no wonder that Harriet wouldn't stay in her class. She sensed Mrs. N.'s contempt, even if Mrs. N. was completely unaware of it herself.

I always have hated the word "respect," as used in schools, anyway, because ordinarily it works only one way. Students are supposed to respect teachers simply because they're teachers. But teachers aren't usually expected to reverse the procedure—and all too often don't.

Another facet of my job became clear. Teachers had to be made aware of their own feelings, and being made aware, either their feelings would have to change, or they would have to leave. But not right away; I could hardly come in to a school and fire over half my staff within the first month. To begin with, some of the teachers were permanently appointed, and I would have union trouble if I asked them to leave. I would have to prove that their attitudes were damaging to the girls, and attitudes, like feelings, are impossible to prove. Second, where would I get competent teachers? There was a teacher shortage in the city. I had one vacancy that was still unfilled, and I had asked a Mrs. B. to substitute.

Mrs. B. was a retired teacher who supplemented her pension by substituting several days a week. She had a reputation for being an excellent disciplinarian. I didn't know whether she was a good or a bad teacher in her old school, but she was a disaster here. She demanded respect, too. She was delicately proper.

"Dr. Rothman," she called across the lunchroom one day as she ate lunch at a table with her class, "I cannot eat in this atmosphere." It was the beginning of my second week.

Seventy girls in the lunchroom stopped their yelling and scuffling and pushing and listened intently. She continued, completely insensitive to the storm she was creating. "These girls and their filthy talk make me too ill to eat my lunch."

I didn't know what atmosphere she meant, or what filthy talk. The only thing I observed was Lillian huddling with three other girls at a corner of the table. They were all obviously laughing, but not particularly raucously.

Lillian straightened immediately and pointed her finger in Mrs. B.'s direction. "You can take your lunch and stick it up your ass and see how you like to taste it then, for all we care," Lillian called out. "Don't nobody give a good fuck whether you get fat from eatin your damn lunch or not."

I must say I did not blame Lillian, but of course I could not condone her condemnation. Everybody turned toward me, and silence fell.

If I went through the expected routine, I would first scold Lillian and tell her how bad she was, second, get her to tell me she was sorry for her rudeness, third, grandly forgive her freshness, and fourth, ask her to apologize to Mrs. B.

I couldn't do it. I could not perpetuate that particular system of hypocrisy. Lillian was not sorry, and I could not get her to say she was sorry, even if I wanted to. Besides, what should she be sorry for—her lack of respect? Mrs. B. had not earned respect.

I turned and walked out of the lunchroom and left them all staring.

The gasp was from the teachers, the derision from the girls. I had lost both. The teachers thought I was weak; the girls, that I was afraid.

Mrs. B. left the school immediately, in mid-afternoon. She gathered up her things and left, but not before she told me in no uncertain terms that if I did not back up the teachers, I would run the school down to the ground.

Where did she think it was, anyway?

"And what's more," she seethed, "who is going to teach respect to these—these animals!"

I didn't bother to tell her that I was. But not in her terms. I was not going to perpetuate the spurious sentimentality upon which this school was based. I was not going to be the all-accepting model of false forgiveness and equally false love. I was going to make demands of girls that showed them I respected them even if I did not like them. And I didn't like them—not then I didn't.

The riot occurred a few weeks later. It happened one afternoon during the showing of a film at an assembly that all the girls attended.

I was opposed to holding assemblies right after lunch. It held the girls together still another hour, heightening the tensions they had already built up during the confinement of mealtime. I was opposed to showing films during assemblies, especially those as ridiculous as this one on pineapple processing in Hawaii. But the picture had been scheduled a long while ago, and to cancel it or the weekly assembly might further upset the teachers and the status quo. It was absolutely incredible to me how everybody seemed conveniently to forget that the girls were here in the first place because they couldn't function within the status quo, and here we were, doing things exactly the way they had always been done in the school system, holding assemblies the way they had always been held, showing irrelevant educational films the way they had always been shown, as a consumer of time. Our girls from Harlem and Brooklyn and the Bronx couldn't care less about pineapples or Hawaii.

There was a lot of snickering and whispering during the film. The girls giggled and scuffed and moved their unfolded chairs close together in tight little groups. Lorene snickered and whispered a lot louder than the rest.

Suddenly she stood up and pointed toward the screen.

"That man's got a mosquito for a pee-er," she jeered. Everybody howled; I should have, too, and let it pass, but I didn't. I practically wrote the script for what happened next.

"Stop it," I told her in front of everybody. Loudly, too.

"Make me," she said. She turned and faced me, and suddenly all eyes were turned toward us. The film was still going on, the sound track blaring; no other sound was heard. The girls were completely silent. It had never happened before.

I then did the one thing I should not have done. It was not the time to touch, and completely ignoring the warning signals that were flashing in my head, I put my hand on her arm and told her to come with me to the office. As soon as I made it, I realized it was the worst move I could possibly make.

"Take your fuckin hands off," she threatened menacingly.

I didn't. I wasn't just saving face. I was frightened, one of the very few times I ever have been. I sensed that the teachers would be delighted at my downfall. They were almost eager for me to be a loser. I played right into their hands.

I tightened my grip.

Lorene stepped back, knocking over her chair. She slapped me on the arm and I stood there. I simply stood. If my life had depended on it, I don't think I could have moved forward or backward or one iota from that spot. Mr. Cohen saw my panic and immediately rushed over to me. The teachers just watched. They made no effort to relate to the girls, and the girls went berserk.

Chairs went flying—girls began to scream gleefully. It was directed at me, and then it turned. One girl hit another, and the fuse was lit. Old feuds, new feuds, undreamed-of, later-to-be-developed feuds erupted. Girls clawed at each other and tore at each other's hair. Clothing was torn, faces and hands were scratched to the point of blood.

We needed help. It was the only knowledge I seemed to have at the moment. It was as if all my education and training had ended in only one word. Help! I asked one of the teachers to call the police.

They came to a halt in front of the school, four squad cars full, sirens screaming. The girls recognized the sound and focused all their anger, which really should have been directed at me, upon each other. They fought more fiercely than before. It was a fight of frustration. Everything in their lives that was wrong, everything in this school that was wrong, was in that fight.

It really was not the police who quieted them down; after a while the anger just seemed spent. Girls were separated from each other by the police, who were unusually gentle, and the girls, individually and in small groups, were sent home.

But Lorene, what to do with her? I felt I had to arrest her. She could not assault me in front of everybody and get away with it. I knew it would be wrong for her and wrong for the rest of the school to feel that anyone could hit a teacher and go completely unpunished. The problem was that I really did not want to arrest her. It had not been entirely her fault. Equally at fault was my mishandling. We had both been frightened; she had gotten carried away by her own bravado; I, by my fear. Unfortunately, though, I knew of no other way. I had to arrest her. It would set an example—girls would learn that we would not tolerate assaults upon teachers.

Lorene was arrested and taken to court. The hearing was set for the next day, when Lorene's parents would be able to appear with her.

How naive I was! I had no idea that the story—*Principal Assaulted*—would make the evening news both on radio and on television. I hadn't realized that when we telephoned for the police, newspapermen would get the story. That evening I was besieged at home by newspapermen. Lorene, it seemed, was turning out to be some kind of beast. I was badly beaten, I was hurt, I was in critical condition—the stories were wildly exaggerated.

That evening I resolved to ask the judge to drop the charges when we got to court. The arrest had been a mistake.

My naiveté again.

When we got to court next day, the judge asked me to come up to the bench.

"You don't have a lawyer, do you?" he asked kindly.

"No, your honor." It had never occurred to me that I should have one.

"You should," the judge informed me. "If you drop charges now, you are holding yourself liable for a false arrest suit."

"My God!" The words were out of my mouth without my even knowing it.

"Did she assult you?" he continued.

"Well—technically, yes," I answered.

"Perhaps you might want to ask for special consideration for her," he suggested.

I did. Oh, yes, I did. I felt as if I were caught in a trap of my own making. I was protecting myself in going ahead with the assault charge. I was thinking of myself first, and only secondly of Lorene, but I did not know what else to do, and the fact was that she had hit me.

The hearing lasted only a few minutes because Lorene admitted freely and frankly that she had assaulted me.

I asked the court to put her on probation so that she might come back to school.

But Lorene did not want to return to school. Her own behavior, which really had started merely as play, had startled and upset her as much as it had me. She was almost seventeen and wanted to work. She asked me to help her get a job, which I did. It was a shattering experience for us both, but somehow it drew us together. She still calls me occasionally.

After my one evening's notoriety, the Board of Education decided to notice me.

No one from the Board had been near me during that first month, but now was the time. The day after the so-called riot, the superintendent descended, the assistant superintendent of the district, the associate superintendent at the Board, the Director of Socially Maladjusted and Emotionally Disturbed Children and several assorted and sundry assistant directors of various bureaus. Singly, together, in teams, they came to school. One wanted to know why the girls didn't walk in lines when they changed classes, and another why I permitted the girls to curse. Yet another asked why I didn't have experience charts posted in the classroom.

Permit them to curse? How could I stop them? Experience charts? Did the superintendent know what he was talking about? Experience charts were just that, experiences dictated by individuals. I could just see Ellen's.

The girls were enthusiastic over the visitors and the trouble I was in. They had got rid of the previous principal, Mrs. Z., and now it was my turn. The teachers were not overt, but they were clearly waiting to see if I would stay or go.

But I knew I would not go. I also knew that I would not permit officialdom at the Board to chastise me and get away with it. What did they really know about these girls? All that they needed to label a school "good" was silence from the community.

But I was not going to be silent. I was going to protest—loud and clear. I needed teachers, not hand-me-downs, but teachers I could select and work with. If there were some who would stay and work with me, well and good. If not, they had to go.

I stayed up all that night nursing my anger, steeling myself for the confrontation I was planning. I had to do what I believed in, for if I couldn't do it for myself, then I could never teach girls to fight against the injustices of their own lives.

The day after the celestial visitation from the powers-that-be

I walked into that cradle of education at Livingston Street, up to the Superintendent of Schools who had chastised me for my lack of experience charts, and told him out of the language of Chaucer and the Livingston girls that when a girl is saying *shit* to a teacher, neither she nor the teacher wants to print it on an experience chart.

I will say this for the Superintendent. He listened, particularly after I showed him the reports teachers had written about girls. These anecdotal reports clearly indicated not only how the teachers felt about the girls, but also how they felt about me. One did not have to be a psychologist to see below the surface.

Mrs. N. wrote of Shirley:

Has extremely short hair, for which she is constantly teased by the other girls, and when they say 'Liver Lips,' they are referring directly to Shirley in our class. Has big eyes and is almost a pure African type. In class there seems to be no trouble. Out of class, that is another matter, as she will quickly inform whomever it is, "I ain't in your class now and you got nothin to do with me." Formerly such remarks would have earned her a good talking-to on the subject of cooperation and the respect and obedience demanded BY THE OFFICE (The Principal). There was never any doubt allowed to remain about whether they had to comply with requests, nor about how long they would have to wait to get told about their derelictions IF such occurred.

Has been warned about not staying with class, when travelling to classes. Shirley arrives as much as half hour late, although leaving with the others on the bell. Has been told that a repetition of this will result in her remaining a while after school the next time it is found out (and they ALL love to tell on one another). Says Sandra doesn't get laid out, why do they fuss at her and not at Sandra, "becos she white, I guess."

I don't know *why* something is not said to Sandra, but I intend to

find out because Lois and Ruth are also following her lead of not returning to official class at dismissal time. They say, "Sandra don't
hafta, why do we?"

Mrs. N. was openly accusing me of bigotry. Okay, maybe I
deserved that, particularly after my poor judgment in imitating
Sarah, when I did not know that Sarah was black.

After reading the anecdotals, the Superintendent agreed with
me that I had to choose my own staff, whom I could train.
People at the Board will accept natural leadership, not, of
course, when the leader is far out front, but only when the
leader is behind the leader in front of him. Thus, a superintendent must have his principals behind him. A principal must
have his teachers. They perpetuate the incompetencies by
creating everyone in the image of the biggest superintendent of
them all, the ninth floor, the Superintendent of Schools. And
even if they didn't think I knew what I was doing (I didn't
always), the Board of Examiners had licensed me, the Board
of Education had appointed me, and besides, they had almost
no choice. They could not rescind my appointment.

Word must have gone down. *Let Rothman alone.* They did.
They let me work my own way.

My so-called riot did it. The teachers and the girls knew I
was staying. Like the seven-year plague, I was here to stay. I
had proved I could take it. I was tough. And mean.

It earned me a certain respect from both teachers and girls.
Oh, what a hard way to earn it! I wasn't reaching either the
students or the teachers, really; they weren't liking me, but they
were beginning to listen to me, because they were afraid not to
listen.

"You fuckin bitch," Anna screamed, "all you wanta do is
send girls upstate."

"It's not what I want to do," I answered, "it's what I will have to do if you bring in wine again. I will have you arrested."

And within a week, Anna did. She and six other girls brought several bottles of wine to school and had a party on a fourth-floor stairwell. I asked Mr. Cohen to arrest them all. I pressed charges. I didn't like doing it, but I had to. I could not permit girls to get drunk in school. We could not teach drunken girls. It was as simple as that.

Mrs. T. was critical of another arrest.

"Was it really necessary to have them arrested?" she asked, not ungraciously.

"Yes, it was," I answered her.

She was silent, and started to leave. But she came back.

"I have to be frank," she said. "I don't want to say it behind your back. Would you arrest them if they were white girls?"

There it was out, and I was glad it was.

"Mrs. T.," I said, "I'll arrest any girl of any color, of any religion, of any sect, if I think it's the right thing to do. We can't help girls if we permit them to destroy themselves. I don't like arrests, I don't know any other way, but we have to begin to have a semblance of sanity here. We have to structure, we have to say no, we have to set limits, we have to give them strengths they don't have."

She didn't say anything, but I knew she believed me. Mrs. T. was black.

By February, several teachers left. I hired new ones. A few old ones decided to stay. We began to work. I began to reorganize the school. I abolished the system of putting girls into classes by their reading grades, and I threw out most of the readers that were in the classrooms.

For instance, Antoinette, being an intelligent, sixteen-year-old non-reader, had been placed in a class with other intelligent non-readers. This meant that Antoinette, as well as the other girls, was bright enough to recognize how stupid they really were and sensitive enough to recognize that the teachers felt they were helpless and therefore hopeless.

"Retards, that's us," Antoinette said.

The teachers said she was a classic reading disability case.

To add to Antoinette's discomfort, whe was given a first-grade reader about Dick and Jane in which Dick, who was six years old, said to his sister Jane, "Look, Jane, look, see Sally run."

Antoinette thought the story slightly dull. "Shoo," she asked her teacher, "don't Dick ever fuck Jane?"

It was time to change. Dick and Jane were both thrown into the rubbish heap, and the system of organizing classes on the basis of how well girls did or did not read was also abolished. I pointed out to the teachers that grouping girls according to their ability also meant grouping them according to their disabilities, and disabilty grouping is not only ineffectual, it's cruel.

"But it's easier to teach if everyone is on the same level," the teachers protested.

"Only if you teach to a group," I answered, "but as there are only seven to ten girls in a group, all teaching should be completely individualized."

The teachers began to like the idea. Teaching became easier, not harder. Behavior improved, as no girl was humiliated at the indignity of having to read, "See Spot. See Fluff."

But how to group? The answer was obvious to me. We would organize classes on the basis of interest. And what interested girls? This, too, was obvious. Dance. Cooking. Music. Typing. Beauty Culture. These became our official classes. It really didn't matter whether a girl was thirteen or fifteen, if she was in the seventh grade or tenth, or if she read on a ninth-grade level or was a non-reader. When she was in the Dance class, she danced. The program was organized so that girls spent a part of each day studying their particular areas of interest; the rest of the day, each class was scheduled for other subjects. Thus, girls in the Dance class also went to Music, Typing, and Beauty Culture. In addition, every class was also scheduled for English, Mathematics, and Social Studies. As the academic work was completely individualized, the level at which each girl was working really didn't affect any other member of the class. Girls could proceed at their own rate of progress.

The school began to work because we did not have to follow the prescribed curricula or organization, we were able to experiment and fail, experiment and try again, experiment and learn—not only the girls, but the teachers also, and isn't that what education is all about?

We tried forming an official class around Mathematics as an interest; it did not work. We formed classes based on English as a center of interest; they did not work, either, even when we euphemistically called them Journalism, Creative Writing, or just plain Academics. Neither could we form an official class around Social Studies, calling it Anthropology, Human Relations, or by any other name. We settled for academics fed in small doses, and not around a core or center of interest.

Then we tried nursing as an official class, but anxieties were too deep, and personal experiences were too emotionally charged for the class to be successful. Taking a body temperature became a source of ribald jokes. Care of the sick aroused fears of death and fantasies of dying and stories of deaths they had witnessed. When we switched the emphasis of the course to child care, the same thing held true. The whole topic of babies presented emotional challenges. Some girls who had babies didn't want other girls to know, but found it hard not to talk about them; other girls who didn't have babies pretended they did. Still others were bored with the whole thing. Their mothers had babies at home, and they were tired of caring for them. And a girl like Pat, who had delivered her mother's baby at home, couldn't even face up to a classroom discussion. Her trauma was so great that she needed individual help. And this was the conclusion we finally reached: babies, sex, family life, and nursing were areas that were best handled individually in counseling and therapy.

Experimenting was exciting and rewarding. I was learning constantly. Mostly, I learned how to listen to the girls—to listen, listen, and listen. It was exhilarating. Not so exhilarating was learning how to unlisten to the Board of Education and New York City officialdom, to unlisten and to ignore.

For instance, I learned soon after I became principal that the fire alarm box, which was located on the third-floor landing of the main stairway, and therefore a source of constant stimulation, had to be relocated to a place where it could be better supervised.

I knew nothing about its attraction for the girls until one day, without apparent cause, without fanfare, in fact it was a relatively quiet day, three truckfuls of firemen came dashing up into the building, five steps at a time, axes in their hands, shouting, "Where's the fire? Why aren't the students in the street?"

I looked at them as if they were crazy.

"Fire here? I didn't hear an alarm."

They looked at me as if I were crazy.

"Lady, when a fire alarm rings, it rings in the firehouse, not in the building where you have the fire. When you have a fire, lady, you don't need an alarm, you know you have a fire."

I admit that they had logic on their side. They left, sadly

shaking their heads at my stupidity. I was joyful that we didn't
have a fire, but that week they arrived five days consecutively.
They heard the alarm, even if we didn't. Someone was having
fun, although we never found out who. After a week of it the
someone stopped having fun, and all was calm again. Well, at
least no fire alarms were sent in. It was obvious to me, however,
that the firebox had to be relocated to a spot where it could not
be tampered with. This meant directly outside the general
office.

It seemed logical to call the fire department and ask them to
do it.

At the other end of the phone, the official sounded as if it
were the strangest request he ever had heard.

"Madam, the fire department does not relocate boxes," he
told me.

"Are you sure?" I asked skeptically.

"Yes, ma'am."

Nevertheless, I asked him to switch my phone call to another
official. He did. I received the same anwer. I got endlessly
switched and answered in the same way.

Finally, I asked the next question that seemed appropriate.
"Who does?"

No one knew. Certainly, no one at the Board of Education
knew. Two months later, and after what seemed endless phone
calls and letters to every major department the city of New
York had to offer, I had the answer.

I called the fire department again to tell them what I thought
they should know, in case anyone asked them the question
again.

The relocation of a firebox is not done by any department of
the city of New York. It is done by any private company who
submits a bid to the city for the privilege of doing so.

Now, that was one bit of information I could never as pre-principal have foreseen the need to know. As principal, and knowing it, I was still annoyed that it took one whole year for the specifications to be written, bids to be received, contracts to be awarded. Finally, it was done. But it didn't seem to matter, because ever since that week of alarm-ringing, no alarms have been sent in, falsely or verily.

Berenice came closest to it, and that was nine years later. She merely began to break the glass of our internal fire alarm bell system. This one doesn't even ring at the station house, only in school, and is used for fire drills. Before she could do her damage, however, her teacher saw her. Berenice quickly became very interested in studying the redness of the box.

"She get on my nerves," Berenice yelled when the teacher finally got her to come into my office, "always pickin on me, sayin I gonna ring that bell. Why I wanta ring that old bell?"

"I don't know why," I answered, "but come on, Berenice, your teacher didn't accuse you of anything. It's your guilty conscience speaking. You know you were going to ring that alarm."

Berenice grunted and looked at the floor.

"Berenice," I said, "there must be a reason you do these things."

"Ain't no reason."

"There must be," I insisted. "Only maybe you don't know it."

"Nope."

"Maybe something inside you tells you to do these things."

"No devil inside me," she said.

"An angel inside you?" I tried again.

She was truly beautiful when she smiled.

"My angel inside went sour."

"Well, we'll have to fix that," I said, "and unsour you."

"Nope." She was negative again.

Then, as she so often did, she changed the topic abruptly.

"When can I go back to regular school?" she asked.

"Whenever you and the teachers and I decide you're ready," I answered.

She laughed. "I'll never be ready."

"Maybe so," I answered.

"I'm stayin right here."

"Okay."

There was a silence as she studied me. Then, "When you goin back to regular school?" she asked.

"Me?" She took me by surprise.

"They kick you out, too?" she asked.

"No," I answered. "I want to be here. I chose this school."

"You don't want to go to regular school?" She was incredulous.

"Listen," I told her, "when I was a little kid, much younger than you, in fact, I used to play hookey. So why would I want to go now, if I didn't go then?"

She studied me.

"You're not loudmouthin?" she asked.

"No. For real."

"Well," she thought that over, "I guess we belong here."

We did. And we do.

chapter two

The Route to King Street

A Mexican movie star's red Jaguar draws up to the psychedelically painted front doors of the Livingston School and out steps his fifteen-year-old protégé, Miss Boom Bang, delight of the *à go-go* cave dwellers, but known to us as Nilda, girl student, late-morning comer, sleeper-in-classes, and very serious.

Two blue-jeaned ersatz boys angle slowly down King Street, caps half-slanting on their heads, cigarettes dangling from the corners of their mouths, and Annie and Diane are welcomed at school.

Fran, a finely sandpapered sirloin steak bone hanging like a pendant from a string of silvered leather around her neck, comes to school—all two hundred and twenty-five pounds of her.

Delicate Miriam, who walks and dresses as if she worked at *Vogue*, comes to school.

And Muriel comes, saying matter-of-factly, "I was absent yesterday because my mother died."

Vera isn't absent at all the day of her mother's funeral. Neither is Nita, whose mother is being arrested for murder. Nor is Linda, whose father is being sentenced. It hurts too much, not coming.

Joy runs down the block, catches up to me, and asks breathlessly, "You the principal?"

"Yes," I tell her. "And you're a new girl."

"You really the principal?" she insists.

"I told you the way it is," I answer.

"And you let the girls talk to you that way?"

"Well, words are only words," I say.

"Shit, I can't stand it."

And Joy enters school . . .

Marion, clothing torn, bruises dark on her arms and around her face, where her mother had beaten her the night before with an iron cord, comes to school.

And Lucy, undernourished, undersized, who, barely above a whisper, weeps, "I tried to kill myself this morning," comes to school.

Lenore, who spends every cent she can earn on heroin for her mother, because "God, who else but me can help her?" comes too.

And to my good morning, an angered Denise greets me with, "Suspend me, Dr. Rothman, go ahead and suspend me, I don't care, I'm gonna get that fuckin Iona."

I accept her anger, tell her I'm not going to suspend her, she's done too well and come a long way, and furthermore Iona sometimes gets on my nerves, too. Besides, what did Iona do?

"How would you feel," Denise explains, "if she be on you and say—excuse the expression, Dr. Rothman—you're in a house of prostitution?" Denise looks away from me. I have never known her to be embarrassed before.

I admit, not so good. But on the other hand, not so bad, either. If I know I'm not a prostitute, anyone saying so doesn't make me one. So why should I care what some stupid person says about me? "They're probably jealous," I say casually, "when they say things like that. Iona is probably jealous of you."

Denise calms down. "I may fuck once in a while," she says, "but I ain't running a whorehouse. I'm friendly, I'm a friendly girl, can I help it if I'm friendly?"

With that unacademic question, Denise starts her school day.

Alma starts, also, burdened with the horror of watching both her parents die of cancer, and suffering intolerable guilt because she can't stop them from dying.

Ophelia arrives, wearing around her neck a baby's pacifier on which she intermittently sucks during breakfast—the "in" thing with her group on Staten Island this year.

"Ophelia," I order, "take that pacifier out of your mouth. The girls are going to laugh at you and before you know it, there'll be a fight and then I'll have to send you home early."

She looks up at me, superiority written all over her very beautiful face. "There won't be a fight, Dr. Rothman. If anybody says anything to me, I'll just tell them there is such a thing as individual differences."

Her glance slides down to the heavy load of books she carries, for effect, not for reading. Freud is prominent on top.

"Okay," I say, "but I don't think Freud means for you to suck that silly pacifier."

Suddenly she laughs. "Well, you do your thing, and I'll do mine. But," and she emphasizes the word, "when Ophelia and her butt come to school, they come to stay, and not to be sent home early, remember that, Dr. Rothman."

I decided to remember.

Savannah comes to school, too . . . Savannah, whose mother was murdered, whose brother is awaiting trial for armed robbery, whose father has deserted her.

Pat appears two hours late; she had been arrested for purse-snatching on the subway. She didn't need the money. Her stealing goes much deeper than that.

They live with tragedy—our girls of the Livingston School —tragedy most of us stronger mortals, the professionals, could not transcend. I know one thing, I could not come to school, even now, as principal, much less as student, if my beloved sister were in the hospital having her arm amputated. Yet Andrea did. She come to school to go to her classes and to see her counselor and to talk and talk and talk.

No tears. They survive, and even laugh. What achievement! What colossal achievement for Pat to concentrate on math when just the night before, the little boy with whom she baby-sat bled to death when a loose glass door unhinged and fell on him, piercing an artery in his neck. Two days later, Pat herself was stabbed in the back by an irate friend who claimed Pat had stolen her boyfriend; in that same week, Shirley's mother died of cancer, Gloria's father was rushed to the hospital with nephritis, Constance's father collapsed on his job, Pauline was hospitalized with asthma, Esther's six-month-old brother was rushed to the hospital with acute pneumonia while Esther's mother, refusing to release her baby from her arms, violently attacked her husband and the doctors, accusing them of trying to kill her baby. And except for Pat, who was physically incapable of attending, all the girls came to school.

Call them what you will—socially maladjusted, or emotionally disturbed, or delinquent, or neurotic, or psychopathic, or psychotic, or underprivileged, or troubled, or angry, or spoiled, or victims, or sick or culturally different, or behavior prob-

lems—the fact remains that they cannot be commonly pro-
cessed and commonly labeled, for they have only three things
in common: they are girls, they are adolescents, and they have
been in, created, partaken of, and caused trouble in the public
and private schools of New York City. One thing for certain.
They are not the quiet types.

They are committed to rebellion against the facts of their
lives, and beyond that, they fit no mold. They cannot be sieved
to fit the perforations of an IBM card. They are inspiring
examples of outrageous individualism. They dare to be different. They will not be stifled. This is the main reason they are at
Livingston. They think divergently, see things differently from
the way most people do, reconstruct their perceptions in a way
that most people do not. They are truly creative. This does not
mean that they are artists or talented in the conventional sense.
Some girls are; many are not. Talent and artistry are rare.
Creativity is not. We are all born with a potential and a
capacity for creativity. Catastrophically, this potential is
crushed out of most of us at an early age, first by our parents,
later by our teachers. "What—you drew a red horse? Who ever
heard of a red horse?" The five-year-old soon learns adults
don't like it when he's different. Our girls, however, continue to
be creative because they have survived the conformity process,
because they continue to diverge from the norm, despite all
pressure to stop.

Being creative is wanting to be tickled and not finding
someone to tickle you—you cut off the mink tails from your
teacher's coat and tickle yourself under the chin. Being creative
is not following the straight and narrow line to a goal. Many
curves and detours to that goal. The whole concept of emotional disturbance or mental illness can be viewed as the ability
to be divergent. It is a refreshing thought because it is really a

hopeful outlook without fear. How wonderful to be Napoleon at times!

What is more wonderful than being fat Lillie for one moment of her life, when puffing and huffing up the main stairway, with a taxi driver behind her demanding his six-dollar fare, she flung her directive at me. "You want me to come to school, you pay."

What is more creative than Judy tearing her blouse off her shoulder and running out of the classroom screaming that Mr. O. was trying to rape her.

"In the art room?" I said. "I don't believe you. He's not that hard up to need a kid like you. You just want to leave early. It won't work."

She quickly pinned her blouse back up with a safety pin I gave her and was ready to go back upstairs to Mr. O., but he came flying into my office before she could leave, gesticulating to me behind her back that he didn't want her back in his classroom. Not many things shook Mr. O., but Judy certainly had. For some reason, he didn't like being accused of rape. Later I teased him and told him how uncreative it was of him to be so upset. But, of course, I didn't send Judy back to him—that day, that is. It was a new switch to Judy when I told her she couldn't go back to the art class that day because Mr. O. was too busy to have to put up with every girl who was going to accuse him of rape.

"He too damned smart," she said with not too much sullenness.

"And sexy, too," I added.

"Naah," she made a sound that could only be described as derogatory, which of course is why I had said what I did. I wanted her to deny it. One always has to be worried when an attractive thirteen-year-old impulsive girl accuses a teacher of a sexual advance. There is always the chance that someone, somewhere, would believe her, particularly if she started to cry. Not her mother, of course—nor us—we knew her too well. But some well-meaning sentimental professional idiot who sold love as a worldwide cure—well, you never could tell. Judy stayed and chatted with me, and in talking about the incident became pleased with herself. After all, she had tried a meandering approach to get what she wanted. She knew the straight one wouldn't work, not when her mother had told me that Judy was never to be given permission to leave early. She had too many boyfriends.

Judy was creative all right, as creative as the sixteen-year-old boy I had taught at Bellevue who had masturbated with a typewriter ribbon.

I remember George well. In fact, I shall never forget him. I remember asking him to wheel a typewriter down a long corridor from one classroom to another. I went ahead of him, but since then have learned always to stay behind patients when walking down long corridors in psychiatric hospitals. George, typewriter, and typewriter table had disappeared when I got to the classroom. Finally they arrived, typewriter table and typewriter, sans ribbon. I asked what had happened. He looked at me almost condescendingly, certainly not unkindly, and without a word he fished the unwound, tangled, damp ribbon from his pants pocket and proceeded to show me how a ribbon could slide.

That was almost twenty years ago. I probably was too stupid to be shocked. Numbed was more like it, but after my feelings returned, I began to appreciate his ability to use a typewriter ribbon in a way that no one, absolutely no one in the educational hierarchy, could ever have conceived.

I learned then to cherish creativity, unacceptable though it

sometimes may be in terms of social behavior. At Livingston, I
continued to cherish it while at the same time trying to direct it
so that the behavior would become acceptable while the creativity remains deliciously alive. The teachers and I are dedicated to this concept.

A girl caught sneaking out of the building without permission hurls at me, "If I left this building, then my mother is a
whore, and my mother ain't no whore, and I never left this
stinkin building."

Or another girl, caught with cigarette in hand in the bathroom, may scream, "If I smoked in the bathroom my mother is
dead and my mother ain't dead, so you're a fuckin liar, I didn't
smoke in no bathroom."

A girl refusing to follow instructions taunts, "If I do that my
mother is a faggot and my mother ain't a faggot so I'm not doin
it."

Should I blame them for being more creative than I, or
should I somewhat envy them their existing powers? I envy. I
also fervently hope that I can give them some of my social
judgment in exchange for some of their creativity. We have a
lot to teach each other, and we do.

"That's very creative," I respond. "You have an unusual way
of saying things. You also have an unusual way of seeing
them."

Each girl gets the point, namely she and I both know that
she has lied. We also know that her lie has not worked. A new
and exciting idea, however, has hit her—the concept that she is
creative, and while she had been creative in a way that has not
served her purpose, she might try to utilize her talents in more
socially acceptable ways.

And she does begin to try.

But let's face it, creativity, because it's frightening to those who have been molded to the concept of the norm, often leads to diagnosis, and our girls have been through the diagnostic mill.

Some of our girls have been diagnosed as mentally ill; some have not, although they may or may not be severely mentally ill. Who really knows? Who can be so definitively wise?

Berenice, for instance, had been born with barbed wire for teeth. She slashed into her environment with fury. No teacher in any of the four schools she had gone to could contain her, and the Board of Education assigned a teacher to go to her home twice a week.

One day when Berenice and her teacher were sitting at a kitchen table in her father's apartment, two teenage boys climbed in through the fire escape window, which opened into a bedroom, and lunged at Berenice's father, who was sitting with his back to the window, watching television. At Mr. A's screams, Berenice and her teacher came running into the bedroom and the two boys fled past them and out of the door, but not before they had slashed Mr. A. with a knife. Berenice and her teacher called for an ambulance, and Mr. A. was taken to the hospital in critical condition. He was released after several months with permanent partial paralysis of his hand and leg.

Mr. A. identified one of the boys—Walter, his wife's sixteen-year-old son by a previous alliance—as the attempted murderer. Walter was charged with attempted murder. Mrs. A., in turn, preferred countercharges against her husband. She claimed Mr. A. had sent a hired gunman to shoot her, Walter, and her new paramour, with whom she was living. Mr. A. denied this vociferously. Walter was released on bail. He was most cavalier about the whole situation, forgiving Mr. A. for being alive and visiting his home frequently.

This was the point at which the home instruction department made a profound decision. They referred Berenice to the Livingston School because they decided that for some reason she was now emotionally equipped to attend a school.

Berenice alternated between sleeping at her father's house and her mother's new house. Sometimes she slept at neither one; she stayed with her boyfriend. She was as uncaring about him as she was about everybody else. His room was just another place to go. He was just another person to give her money. Both her parents gave her money to buy clothes. So did he.

Berenice was an emotional isolate—an alone child—isolate, not meaning silent, withdrawn, huddled-in-the-corner child, to whom the observer instinctively offers heart and warmth. This kind of isolation is recognizable, and often the barriers guarding it can be broken by people willing to make the effort to do it. Berenice was the other kind of isolate, the vociferous isolate, the angry, loud, boisterous, aggressive child, the nasty child, the mouthful of obscenities, cursing child who could not share her deep feelings or her real thoughts with any person in the world. Come near her emotionally, and she struck out. She built her own walls, and because reaching her meant absorbing an incredible amount of abuse, very few people had tried. Even we professional people, who train ourselves to know better, couldn't get past the obscenities, past the anger, past the sullenness, to the girl underneath. Our own feelings of repugnance and resistance were as much obstacles as was Berenice's own terrifying defense of impenetrability.

Walter was apparently very fond of Berenice, for he would call school anonymously to threaten me whenever Berenice had some difficulty in school, and this was frequent. After the initial two-minute panic of the first call, I got to know Walter's voice, and after the first few threats were got over with, we would discuss Berenice's problems quite pleasantly and openly, and Walter would agree that Berenice "had a mind a her own."

She definitely had, and she had no difficulty in letting me know what was on it. Another girl looked at her funny. It was raining. Her brother had hit her. She was tired. Her ear hurt. What was bothering Berenice was all of these things and none of these things. What was bothering her was her total reality. She could not change it. Neither could we. We could only give her the strength to withstand it, and give her alternative courses of behavior that would begin to make her feel better about herself, for underneath that wildness was a deep depression. Berenice did not want to be the way Berenice was, but she had no other techniques of behaving. It was up to us to teach her how to be the kind of person people might like—not abrasive, not abusive, not nasty, but Berenice, whose angel inside need not be sour.

Was Berenice mentally ill? What yardstick could one use in making judgment? Who wouldn't be mentally ill living under the conditions she did, but was it illness or was it strength that made Berenice come to school every day always well groomed, invariably bringing bagfuls of hero sandwiches, soda, and candy with her, invariably with money. It took strength just to get to school. It took strength to acquire enough money to buy all the food with which she was always stuffing herself. She ate like an infant, grabbing it all in—there was no other gratification in life for her.

Berenice was a delinquent by all social standards, although by legal definition she was not. She had never been arrested. Some of our girls have been brought to court and adjudged delinquent for assaulting others, shoplifting, or joyriding in stolen cars. Some have not, although they may have committed exactly the same offenses or worse. Still others are brought to court by their own parents, who no longer want them, or wanting them, cannot control them. The obvious question, who is the real delinquent, parent or child, is often smugly asked by the unknowing professional. The fairer question, less damning by implication but certainly more insightful, should be—who is more in need of help, parent or child?

Some girls come from homes that are superficially labeled "good"—intact families, self-supporting, clean; some others come from homes that are undeniably bad—what father? where is the mother? who pays the bills? Of one thing there is no doubt; all come from homes that have failed them emotionally.

It is easy to believe that parents are rejecting, that they are brutal to their children simply because they never wanted them or simply because they hate them. It becomes easy to put the onus of their children's behavior upon their absolute rejection. It makes my job easier, but it is simply not true.

The parents—most, if not all of them—are deeply troubled, not only by their own children, but by the confusions of their own feelings and the circumstances of their own lives. It is the function of the school to help them, for if we are to help a girl, we must often start by helping her parents. Sometimes, it is hard to offer that help. We have to push ourselves to be therapeutic. We have to look beyond the rejection, beyond the punitiveness, beyond the emotional brutality, and see not a villainous human being, but a harmed or destroyed one. It's hard. I had no difficulty recognizing that when Margaret brought a knife to school, slipped unsheathed in her knee sock, and told every girl in school that she was going to fight on the subway, she was saying, "Help me before I kill someone." But I had the greatest difficulty accepting Margaret's mother, who when I offered her coffee said, "What's the matter, you think I'm drunk?" I could understand the years of hurt that lay beneath the question, but I still had to muster all my training and skill not to act startled. And if I—the professional—am unsettled at her toughness, what must Margaret feel when she faces the same granite? Is this mother? How Margaret must suffer! But even as I think of Margaret's hurt, I know I am not completely right. I must force myself to think of her mother's hurt, too. I cannot afford the luxury of my own reaction, nor even the luxury of sharing Margaret's. What I must really do is understand the depths of despair that led Margaret's mother to ask her question.

And it's no different with Mrs. P., who is even more blunted emotionally and much more brutal to her children than Margaret's mother. Mrs. P.'s husband was entirely out of the picture when we admitted first Alice, age fifteen, and a few months later, Amanda, age fourteen. They both had been referred to Livingston by two different schools in their neighborhood. Neither school had known the other sister was also being referred. Each girl was incorrigible, assaulting other children, cursing and shoving teachers. Amanda had hit the assistant principal. Alice had been drunk in school. Two angry girls.

And they had every right to be. Mrs. P. had not once in their lives ever kissed or fondled them, ever given them a birthday present. "Oh, yes," said Amanda, "she kissed me once when I was about six. I was sick."

Mrs. P. concentrated upon each of her children, one at a time. When she was told that Willie, her nine-year-old son, needed heart surgery, she signed him into the hospital. Just at the point of surgery she signed him out because she didn't want him "to be a guinea pig." After the doctors spoke with her at length, she signed him in again. Then she changed her mind again. She made Willie go through the horrendous experience of facing heart surgery four different times. Finally, she did not change her mind. But at what expense to Willie! Later, when he was sent to a convalescent home, she concentrated on Alice.

Alice, too, had a congenital heart condition, as well as asthma. Mrs. P. consistently refused to admit it. Therefore she consistently refused treatment. The day Alice called me at school to say she couldn't come to school because she was having trouble breathing, I signaled to Mr. Scarcella, the patrolman then stationed at our school, to call the police and have an ambulance sent to her home in the Bronx. Alice's gasping breath on the phone was very real and very frightening. I kept Alice on the phone while she waited for the ambulance. I tried to reassure her, telling her she would be all right, that the ambulance would be there any minute, that we missed her in the school, that I would go up to be with her but that I could never get up there in time right now. She told me between gasps that her mother had gone out earlier, even though she knew Alice didn't feel well.

"It's just gas," Mrs. P. had told her. But as Alice spoke I began to feel that her breathing was somewhat easier. But she certainly needed to see a doctor, of that I was certain. Even as I was speaking to her, Alice hung up on me. For a half-hour I didn't know what had happened. No one answered when we called back. We called the police and the hospital, and they didn't know. Finally we learned that Mrs. P. and the ambulance had arrived simultaneously, that Mrs. P. had met them downstairs in the street, and that she had refused to let the attendant upstairs to see Alice. She sent them away, but she was overcome with anger at Alice for having called me. That was the point at which Alice had hung up, when Mrs. P. had come barging in, accusing Alice of disobeying her.

And then Mrs. P. really got even with Alice. She called the police, told them Alice had threatened to kill her, had, in fact, assaulted her, and that she wanted her arrested. Alice remained silent during her mother's barrage and she was arrested and sent to Youth House. My rage at Mrs. P. was almost uncontrollable when I heard the story, but in another sense, I felt relieved that Alice was in a place where she could get medical attention. At least, we saw to that. We called the juvenile detention center and insisted that they give her an immediate and completely exhaustive physical examination, including a cardiac examination, something they do not do routinely.

When Mrs. P. is being so cruel and manipulative, it's hard to remember she is as emotionally ill as a third daughter, Barbara, who revolves in and out of mental hospitals. I want to reach out and throttle her. My feelings are pointless, of course. They should be directed against the city of New York for not providing a Livingston School Residence—a residence attached to this school, run by our staff for girls like Alice and Amanda, who need to come to our school, but who also need a place to live away from their own pathological and damaging homes.

But all parents are not like Mrs. P. Not all are so disturbed. Many are merely powerless to provide the nurture their children need. Inez and Marie, for instance, two other sisters who attended Livingston, demanded more than their mother could give. And not getting it from her, they drank, sniffed glue, eventually became pregnant, Inez at thirteen, Marie at fifteen. What did Inez and Marie really want—the alligator shoes they admired? No. To feel important. The shoes and clothes and glue-sniffing were escapes into status. But they couldn't feel important, not when the welfare worker, unannounced, came into the apartment and berated Mrs. C. for having had a telephone installed.

"Honest to God, Dr. Rothman," she rasped (her voice was

always harsh), "you're like a mother to me, I tell you things I couldn't tell my mother, but what that woman want? I need a phone. I have two teenage daughters, you know what kids are like, they need a telephone, all kids want a phone. If I don't get it, they say I'm not doing right by them. I don't want them to hate me—I don't, I don't."

She began to sob. I watched silently. There was little help I could offer, although a plan began to emerge. If I were to write the department of Social Services and tell them her two daughters were in a school for emotionally disturbed girls and that it was necessary for us to contact Mrs. C. by phone frequently, it would probably work. It did. I stressed the fact that Inez and Marie were disturbed, although in fact they were not. They were just plain angry, and they had a right to be. They wanted the material things the rest of America had. They were entitled to them.

Mrs. C. finally got her telephone. Other people just have to call the telephone company to get one. Mrs. C. had to beg. Mrs. C. cared, all right, and she tried, but she did not have the strength to compete against the slums or to survive. She died.

And what about Dolores's mother? Where had she failed, producing Dolores, who was a compulsive thief, and Dolores's three brothers, who according to Dolores were " . . .not fairies exactly, but they go with fairies, so I guess they're fairies."

The psychologists, social workers, psychiatrists, of course, argue about diagnosis—who's ill and who isn't. And they spend endless hours in conference time and research exploring the dichotomy between those who believe that deviant behavior stems from inner pathology and those who believe that deviant behavior is merely unsocialized behavior and stems from social ills. Many of these professionals are our severest critics. They do not like the school because we do not make a careful, useless distinction between social maladjustment and emotional disturbance. As if anybody could! Furthermore, they feel we should have a different program for different diagnostic categories of girls. Of course, they're wrong. What does it matter what we label a girl? She's the same girl with or without a label. The Board of Education hypocritically states that we do not take psychotic girls, even while they know we do; psychosis is a label with very little real meaning and with no reference to whether a girl should be attending a school or living in seclusion in a closed wing of a hospital.

We simply have no way of knowing, except by trial, whether a girl can profit from coming here. We do not know enough about human behavior or predicting human behavior to know what will happen. I would have sworn that some girls would adjust well. They didn't. I was skeptical that others could make it. They did. Clinical judgment on my part or the combined parts of clinical personnel, the psychologists, psychiatrists, guidance counselors, and social workers, is often unreliable.

So we don't really screen, although we call it a screening interview; we interview and admit. Screening implies running girls through a sieve. Some come in and some stay out, and the sieve, by the very nature of its organic structure, standardizes the sifting. This implies that we have some measure of knowing who should come in and who should not. The fact remains that we do not. We simply have no valid way of predicting with certainty who could profit from attending. We do know, however, that there are three categories of girls we cannot admit, not because they could not profit therapeutically or educationally from our program, as indeed they might, but because their presence would be dangerous either to themselves or to others.

We cannot accept girls with severe heart conditions, or

crippling physical conditions where traveling to school itself presents a hazard to health. We also cannot accept drug-addicted girls or girls who have been known to sell drugs. Neither can we accept girls who are overt homosexuals. Drugs or sex, rampant in a school, can ruin it. We can't have it. If at an initial interview, the girl looks like a boy and makes it quite clear by her responses, although she may not know she's making it clear, that she wants to come to Livingston School for a sexual field day, we must refuse her. Similarly, we are not going to give any girl whom we can recognize as an addict or a pusher a marketplace for drugs.

We generally receive over two hundred referrals a year. We admit approximately fifty or sixty girls during the year. Because discharge from Livingston, like birth, marriage, or death, is a distinctly personal affair, girls leave the school at any time during the school year when it is right for them to leave. We therefore have openings during the course of the year for other girls to be admitted.

We usually admit in groups of five or six, approximately once a month. We keep our admission rate equal to our discharge rate, maintaining an equal number of girls on register, no more than one hundred fifteen at any time.

Because there are so few facilities in New York City for difficult adolescent girls, and because our reputation is spreading, many schools, courts, agencies, and hospitals refer girls to us even when they know the referral is inappropriate and that the girl really needs residential treatment facility, not a day school.

"Look," said one prominent lawyer to me, "I don't believe in the whole damn school system. It's rotting, it's no good, but Theresa has been out of school for six months and she needs to be in school."

"Not in this school, she doesn't," I said. "She's mute, she can't relate at all. We're a school, not a hospital."

Even as I spoke, I knew we would take her, we are not just a day school. We are the Livingston School, a school and treatment center, and who knows, maybe Theresa would love the school so much she would begin to talk, to respond, although I strongly doubted it.

But I wasn't going to give in to him that easily. He had been a bombastic critic, claiming we set no standards for admissions, therefore we were serving no purpose and we were no good.

"Mr. R.," I said, "you have called this school a dumping ground. You have been critical because we admit almost everybody. You believe we should admit only girls who are not severely disturbed. And yet here you are, dumping. You know this girl is severely disturbed and probably needs a hospital, yet you are practically threatening to sue me unless we admit her. Well, you can't have it two ways, you know."

He sputtered a lot because he was caught with his flaws down, and I had my minor victory.

Ninety percent of the girls who are referred are black. The remaining ten percent are divided between white and Puerto Rican girls. Actually, if we were truly representative of the social distribution of New York City, we would have only fifty or sixty percent black girls at the outset. Yet the answer is simple. White girls in trouble most often get picked up by social agencies before they are referred to us, and they often are referred to residential treatment centers.

Most social agencies are organized along religious lines. The Catholic and Jewish religions have developed a hierarchy of services. The Protestant religions have fewer among them. If a girl is Jewish or Catholic, she has a better chance than a Protestant girl for receiving residential treatment. Thus, many Catholic and Jewish girls never get to us. The Protestants do, and as black girls are predominantly Protestant, there are very few facilities open to them.

Social agencies are supposed, of course, to offer services across racial and religious lines. They are supposed to be nondiscriminatory. It just is not true—many agencies remain highly selective simply by making their criteria for admission to their residences so restrictive that it cancels out many children. They take in their token number of blacks. If a girl is Jewish or Catholic, moderately retarded, with an intact family, or adjudged delinquent and of normal intelligence or brilliant and schizophrenic, she has a good chance of receiving residential treatment service in New York City. If she's a black Protestant, retarded or brilliant, schizophrenic or delinquent, intact family or not, forget it. There is no place for her. Reality is reality, despite the fact that this is denied. And the fact is, a referral often reads, "Girl needs residential treatment," or "Home too pathological to be worked with," but because there is no residence available to her, the girl comes to Livingston.

It is my most definite impression that when we do receive a referral for a white girl, it is a good indication that she is an extremely disturbed, possibly psychotic girl who has been turned down by every treatment service as a bad therapeutic risk. Our white girls are definitely our sickest.

Many community agencies, of which the schools are a part, stupidly give the impression to the girls themselves that they are being ostracized, isolated, put down, imprisoned, punished, by the referral to Livingston. Anything but treatment. In the early years, our girls accepted the banishment as complete, themselves as hopeless. We were a prison. And then, as our reputation began to spread and as girls began to feel that they had achieved status in coming to Livingston, they began to want to come.

"Does Susan attend this school?" asked a fourteen-year-old visitor who strode into the building with two other girls. The three of them wore tight blue jeans, black pea coats and black kerchiefs wrapped tightly over their foreheads, as if they were suffering from headaches. Each girl also had a large gold hoop earring pierced through one ear.

"Who are you?" I asked.

She identified herself as Susan's friend, and I identified myself as principal, but I didn't know her Susan.

"You sure?"

"Yep."

"Howdya like that?" she asked. "Howdya like that? Tryin to be big, and she told me she had finally made it here. Howdya like that?"

She left disappointed in her friend Susan.

Some girls do make it here, though, not even waiting for their schools to refer them.

Iona, for instance, visited the school during one summer session and informed us that she was going to be so bad in her own school that they would send her soon. They did.

Then there was Betty, who walked unannounced into my office one day and pleaded with me to let her come.

"I hate my own high school," Betty said grimly, "and I want to come here. They threw me out."

"Why?" I asked.

"Because they said I was a trouble-maker," she answered.

"Were you?" I asked.

"No," she cried. "How could I be a trouble-maker when I didn't even go?"

I called the school and spoke to the dean of girls.

"Betty?" she asked. "Why did we discharge her? She was a trouble-maker, my dear, a very difficult girl."

I hung up and looked again at Betty. Somehow, she did not

impress me as a trouble-maker. I told her what the dean had said.

Betty was genuinely surprised. "She said that? How could she say that, when most of the time I didn't even go to school, I was truant."

"Why?" I asked.

Her story was persuasive.

She didn't go to school, she said, because boys were waylaying girls outside the school building and extorting money from them. Inside the building, it was not much better. Both girls and boys were smoking reefers in the bathrooms; many were selling narcotics. It was too much for Betty. She was afraid.

I must say I believed her, and I could not blame her. The school situation was particularly bad, because the long teacher's strike had just ended, and students were angry. They were also taking advantage of the situation. Teachers were losing control. I called the school back and again talked with the dean of girls. She readily admitted her mistake. She was sorry, she had been wrong. Betty was no trouble-maker, she was discharged because she was pregnant. "Didn't she tell you?"

I looked at Betty opposite me. She was a really beautiful girl, petite, light-brown skin, large eyes, and certainly not noticeably pregnant. But, of course, I couldn't be certain. I decided to be direct with her.

"Betty, are you pregnant? That's what the dean said."

Betty was stunned. "She knows I had my baby over one year ago. And I came back to school. I want to finish my education."

All the time she was speaking she was going through her purse.

"Here, here's a picture of my baby. And here," she threw a packet at me, "my birth control pills. Do you think I'd make a mistake like that again?"

No, I didn't. I called the high school again. I was indignant.
Did the dean of girls have the right to give misinformation
about a girl? But I never reached the dean. Instead I spoke to a
guidance counselor, and I told her the story, ending with would
they transfer Betty to Livingston? That school was no place for
her.

"To tell you the truth," she said, "but I'll deny saying this to
you if you ever quote me, I don't blame Betty. The girl is right.
I'm afraid to come to school myself. It's terrible here. I wish I
could get a transfer." She laughed ruefully, "Got a place for
me, too?"

I didn't have a place for the guidance counselor, but I did for
Betty. I arranged for her and her mother to meet with Mrs.
Landsman, who generally conducts the initial interview before
admission. It is our so-called screening interview. Actually, it is
much more. It is the beginning of the therapeutic process. Each
girl has to face up to one basic fact, that she has been in trouble
or she wouldn't be here now sitting in Mrs. Landsman's office
at the Livingston School. Many girls try to deny their own past
behavior, but through Mrs. Landsman's adroit questioning and
reflection of their feelings, the girls begin to ask themselves the
questions they have not dared to ask before. Is it really
everybody else's fault but theirs that they are here?

The choice to accept or decline the school rests with the
parent. Mrs. Landsman makes it quite clear that while we feel
we can help many girls, we can't help them all, and we
definitely can't help if either the girl or her parent really does
not wish her to attend. In that case, the decision is theirs to
come or to leave. This is not what they had expected. They had
anticipated coercion, not invitation. It is a totally unexpected
situation for them, and the defenses peel off—the hostilities, the
fears, the anguish. By the end of the interview, most of the girls
openly beg to be admitted. Some parents do, also, but most

merely smile. It is a pleasurable thing for Mrs. Landsman to see, for while they are not putting their feelings into words, we know that it is the beginning of a therapeutic process for them, too. The parent, often for the first time, begins to believe that the child is not the worst child in New York City. It is the beginning of hope. And both the girl and her family wait eagerly for admission. The wait is generally only a month or so. But to the girl it is interminable.

Only once has a parent refused admission, and it was a parent Mrs. Landsman had not even interviewed. Mrs. D. came storming one day into the second-floor lounge, where she litterally bumped into Mrs. Landsman as we stood outside my office. My first impression was of wild gesticulation, tightly clutched papers, contorted face, screaming, followed by a wizened apparition who turned out to be her daughter. All I could see was huge eyes on wire legs.

"Oh, no!" Mrs. D. flung a piece of paper at me, not even knowing who I was. "My daughter isn't coming here, not to this school, this school is for delinquents. My daughter is not a delinquent, this school is for bad kids, my girl isn't bad, oh no."

I had trouble breaking into her barrage to introduce myself, but I finally did. I told her that I had no intention of admitting her daughter if she felt so strongly against it.

It took a while, but she quieted down when she decided that I was telling the truth and that I was not going to ensnare her daughter with a huge net. She told me that a superintendent had referred her to Livingston and that while at first she had agreed, she now had changed her mind, her daughter was not bad, everybody had lied.

I tried to reach her; so did Mrs. Landsman. It was hopeless. We could not maintain a two-minute plateau of quiet calm before she became hysterical again. Finally, she left, irately dragging her daughter with her. The daughter had not said a word. I guess the superintendent made other plans. He had to. We could not keep a girl whose parent could not be reached, no matter how special we are, and the Board of Education does call us "special"—special because we serve girls no other regular day school wants or can handle, "regular" being equated with "normal" or "usual" or "typical." Livingston is the a-normal school. Special. Unusual. Atypical. Girls come because they are referred. No other school will have them. They stay because they want to.

In what other school can an angry girl sit at the principal's desk and write:

> Dr. Rothman
> Well Well
> What the hell
> the name ring a bell
> I used to call her hags
> and old bags
> But one of these days
> I must say
> I'm in Livingston
> to stay
> If I must go all the way
> and get along with her all day
> Well Well
> What the hell

In what other school can Martha smoke a cigar in the bathroom and feel that she kept her word at keeping to school regulations because all she promised me was not to smoke cigarettes in the bathroom?

There's logic to this line of thinking, and if I want to keep up with Martha, I have to think like her. I can't afford to think Board-of-Education, out-of-Teachers-College style. That's requisitioning trouble.

I learned this the day I had two appointments. One was at 9:30 in the morning with Miss Weng, a prospective arts and crafts teacher. The other was at 10 o'clock with a visiting woman psychiatrist.

At 9:30 a lady walked into my office, and before she could introduce herself, I welcomed her. But I thought, "Funny, I expected Miss Weng to be Chinese."

"Oh," Miss Weng said. "Is it all right to park my car in front of the building, or will I get a ticket?"

"You'll get a ticket," I said.

"Even with an M.D. license plate?" she asked.

And while I answered her, I thought, "Uh-huh, she's not Chinese, but her name is Chinese so she must be married to a Chinese and he must be a doctor if she had M.D. plates on her car."

So I went ahead with my interview. I asked her how long she had been working with aggressive children, what her educational philosophy was, what she said to a child who said "fuck" to her, and how she felt arts and crafts should be taught.

I must say she seemed rather evasive. Oh, well, I thought, this arts and crafts teacher who is married to a Chinese doctor doesn't have too much teaching experience.

And then at 9:45, my secretary ushered in a panting Miss Weng who had been delayed in the subway.

This was not an arts and crafts teacher I had interviewed. That was my early psychiatrist.

Agnes laughed when I told her the story. Agnes visits me regularly, although she left Livingston over five five years ago and is now almost twenty-two. The weaning process is a hard one. Agnes put it simply. "Growing up isn't so easy. Why couldn't they leave me in my little shell? It was a nice world."

"Because, Agnes," I explained, "I never heard of pregnancy being a state of permanency or school being forever."

"Everyone has to live on the outside?" Agnes demands, and to my nod, she adds, "When I finish growing up, I'll be ready to die."

But Agnes doesn't really want to die. She wants to be noticed. Not loved, she has given up hope of that. Not accepted—but seen.

"Here I am, see me," comes out of tumultuous thirteen-year-old Marie as "You're no better than me. Your shit is the same color as my shit."

When I told Marie that I was not impressed with the color of her speech, she muttered, "Go fuck your mother."

Joanne, who was quietly observing her, asked most innocently, "But why should Dr. Rothman want to do that?"

As Marie had no obvious answer, the matter was dropped. But Marie was definitely noticed. And she was pleased.

Poor Iona, however, when she first came to school was inadequately noticed. She reminded me of Brenda, her sister who also attended our school, and stupidly, I kept calling her Brenda.

When I apologized to Iona, she was magnanimously forgiving, "I ain't crying because you called me something else. I knew who I was," she said. But did she?

Does any girl who comes to Livingston? For she comes via one of four routes, from reform schools euphemistically labeled training schools, from mental hospitals, from home instruction, and from the regular schools from which she generally has been suspended. And she's troubled. She really doesn't believe she's

attractive or smart or worthwhile or beautiful or genuine—
sometimes even human.

Pat said, "I'm me. I'm an original." The trouble is that she
really doesn't believe it.

Linda dreamed of when she was born. She saw the doctor
hold her naked body upside down and slap her on the behind.
Said Linda to Mrs. Langness, her guidance counselor, "I
looked him straight in the eye and slapped him back." She
hasn't stopped slapping.

June expressed the nothingness when she said of her life,
"All that static for nothin."

The psychologists and psychiatrists call it a lack of a prime
sense of identity. And many of the girls show it not only by
their confusion and their anger, but by the way they cling
physically to adults. Iona, for instance, would frantically wrap
herself around a teacher's body. She practically crawled in. She
clung and touched and intermingled with the teacher's physical
presence. Other girls fight this tendency. They are fearful of
admitting their need to be part of another individual's life.
Hands off. They don't touch and are fearful of being touched.
But oh, how they want it and need it! Progress indeed when
Elaine, aloof, guarded, straight and distant, bent over me
and tenderly tightened my earring. She was truant for five
days afterward. The closeness frightened her. She couldn't yet
admit she wanted it or even needed it.

The girls communicate in silent ways. Oh, they are loud
enough. But they speak only of frustration. They don't go
beyond. And the words are limited, not just because girls don't
trust words, because people have lied to them so often, but
because they really don't know enough words to express their
rage and helplessness. If Dolores has trouble reading, "It's the
fuckin books' fault." If Ophelia misses a beat on the piano, "It's

the fuckin keys are stuck." If it rains, Audrey doesn't have a "fuckin kerchief." They feel helpless and inadequate, and after a while, the helplessness and inadequacy permeate all situations. The important, the nonimportant, home, mother, book, piano, rain. It's all the same. Everything and everyone is against them.

Margaret couldn't tell me in words how fearful she was of her desire to kill, so she brought in a knife. Not only because she didn't know the words, but because no one had ever listened before. No one.

Margaret was a chronic runaway from home. Her mother ran a numbers racket in a candy store. The store was constantly filled with strange men who came and went. Nights, the store was open until three and four in the morning, and Margaret had to stay in front while her mother played cards and became drunk in the back. Finally, her mother got annoyed that Margaret seemed unhappy enough to run away so often, so she brought her to court where a petition was carefully filed and the case was carefully heard in three or four—no, that's not fair—maybe seven or eight minutes. Margaret was clearly defined as a "person in need of supervision" and sent to the New York State Training School, "Upstate," where she was supposed to be "rehabilitated" and to live in a "therapeutic milieu" with other delinquent girls, who largely were counterparts of Margaret. Sure, Margaret was delinquent. The law says she was, even though the law didn't say anything about her mother, and sure, she needed—desperately needed—therapeutic living milieu where she could learn to understand her own feelings—learn that while her mother had problems of her own, problems which seriously affected her, Margaret need not succumb. She, Margaret, could make something of her life.

Instead, Margaret became angry at her cottage parent (cot-

tage jailer would be more accurate), and instead of therapy
and being able to talk out her crisis, Margaret was placed in
isolation, in a cell without bed or lavatory. Mattress and
blanket on the floor. That's all. The Training School trained, of
course. They neglected to ask, for what? Margaret was smart
and she learned—learned not to show that she was upset or had
problems or was unhappy. And so, "cured" of her upsetness,
she returned to the cottage she shared with fifteen or so other
girls. She further learned to be silent and to say only what was
expected. So, "cured of her rebellion," she returned to her
home and to us. But before her return, she wrote a letter that
could not be mailed:

Dear Someone:
    Just a few lines to let you know that I do not know who I am writing
this letter to. You know something, someone, I haven't wrote a letter
like this to no one but you so you know how I feel. A very simple nut
like me can feel for a really no one at all. So why don't you stop trying
to pretend that I am a nut writing a letter to a no one at all. So I have
to stop being a nut now. Someone, I am going to close this letter with
all the none feeling I feel for you. Now, someone, now that you know
how I feel about you, why don't sometime in the future, you find a
place in the King's Castle for me?

    Margaret, no one listened. No one understood, certainly not
the court, that when Margaret ran away from home, she wasn't
running away from something, she was trying to run to something. The King's Castle? When Margaret fought other girls,
threatened teachers, used obscenities, she was crying for salva-
tion. At the Training School, she got an empty room, a bed,
and a blanket. And from the Traning School—where? Home,
of course, to the same conditions, the same feelings.

But this time, no neighborhood school. The authorities at the Training School recognized that she could never make it. She had learned to conform—but nothing else had changed. And Margaret would be more upset, more unhappy, and thankfully, more rebellious. She was not going to give up making someone listen.

The Training School referred her to us, and we took her. How unhappy she was—and how difficult—one of the angriest girls we have ever had. She was typical of the girls who return from the Training School, clearly more damaged upon coming out than upon going in. Survival at the Training School is a clear indication that she had found a way to survive, and the way is often homosexual. Perhaps it is a temporary way, but it is a pattern that sometimes becomes confirmed, if not entrenched. The girls coming from the Training School are among the saddest we see. They are so untrusting. Who can blame them?

Margaret trusted no one at first. But she did begin to smile and even laugh, particularly when she met Jeanette, a girl who made us grit our teeth even while we laughed.

Jeanette was a mixed-up girl with scope.

"That's a fine psychological diagnosis," Miss Miller, the reading teacher, told me after I described her in just that way.

"Would it be better," I asked, "if I quoted the psychiatrist who felt that her lack of 'ego structure strongly suggests schizophrenia'?"

"Go back to mixed-up, with scope," said Miss Miller.

It wasn't Jeanette's fault that no school could help her. Jeanette couldn't help it if teachers were so unreasonable that they didn't appreciate having their hair snipped off at the edges. Jeanette couldn't help it if the principal was so mean she expected her to leave the building during a fire drill. The Board of Education, of course, had no choice—they couldn't provide Jeanette with a school all her own, so they had to provide her with a home instruction teacher. Nine years' worth. For nine years, the Board of Education assigned a teacher to go to her home weekly. Then she came to Livingston and she met her match—a school with scope.

Jeanette's grandmother, with whom Jeanette lived, came to see me one morning, very irate because Jeanette had come home from school the night before at nine o'clock with swollen feet.

I immediately sent for Jeanette, who told me that two days ago she had met a teacher with green eyes and a cat's face who stopped her outside of school and told her that Jeanette's name was on a list. The teacher told her to be in school the next morning at seven o'clock.

"What's the teacher's name, and what list?" I asked.

But Jeanette didn't know. All she knew was that she arrived at seven yesterday morning and met three Spanish-speaking girls and the teacher with green eyes and a cat's face. They all went upstairs to the fourth floor, where they did arithmetic and writing and read a book about sex.

I stopped her again. "You read a book about sex? Why?"

"The teacher wanted to know what I read and to tell her the facts of life."

And did you?"

"I'm too young to know them," Jeanette said primly.

"How come you came home at nine at night with swollen feet?"

"Because," Jeanette explained, "she made us take our shoes off and dance until twelve o'clock noon."

"What happened then?"

"She sent us out with a yellow pass to buy hero sandwiches for lunch."

"And no one in the whole building knew this was going on? No teacher on the floor saw you?"

Jeanette insisted they didn't.

I pursued it further. "And then what happened?"

"We danced some more until half past two, and then the teacher took us to the subway and we rode on the subway for about an hour, and then we came back and danced until eight at night."

"But, Jeanette," I insisted, "there are no lights in the building at night. The electricity is cut off every night."

For a minute, I thought I had her. But my faith in her was restored quickly.

"We danced by candlelight," she said.

I looked at her grandmother's face. I knew I could never convince her that I didn't have a teacher on staff who had green eyes and a cat's face. And, of course, we had candles. Doesn't every school? I threw in my mighty bolt.

"What did you do, Jeanette, when we had the fire drill right after lunch?" I asked her.

"Oh," Jeanette said smugly, "we all left the building."

"You and the teacher with the cat's face and green eyes and the three Spanish-speaking girls?"

"Yes," she said, and corrected me nicely, "the teacher with the green eyes and the cat's face."

"But, Jeanette, we had no fire drill."

"Of course we did," said Jeanette, "that's how come my feet got swollen walking up and down the stairs so much."

So—

I called the assistant principal, who stated we had had no fire drill.

And I called the guidance counselor, who verified that we had had no fire drill.

And I called the secretary, who swore we had had no fire drill.

And I called the custodian, who affidavited that we had had no fire drill.

And I called the custodian's helper, who notarized that we had had no fire drill.

But Jeanette stuck to her story. "You're all storying on me," she cried. Her grandmother apparently agreed.

We all enjoyed Jeanette. She was so creative, as indeed are all the girls who have been for years on home instruction. They have to be, to manage to make a career out of having personalized teachers.

Phyllis, for instance, straight from six years of home instruction, enjoyed crying incessantly every time girls accused her of talking about them. Yet this did not stop her from talking about them.

"She said," or "That girl said," or "That girl I don't know her name said," or "That girl's I-don't-know-her-name brother said," was Phyllis's conversational style.

Henrietta, who didn't go along with all this "hesaying-she-saying" and who advised me to suspend Phyllis after the tenth girl in a week had hit her, said the trouble with Phyllis was "she had her attitude."

Phyllis didn't deny the fight. But she denied that she had her attitude. She said it was fate she had. In a letter of explanation to me, she wrote:

I am a girl of cause. And like to be Friendly. But I say things to Others that are not to friendly. I don't mean any Harm but they take it that way. My next probem is that I talk a lot and sometime the Wrong things come out.

The wrong things were frequent. But the amazing thing was that while Phyllis said many wrong things, she couldn't extend the privilege to others. "Don't curse at me, girl," she once screamed at Jeanette, "I have virgin ears."

"That's all you got that's virgin," Jeanette answered.

"You callin me a whore?"

It took several men teachers to separate them.

Jeanette later went to a treatment center. Her fantasy life, which she could not separate from the reality of her life, made it impossible for her to function either at home or at school. And to get a girl into a hospital when she needs hospital treatment is a great success for us, although some foolish people consider it a defeat. They refuse to accept the fact that we cannot be the panacea for everyone, and that when a girl needs intensive psychiatric treatment in a closed setting for a period of time, we should be able to see that she gets it. We do—no small feat, because hospitals are reluctant, all of them, to accept school referrals; even reluctant to accept a girl who attempts suicide, or is obsessed with it, because suicide under the age of eighteen is not legally a crime in New York State and treatment therefore cannot be mandated by court. The girl has to go for treatment voluntarily. If she cannot be motivated toward treatment, none is offered.

Our mobility is high if we are to give each girl the help she needs, and when Jeanette went into the hospital, Lottie came out. Even after her release, Lottie was still very sick—too sick for speech.

She had first been admitted to a psychiatric hospital when she was nine. Although the psychiatrist's diagnosis was childhood schizophrenia, her mother took her out of the hospital against medical advice. Lottie was then admitted to a public school.

She was, however, extremely fearful of attending school and

became a chronic truant. Accordingly, she was placed on home instruction. Lottie's emotional problems, however, did not subside. She was an extremely fearful child; even people whom she knew well frightened her. She cried when relatives and close friends came to visit. She was soon re-admitted to the State Hospital, where she remained for over a year. Upon her release, she was offered a chance to attend another school, but again Lottie could not muster up the strength to attend. Her old anxieties returned. She was placed on home instruction again, but her anxieties were too great. She could not sleep, could not eat, and within a year was returned to the hospital. This time she was released within six months and was admitted to the sixth grade of her neighborhood school. She attended, much to the sorrow of the teachers and her classmates. She fought constantly with teacher and children and had severe temper tantrums. She was defiant and refused to attempt any academic work, mostly because she was ashamed that she could not read and could do arithmetic only on a second-grade level.

Lottie's ego was nil. Her controls were nonexistent. One day while her mother was marketing, Lottie poured a kettle of soup on a bedspread, smeared linens with cosmetics, and put black paint on the furniture. In desperation Lottie's mother rushed her again to the hospital. This time she remained over a year. When she was released, she was fourteen and the hospital felt that she needed Livingston, not a trial at a regular school.

And she made it. Despite her problems, she made it. She began to speak, began to read, began to relate.

Not so Lorraine, who came at the same time. She had been suspended from four schools because of lack of self-control, fights with classmates and teachers, writing improper things all over desks and chairs, wandering through halls, vandalism. She was diagnosed by the assistant superintendent as "very nervous

and jumpy." Furthermore he made the following recommendation: "Lorraine needs a complete comprehensive medical
examination and possible encephalogram. She is suffering from
malnutrition and severe emotional disability. She should be
placed in a residential treatment school with special services.
Please explore brain damage possibilities."

The superintendent must have thought we had the facilities
to do these things. We don't, but we accepted Lorraine because
not to have accepted her would have left only the Training
School, and Lorraine needed observation, diagnosis and treatment, not punishment. And while we are only a day school and
not a residential one, partial treatment is better than no treatment. We are not a hospital; we cannot explore brain damage
possibilities ourselves. We can only refer and nag every hospital
and agency in New York to see that it gets done. Eventually,
we were able to get Lorraine what she needed—placement in a
treatment center away from home. Eureka!

It made sense for Lorraine to attend Livingston, but I
could never figure out why Kathy came to us. There wasn't
a thing wrong with her outside of the fact that she was about
six months old emotionally, counting from the time of con-
ception.

Kathy drooled, dripped, dribbled, gurgled, and gargled. Her
hair went in one direction, her toes in another. Her clothes
seemed to have a will of their own. They apparently had the
urge to travel—mostly off her. She went in twelve directions all
at once. And she relished saying "No," followed by the refrain,
"make me."

"Kathy, please go to your class."

"No."

"Kath-ee."

"Make me."

"Kathy, sit down, please."

"No."

"Kath-eeee."

"Make me."

It became our song.

"Kathy," said Mrs. Gray, the assistant principal, "get out of this room immediately and go to the office. You don't belong here because you're causing trouble."

"No," said Kathy.

The Kath-eeeing didn't help, so Mrs. Gray called me on the intercom. I knew I wouldn't budge her. I turned to Agnes, who was visiting, and she went to fetch her. In a few minutes, a docile Kathy came trotting into my office following Agnes.

I looked at Agnes in admiration.

"Nothing to it," she said. "I told her to move her fucking carcass out of the fucking room and into the fucking office."

Kathy beamed and agreed.

Well, there is communication, and then again, there is communication.

I always thought of Kathy as a neonate—a child unborn. Loretta, on the other hand, was merely ungrown, and not nearly as overtly charming or as seltzery. She had been transferred seven times before she anchored at Livingston.

Each time a new school was tried, it was with the hope that she would like them better and they would like her better than the one before. It never happened that way.

She was pleasant enough. She'd only say to her teacher, "So help me I wanta kick your butt in." She never did.

Loretta was real tough, man. She never talked, man, unless she said "man." But she really never talked. She fenced—she surveyed—she sized up. She never committed herself. She was tentative.

"Why are you coming in late, Loretta?" I would ask.

"Why you wanta know, man?"

"Because this is a school, and I have a right to know why you're late."

"If you got rights, man, then I got rights."

"Oh, come on, Loretta, all I'm asking is why you're late."

"And, man, I'm not tellin."

"So I'll call your mother and find out where you've been."

"Don't call my mother, goddamn it, man, and don't write her, either."

"Is that a threat, Loretta?"

"If you say so."

"I don't say it is. I don't say it's not. I don't know."

"Well, man, if you don't know it, I don't know it. You're principal, ain't ya?"

And all that, to find out later, via the radio, that there was a serious subway tie-up on all lines.

Loretta never relinquished her boundaries, never talked of herself, her friends, her family. In a rare moment of real feeling she said she never got close to anybody, especially her family, because she couldn't stop them from doing what they were doing and what they were doing was bad. That's as far as we got, although we knew that Loretta's brother and sister were both homosexuals and both on drugs.

But not Loretta. She's still fighting. At least, she's coming to school every day. Well, every other day.

Loretta put it this way, when I asked her what she did when she didn't come to school . . .

"You think I use pot, man?"

"No."

"You think I use reefers, then?"

"No."

"You think I'm that sick, man?"

"No."

"You should know better, man. You should know I haven't gone up yet."

No. She hasn't gone up yet. Neither have the others. They haven't given up fighting, the way many of their parents have. They are not yet overwhelmed. They are not yet defeated. We go on from there to find hope and build lives.

chapter three

The Teachers: The Acceptable and the Unacceptable

OR

God Save Us from the Teacher-Training Colleges

At the end of her first year at Livingston, Miss Feldman wrote her love letter to the school:

GO KNOW (End term thoughts)

Who would have thought I'd ever buy a kid an ice cream pop for learning the meaning of a word . . . who would have thought that "bad" kids were scared kids . . . who would have dreamed that school could be synonymous with love and caring . . . who would have believed that so much laughter could spill out in the very midst of so many tears . . . who ever would have thought that a skinny girl called "Super-Chicken" would lift me off my feet and carry me into my room . . . who ever thought that a school could run a store . . . who would have dared hope to find an administration that didn't have "Ostrich Syndrome" . . . who ever thought there were so many ways to say fuck . . . who would have guessed that ministration meant getting your period, and "being bad" was good . . . who would have

thought I would enroll my cat Rufus in a school for girls . . . who
could have known Constance would ask me to marry her . . . who
would have thought I'd stay up late every night for a week to finish
Renee's birthday present on time . . . who would have believed someone could call me old and fat without my needing resuscitation . . . who
would have thought that a guidance counselor really can guide . . .
who would have thought with over 60 days' absence last year that I
would come to school even with a fever this year . . . who would have
guessed that teaching art would be one of the least important things
I do with the girls . . . who would have thought that one's anecdotals
are really read . . . and who would ever have guessed there was so
much to learn . . .

And so (as the doctor said to Portnoy), *Now vee may
perhaps to begin. Yes?*

The teachers who succeed at Livingston permit themselves to
be used in many ways. What they give to our girls in the way of
acceptance, appreciation and affection, is more important than
the subjects they teach. They themselves—their sensitivities,
perceptiveness, relationships—are the tools with which they
work.

Unfortunately, I really have no definitive way of knowing, in
advance of hiring them, who can develop this technique of
teaching. I trust to interview and luck. Previous experience and
qualifications, I have found, often have little relationship to
whether or not a teacher will succeed at Livingston. Some
people with doctorate degrees and extensive clinical and teaching experience have failed here; others with the same qualifications and experiences have not. Still others, recently graduated
from college and with no previous teaching experience, have
succeeded, and others in the same category have not. I do not
always know how I am going to get them, but teachers I seek

must be overtly impervious to shock, receptive to emotions freely expressed, and willing to stand the pain of learning.

My interviews therefore are often painful for the applicant.

"Tell me why you want to teach in this particular school, Mr. C.?" I asked.

If he had said because it was within walking distance of his home, as some rather unfeeling teachers have, I wouldn't have bothered to continue. But he didn't. He thought for a moment. I liked his taking the time to think.

"Because I want to contribute to society."

"How can you contribute here?"

"Teach deprived children like these about history and culture, give them something they don't have."

"What do you have, Mr. C., that they don't?" I asked.

"Well—" he found it difficult to answer. "It's like I have so much, this country has given me so much, my education, and I want to pass it on—I owe it to, well, I guess, I owe it to history."

"History is dead, Mr. C. You mean, you owe your good fortune to dead people? You paying back?"

It was a bit unfair, but I sensed layers and layers of guilt. I switched my line of questioning, with really nothing specific in mind, just to give him time to recover. As it was, my question hit another sore area.

"Are you married, Mr. C.?" I asked.

"Well—yes."

It was an odd way of answering. I picked him up on it.

"You sound as if you're unhappily married," I interpreted.

He blushed. I knew that blush would definitely make teaching here difficult.

"Well, to tell you the truth, my wife doesn't want me to teach. She wants me to go back into the business I was in—"

"What was that?" I asked.

"I was a salesman for a paper concern, but—" he smiled ruefully, "it wasn't for me."

I felt sorry for him. He was a man groping to find himself. And I liked him, but it became clear to me as he spoke that I could not hire him. He was relating to me as a patient, and I was relating to him as his therapist. He was too bound up with his own problems to become free of them even during the time he would be teaching. If I hired him, the focus would definitely be on him, not on the girls, and that would be unfair to the girls. I needed teachers with better defenses than that.

I find them.

To my question, "Why do you want to teach aggressive adolescents?" Mrs. Murrain answered simply, "I guess because I like them, I don't know why, but I do. And they seem to like me. I really don't seem to have much difficulty in the class-room."

"Why is that?" I asked. "Maybe you have the secret."

"Well, I don't know about that," she laughed, "but I enjoy working with them, and that's probably why it works."

"What do you do when a child calls you a mother-fucker?" I asked abruptly.

I watched her closely. She didn't bat an eyelash.

"Well, I suppose I survive," she answered.

I knew she would, too. I could always teach a teacher what to say to a girl, but I can't teach that teacher how to survive.

"How do you feel about children, Mr. Henwood?" I asked.

"I like them," he answered simply.

"How about love?" I asked him.

"I have to be honest," he answered. "There have been some children I have loved, and there have been a few that I have found it difficult to like. I know the fault was probably mine,

but something about them—well, they just made it very difficult for me—"

I liked his answer. It was honest. Teachers who gush about
their love of all children are liars. They don't love all children.
They can't possibly. And they shouldn't. They would be emotional wrecks. But they can appreciate all children, and they
can enjoy all children, and they can like all children. Well, almost all. All is asking the impossible, simply because we are
human beings. Appreciating, enjoying, and liking often lead to
love. Love is the end product of the teaching process, not the
beginning.

I remembered conferring recently with a Board of Education
official (Board of Education officials always confer, they never
talk), and Miss F. looked at me and said, "You know, you
really thrive on these kids. Anyone else would be desperate.
But you enjoy it, you love them. You should pay the Board of
Education for having given you the job."

I disagreed with her, of course, about paying the Board of
Education, even though I often misplace my paycheck, to the
unhappiness of my secretary. I am certain the Freudians could
clearly diagnose my aberration, but the feeling I have that
school is fun and children are fun to be with should be shared
by all of us who teach. It is gratifying to believe that what we
are teaching makes a difference. Miss F.'s statement says a
damning lot about the attitudes of most of the Board's officialdom. Desperate? Why? Unfortunately, of course, I know why.
In the regular schools, teachers can't teach—that is, if they
know what teaching is in the first place. Classes are large.
Educators are hypocritical. Creativity is stifled. And the kids
are fighting back. They have inquiring minds. They want the
teachers to open up the world to them by leading them to ask
the meaningful questions; they do not want teachers to supply

answers to questions they do not have the need to ask. Yet this is by and large what teachers are doing today.

And they are doing it because this is still the way they are being taught to teach at the teacher-training colleges, particularly those colleges that like to think they are training teachers or reach our so-called "disadvantaged youth," whatever that is.

The teacher-trainers at the colleges generally infuriate me. I have met and worked with many. I am at the point where I no longer wish to work with any, for they seem to come to their jobs with little understanding of the children in the classroom or the problems of the teacher. They are far removed emotionally from the children they are training the teachers to teach, and being far removed, they do not understand or appreciate them. If these teacher-trainers are personally honest, they spend their time learning about themselves, their own prejudices, and their own preconceptions. They spend time coming to the conclusion that their lives and the lives of many children are far apart, and that they really have little to offer a beginning teacher in the way of training. They have little to offer because they are in the world of the adult, and their selective college milieu is totally different from the world of children in public school.

College personnel sometimes admit their deficiencies. They spend years on themselves, on self-therapy, on changing their attitudes, on learning that their value system and their realm of experience are totally removed from the children. I have no taste, however, for their breast-baring and their self-immolation. It is time-consuming and unproductive. They have little to offer but self-involvement. They call it self-growth. Self-indulgence is more like it, because they should have come to their jobs better prepared to begin with. The teachers they are training are closer to the children in age and emotional experience and often know more than their professors.

Yet the education courses still go on—the lesson plan, motivations, inductive reasoning, and "plateaus of learning" courses. And once in a while the teacher-trainers come up with some new and dramatic finding. Let children write about themselves. Discard old-fashioned textbooks. The trouble is, their findings are always years behind what good teachers are doing anyway.

The result is the mass-produced teacher liberal, the middle-class teacher—who is doing penance for poverty, discrimination, and inequality—and in a sense continues to perpetuate the very values he decries.

Mr. H. was a product of one of these teacher-training programs. I had hired him. He was one of my mistakes.

He came into my office after he had been a few months at Livingston and wearily sank into a chair. He seemed depressed.

"I think Grace is pregnant. The other girls are talking."

"Oh, I hope not," I cried, "oh, I hope not. Not only has she come such a long way, but she's such a thin little girl. She's not physically well, at all."

"Yes," he answered. "It's too bad, because she certainly has improved. Well, she'll have the baby, I suppose, and come right back. You know how these people are—like peasants."

I couldn't believe I was hearing right. I thought I knew Mr. H. I had spoken to him many times about social issues, but I had no idea that underneath his apparently admirable social ideals he relegated the girls to the abyss of "these people."

"How can you say that, Mr. H.?" I asked. "If your fifteen-year-old daughter were pregnant, would you call her 'these people'?"

He was abashed. "You know I didn't mean it like that."

"Well, how did you mean it, then?" I asked. "If your daughter were pregnant, wouldn't she have her baby and come back to school? What would you do?"

He was extremely uncomfortable. "Are you saying I'm prejudiced?" he blurted out.

"You tell me," I answered. "If it were your daughter, if you were teaching in Scarsdale or Great Neck and a girl became pregnant, would you have made the same remark?"

I think he really knew the answer, but he couldn't face up to it, because Mr. H. considered himself an active liberal. But it hurt for him to look deep. I found out he couldn't do it consistently.

He was a good teacher, he was really interested in the girls, and he was able to relate to them most of the time, but every so often, I began to realize, the real self he was hiding from his consciousness and the world was going to come through.

Miss B.'s problem was essentially the same, an inability to accept the girls as equals. There was one difference: Mr. H. was able to accept aggressive behavior and keep it from exploding. Miss B. was not. She suffered.

She was sweet and charming and quiet, but soon after she came, an expression of pain seemed constantly in her eyes. If a girl cursed, the words seemed to pierce her flesh. She told me that if it made a girl feel better to hit her, she wouldn't mind being hit.

"Oh, come now," I told her. "Don't be foolish. I'm not looking for a saint or a martyr. The girls don't need that burden to bear. They don't want to be able to hit a teacher. They want to know that you care enough about them to stop them. If you don't care about them, you'll let them do what they want."

Being principal has some very distinct advantages, I found. I could talk a lot without interruption from teachers. Miss B. listened, but she really didn't understand. She had that bewildered look.

The girls seemed sincerely pleased at first with Miss B.'s fragility and delicate imbalance.

"She's real nice," said Kathy, "but it's not nice the way the girls talk in front of her."

"Well," I said, "they talk that way in front of me, too."

"Oh, you," she said disparagingly. "You like static."

Miss B. didn't. What's more, she was afraid. The teachers found themselves protecting her. It was hard not to, she seemed so sensitive. I found teachers keeping difficult girls from going to her class, chastising girls for cursing in front of her. The men teachers, particularly, were extremely chivalrous; and the more they protected her, the more she relied upon them to keep the immediate area around her conflict-free.

It became apparent very soon that she was feeding upon the girls.

I found her sobbing in her classroom.

"What happened?" I asked. I thought she might be ill.

"It's awful," she said, "how cruel they are to each other."

"Not really," I answered. "They are capable of great friendships, too. Don't listen to the words."

"I'm not," she sighed, "I learned that, but I saw a fight downstairs. Mrs. Gray was downstairs and stopped it, but they're so—so—" she looked for a word, "so vicious."

"They're vicious when they fight," I said, "but tell me, is there another way to fight when you're fighting?"

She waved her hands helplessly. "I don't know. It's just that I want to do something to help—and—I—can't."

"You could have stayed downstairs and helped the girls through it. Instead, you ran away."

She was startled at my answer. It had never occurred to her to stay.

"The trouble is," I told her, "you're using the girls to feel sorry for yourself, when they should be using you to stop them from fighting. It's as simple as that."

"I know I should have stayed," she began to sob, "but things hurt me so deeply—"

"And you hurt more than the rest of us?" I really didn't expect an answer, but she gave one.

"Oh, no—it's not that, but you and the others are used to it and—"

"What you're saying is we're hard-hearted."

"Not really," she whined.

"Yes, really," I contradicted. "You seem to miss the point, Miss B. We hurt, too, but we hurt enough to become angry and to do something about it. We don't just cry. You hurt only to cry. It's not good enough."

I left her to mull that over. I also didn't want to show her how angry I was getting. I didn't enjoy being called callous. Somewhere in her life, in her teacher training, Miss B. should have learned that sentimentality is easy.

Meanwhile, I had a real situation to contend with. Girls really did not want to go to Miss B.'s classroom for typing.

Olivia complained to me, "How come you can't say a little old curse word by accident in her class?"

And Pia agreed, "Can I help it if my ears hear it and my mouth says it, by accident?"

"She don't like us, that's what," Olivia stated, and Pia agreed.

Later, Lavinia cried to me, "Who she think she is? Better than me?"

They were right. She didn't like them. She did think she was better than they. Underneath her apparent receptiveness was a real rejection of their language, their behavior, of them.

"Fuck you," Margaret cried in her classroom after Miss B. had insisted that Margaret could not leave the room.

This was the first time anyone had directly spoken to her this way.

"Don't talk that way to me—"

Margaret needed no further motivation.

"I'll say it again, fuck you, teacher."

The other girls began to jeer, and Miss B.'s mouth began to tremble.

"You're vulgar."

"You're a fucked-up fuckin fuck." It was as if all the obscenities had piled up inside her and could no longer be contained.

"Don't talk that way to me," Miss B.'s voice rose considerably.

"Mother-fucker!" Margaret screamed.

"Don't you dare speak about my mother!" Miss B. was screaming almost as loud as Margaret. "At least I had one to care about me and teach me how to behave!"

Margaret's whole world crumbled. The school she had counted on was no longer sanctuary. She started toward Miss B., but the other girls intervened.

"Cool it, Margaret, don't make Dr. Rothman suspend you."

"Go downstairs, Margaret, come on."

With the help of the girls, Margaret was able to contain herself and report herself to the office.

Miss B. came down later, considerably shaken. Until she had heard her own words, Miss B. had had no real understanding of the meaning of her tears or of how she really felt.

It was up to her now to face herself. She couldn't do it and left before the term was over.

Mr. H. was white, Miss B. was black.

Both were unacceptable because they were unaccepting of our girls and unable to relate to them on equal terms.

Some black nationalist groups feel that only black teachers can relate to and understand black children. Concommitantly, some white groups feel that only white teachers should teach white children. Still others use economics and social class as the base line. The middle-class teacher, they feel, cannot relate to the children of the poor. If we carried the concept to its logical conclusion, we would match every teacher with every child, color for color, tint for tint, economic class for economic class.

If we carry the concept further, we come to absurdity. Only physically ill teachers should teach sick children in hospitals. And who can better understand a mentally ill child than a mentally ill teacher? What about drug addiction and homosexuality? Should the teacher be what the child is in order to understand, treat, and help him learn? No, it's too easy to take this line and too damaging, because it negates the basic condition of humanness that we all have and that teachers must be trained to find within themselves. Call it developing the skills of being empathic, of establishing rapport, of understanding human behavior and dynamics, call it what you will, teachers must learn to find it before they become teachers. Unfortunately, it is not taught in colleges because so few professors are able to teach it.

One day when I was wearing a gold necklace and earrings, as always happened, my skin turned black where the jewelry touched it. Ophelia pointed it out to Virginia and laughed, "Hey, instant black."

Virginia answered, "She's black like us, that's how come she knows what you're goin to do."

"Not instant black or permanent white," I replied, "just chronic human."

"All right," Miss Miller said one day, "so we all have our prejudices, we have to face it, not necessarily against black kids or Puerto Rican kids or white kids—but maybe against aggressive kids, or ones who hit teachers, or ones who have lost their front teeth, or some such stupid thing—"

"Right," I agreed, "and we have to know we have them, if we have them, and know why they're there and know how they cripple us, and work around that knowledge, or we have no business being teachers."

"You're right," she agreed, "but my God, it's painful." She inhaled on her cigarette deeply and said, "Why don't they teach us these things in teachers' colleges, why don't they teach us to *listen* to kids? That's what we do here all the time, listen and try to understand what they really mean."

I agreed, and reminded her of the sign Mrs. Landsman had in her office, "Listen to what I mean, not what I say."

We all listen to the meaning, and listening we continue to learn; because life is movement, and learning moves one, we all change constantly, teachers and girls. Teaching and learning are opposite sides of the same coin. I have learned from the girls, from the rigid institutions of the status quo, from teachers, from parents, from the total environment. Each day I change because each day I try to learn. This I firmly believe, when the principal ceases to learn, so will the teachers, and so will the children. A school must be a place of learning where learning takes place as a dynamic, creative interrelationship of people and ideas from top to bottom.

Phyllis and Geda came up to me in the lunchroom. Geda grinned. "We was just talking about you and Mrs. Gray."

Phyllis interrupted with "We was not talking, we was speaking about you and Mrs. Gray."

I could almost feel the light blinking in my head. I realized that I was going to learn something new, because Phyllis was making a fine distinction.

"Yeah," Geda agreed, "every time I do something wrong, Mrs. Gray says to me, 'Geda, I'm disappointed in you.'"

"And you say the same to me," Phyllis interrupted again.

"You and Mrs. Gray like us," Geda said, obviously startled at her own sudden insight.

"Yeah—" Phyllis agreed, equally startled.

And we all laughed at the joy of our mutual understanding.

Yes, they were right. They were speaking about Mrs. Gray and me. They were liking us for the moment. If they had been talking about us, they might have said angrily, "She makes me sick," or threateningly, "Later for her, bitch," or braggingly, "You shoulda seen the way I laid her out."

Speaking, however, implied approval. A begrudging "She's all right" is speaking. A complimentary "She's becoming to herself today" is speaking. A sympathetic "You sick?" is speaking.

The next time an unhappy girl comes to me and says, "So-and-so is talking about me," I will understand her a little better. I will relate a little more quickly. I have learned. And learning is enjoying, both for girls and for teachers. Many of us enjoy every minute of school, or most of the minutes, because the doubts do come in. The desperateness of not being able to comfort a girl whose mother has just killed her father, the anger of not being able to keep a girl from prostitution, the defeat of not being able to stop a drug-addicted street society from slowly encompassing a girl—these are our agonies.

But there are compensations also.

"I don't know, I'll call you right back." Iona and Ophelia came into the office just as I was hanging up the telephone on my mother, who wanted to know if I could take her to her doctor's office that evening or the following morning.

Iona turned toward me accusingly.

"Teachers supposed to know everything."

"I am?" I answered. "Since when did God resign?"

Ophelia, who by this time had looked over my office and read everything on my desk, said, "That's what I admire about Dr. Rothman. She lets everyone see her mistakes." She picked up a letter of complaint addressed to me and began to read it aloud.

"Yeah," Iona laughed, "and she makes lots of mistakes. Look at that wastepaper basket."

"Stupid, that's me," I said. "But that's a part of learning. You can't learn without making mistakes. So, what's so bad about starting off stupid, if you end up wiser?"

"That's right," agreed Ophelia. "You gotta use your brains."

I turned to Iona. "What's the most powerful weapon you have?" I asked.

"You mean a hat pin?" Ophelia answered.

"No."

"A knife?" Iona asked.

"No," Ophelia answered, "a gun is better than a knife. You gotta get close with a knife—but a gun—"

"Neither," I said. "Your brain. You can think. Somebody's brain thought up the idea of a gun and a knife and all the weapons in the world."

"That's right," Ophelia agreed.

"So your brain is your best weapon," I continued. "It can even keep you out of trouble."

They both agreed.

Of one thing the girls are certain. I can outthink, outcurse, outmaneuver any girl in the school. The Lord knows—and the girls certainly do—I can't outfight them. So maybe brains are good for something after all. Knowledge of this gives the girls a new respect for learning.

Anyone who thinks this is not teaching doesn't know what teaching is. And often the professionals don't!

I remember walking away from a meeting with a principal of a boys' special school.

"Listen," he said, "I took this kid into my office and I said to him, 'Okay, you want to see who is boss, I'll show you who is boss.' I took off my jacket, told him to take off his, and I knocked the hell out of him. He was a big kid, too, but you can't reason with them. They've got to learn you mean business. It has to be man-to-man, otherwise they won't respect you."

I wasn't really shocked. I know that the public schools are full of people who are incompetent, ignorant, unconcerned. Frustrated was more like it. I was frustrated and sick. Going to conferences is like reheating vomit.

I have better things to do with my time, like working with the girls themselves. Working with them and accepting their feelings are the basis of whatever success we have. We never argue with feelings.

"I'm cold," Eva complained to me as she came into my office.

At first I denied her feeling and acted like all the teachers she must have had before me. "But it's warm in here," I said.

"I feel cold," she insisted.

I stopped myself from telling her that the radiator was fully opened. How silly could I be? I could not argue with how she felt. Her feeling was right for her, as mine was for me. Her reality and mine were simply not the same. I had to recognize that she is the greatest expert in the world on her own feelings, as I am about mine.

Sometimes, of course, feelings become confused. What we consider to be hatred is really love. What we may feel as chills may really be a fever. Emotions, therefore, often need to be sifted out before a remedy can be applied. Therapists, and teachers are certainly therapists, must be very certain to analyze the symptoms and sensations accurately before intervention. We accept feelings, and we share feelings, and we often feel compelled to intervene when the circumstances are such that not intervening is an act of criminality.

We intervened when Lucy told us that her father was seducing her; we intervened when Linda told us she was shut out of her house while her mother practiced prostitution. We intervened when Enid's father brutally beat her and broke her nose. These opportunities are rare, and intervention often is impossible in the City of New York—with the civil rights of parents to mishandle their children almost sacrosanct. Most of the time, however, we need not intervene drastically. Accepting a girl's feelings about herself and her life is often therapy enough. She begins to accept herself and later to analyze her feelings for herself and to intervene for herself. She changes, even if the situation does not. How terrible, though, that often it is the situation that should be changed, not the individual.

When Berenice came rushing into my office screaming, "I'll kick Mr. S.'s cold-blooded ass in, see if I don't," and then rushed out, presumably to do it, I heard the hurt. She was one of the few girls the others called "outa her mind." She would never jump rope with them, nor share candy, nor smoke with them in the yard. She never swapped clothes with girls, and she never, but never, let another girl wear her blue coat, trimmed with red binding and punctuated with brass buttons. This is most unusual, for the girls generally swap easily, anything from wristwatches to shoes. But Berenice's coat never left her body, no matter how hot it was. It was as if letting go of her coat, putting it in the closet, or permitting the teacher to hold it, was relinquishing a bit of her own identity.

I had to run faster than she. I waylaid her on the stairway. I was puffing audibly, and tentatively, gently, I touched her on the arm. She did not shake me off, so I let my hand stay there, and we stood silent for a few moments.

"What you want?" she asked angrily.

"Good God, I can't even breathe," I told her, " and you want me to answer? Let me get my breath first." I needed time to study her mood, to know in what direction I should go.

"Look," I finally said, "it's cold here on the stairway and I want a cup of coffee. Come on down to the office where we can talk and have coffee."

"Don't want none," she grumbled.

"Well, if you won't come, I won't be able to tell you that Mr. S. gets on my nerves. Did he get on your nerves today, too?"

"Yeah," she smiled.

I turned and walked down. She started to follow.

"He's a mess," I went on.

"Yeah."

I sensed a bond between us. It was what I had hoped for, but wasn't sure I could achieve. Berenice was so unpredictable.

We were down at the office.

I poured a cup of coffee from the percolator we keep going constantly right outside my office, and she followed me inside.

"Want some?" she shoved a bag of chocolate-covered pea-nut-butter crackers at me.

"No, thanks," I said, without much thought.

She became angry. "It ain't got no faggots in it."

"Oh, Berenice, stop fighting," I answered. "No, of course it doesn't have maggots in it. I didn't think it did. Anyway, the word is maggots, not faggots. Maggots are bugs. Faggots are fairies."

"I know," she mumbled.

"Anyway," I said, "I changed my mind. They look delicious, so just for you, I'll break my diet."

I accepted a handful of the chocolate peanut-butter crackers. My sigh was inward. All those high-calorie chocolate-coated peanut-butter crackers! I would have to starve the rest of the day to compensate. But Berenice needed me to take her offering. I was only fighting overweight; Berenice was fighting rejection of her entire self.

"You miserable, wretched, awful kid, you," I said as I munched my second cracker. "Here am I getting fat while you eat and eat and stay so thin and pretty. I hate kids like you."

Berenice laughed. She felt wonderful. I had entered her world of insults and ended up by complimenting her. If I had been entirely accepting, totally complimentary, she couldn't have accepted it; it would have been too overwhelming. She would have mistrusted me. Later on, much, much later, I will be able to be openly complimentary, and she will be ready and able to absorb it.

It was her turn to comfort me.

"You don't gotta go on a diet," she said, "You got a flat behind."

"Sure," I answered, "but it's the other places that aren't so flat that I worry about."

She contemplated me silently.

Finally, I took a cue from her and abruptly changed the conversation.

"Do you like the school, Berenice?"

"I don't mind it."

That was praise indeed.

"What don't you like about it?" I asked.

"I don't like Mr. S." She rushed her words, and the anger that I thought was temporarily squelched came alive.

"He lies on me."

"What did he do?"

"He make me mad, that's what he do."

"But what did he do?" I persisted.

I already knew what she had done. Mr. S. had called me on the intercom, before she came, and told me.

Berenice didn't answer.

"You were going through his desk, weren't you, Berenice? You know that's not right. Teachers don't like kids going through their desks or going through their things. You know it was wrong."

She became angry again.

"Don't gimme none that old dry talk—who he think he be? He ain't my father."

There, it was out, what she was really telling me. How she wished Mr. S. were really her father, someone who could stop her from the way she was behaving. The father she had was so inadequate!

But I didn't interpret her wish for her. She couldn't have begun to accept it, or even understand that her rebellion was not against Mr. S., but against herself to mask her own yearning for a strong father.

"How about never going to Mr. S.'s class?" I asked.

"Nope. I'm goin back."

I knew she would. It was not only her negativism I was

counting on, it was her need for accepting controls from Mr. S.—the idealized father.

That's why half the teachers on staff are men. Girls need to see men as people with whom they can relate, as stable, permanent people in their lives. Because so many of our girls see their fathers only as sexual partners for their mothers, with little emotional meaning in their own lives, and because so many of them have seen "cousins," "uncles," "friends," "stepfathers," come and go, it is particularly important that they learn that a relationship with a man can be a meaningful one, a comforting and comfortable one, without its being sexual. It's a new experience for them.

Theresa and three other girls were crouched over a table, whispering softly but animatedly. Suddenly, she looked up and raised her voice so that the teacher across the room could hear her.

"Mr. Friedland?"

"Yes, Theresa?"

"Mr. Friedland, does it have a bone in it?"

Immediately, he knew what she was asking. The hushed voices and the sudden silence as she asked her question were revealing clues. He knew they were seriously awaiting his answer.

"No, it doesn't," he answered, equally serious.

"Oh." They whispered some more for a few moments. Then, they looked up again.

"Ready for math?" Mr. Friedland asked.

They were.

It was an honest question and an honest answer. That is one of the traits the girls demand of us. Honesty. The girls demand other things, as well, compassion and acceptance, for instance, and each of us, in his way, tries to meet their demands.

Certainly, we do not all work the same way with the girls, nor should we be expected to. The diversity of our personalities is one of the school's strengths. Each teacher, like each girl, is unique. Thus, each teacher works within the framework of his own personality pattern. Some teachers are more rigid in routines than others; some teachers are more compulsive in setting limits than others; some teachers joke more than others. That is as it should be—we are different, one from the other.

Some things we have in common, however; namely, a belief in what we are doing and a basic philosophy that we have developed. The philosophy is really simple to say, much harder to put into practice. We believe that a school is a place where learning takes place through personal expression and that an expression of a thought or a feeling can never be bad or wrong. Behavior may have disastrous consequences, but an expression of thinking or feeling—never!

Thus, all expression is acceptable, and because it is, each girl is acceptable. We do not demand that girls earn our affection or our approval. We give it freely.

Yet there are certainly times when we feel bogged down by our own limitations or the restrictions of society. At these times I ask myself the question I lightly threw at Iona. "Has God resigned?" No. It is a question I repeatedly throw at a discouraged teacher, for we must remember that we are here because we want to be here, because we can "get in the other person's skin and move around in it," like Atticus in *To Kill a Mockingbird*.

And knowing what the pain is, we remove ourselves from that alien skin and lead the sufferer into learning how to avoid pain, how to choose alternative ways of behavior.

Geda slouched in my office, not speaking, her head low, her feet outstretched, her hands gripped in her lap.

"What's the matter, **Geda**?"

"Nothin."

"Okay. You sure look unhappy, though."

"Yeah, I guess so."

"Why?"

A shrug of the shoulder. No response.

"You worried about something?"

No answer, so I start . . .

"It's something very serious, so does it have something to do
with your mother?"

"Her? No. She don't know nothin."

Two areas left.

"Drugs?"

Her eyes opened wide in anger. "You think I fool around
with that stuff? Shit, no!"

"Well, I don't know, Geda, you might try it. Some kids do.
But if it's not that—boys. Is that it? Boy trouble."

"Yeah."

"He wants you to go with him, that it?"

"Yeah. He comes to my house and everything. My mother
knows him. He even tells her he wants me to go to Washington
and live with him."

"He wants to get married?"

"Yeah, he wants to get married, he told my mother."

"So?"

"I don't wanta get married. I want to get my education."

"That's right, you're right," I told her.

But she still sat. There was more.

"But you really like him, yes?"

"Yes."

"And you're messing around?"

"Well—yeah."

"And you're afraid you'll get pregnant?"

"He wants me to have a baby."

"He does? Why?"

"I don't know. His mother just had a baby, and I guess he wants one, too."

"To make him feel like a man? At your expense?"

"I guess so."

"Well, you tell me why he'd want a baby. Can he support you?"

"Yeah, he can. He works on a truck. He has a good job."

"How old is he?"

"Eighteen."

"And isn't he going to be drafted soon?"

"Yeah, he say so."

"So? Who will be stuck with the baby?"

"Me—that's who!" She jumped up. "I guess he feel it'll make him important. Later for him."

"How about later for you?" I asked. "What about sex? You like it?"

"Sometimes."

"So why do it?" I asked. "To please him?"

"Naw, nobody makes me do nothin. I do it when I want to."

"Well, what are you doing about not having a baby? How about taking the pill?"

"My mother don't want me to. She says it gives people cancer."

"Well, she may be right," I said. "But what about talking to her about taking you to a doctor and getting some other kind of help so you don't get pregnant?"

"I can't talk to my mother about it."

"Oh. Well, how about if I talk to your mother? I'll make some reason to have a conference with her and we'll get around to talking about it."

"My mother would kill me if she knew I talked to you first. Nosiree."

We were at an impasse. I knew her mother saw me as her rival.

"Geda," I said, "there's only one way. You're going to have to learn that there is a word in our language that you must use. The word is *no*."

She smiled. "Yeah."

But I wasn't sure. It was a hard thing I was asking Geda.

As Isabel had told me, "It's the style to get pregnant."

"Some style," I quipped.

"That's because there's a generation gap between us," she said.

"There's going to be a pregnancy gap between us," I told her, "if you wear that dress much shorter. Soon it will be no dress at all, and the boys will come running."

"They come running at parties," she said. "You should see how short my skirts are then."

"Parties, that's where all the action is," I told her, "so lower your skirts at school. You won't miss anything."

"Oo—Dr. Rothman," she laughed, "you know a lot."

But I didn't know what Geda would do until a month later when she came into my office again.

"I told Willard to leave me alone," she said.

"Honest?"

"Yeah, he came to my house and was I mean! My mother says I was evil."

"What did you do?"

"I told him I hated his guts, and you know what, Dr. Rothman, he cried, real tears. Honest to God, real tears."

"Tough on him," I said.

"Yeah, that's what I said, too; but my mother says I was real evil."

"Were you?"

"Yeah." Big smile. "But girls cry all the time over boys. I like to make boys cry over girls."

"What made you do it?"

She became very serious. "You know, after that conference we had, I decided I didn't want none of that. I got me plenty of time until I'm thirty, maybe forty."

Well, I didn't know about thirty or forty, or maybe even next year, or next month, even, but Geda was seeing things a little differently now—and for now, she was safe.

All we can do is work on each day at a time. And I believe in Geda. I think she'll make it. Her education will come first.

We look at each girl and not at her behavior. The behavior may be unacceptable to both the girl herself and to society, but the girl never is. We recognize that behavior is communication, that assaultive behavior is really an individual's cry for help, that a hurled obscenity is often the only way a girl has of expressing herself.

"Shut the fuck up," screamed an irate Denise at me.

"Oh, come on, Denise," I said, "you can do better than that. It's so ordinary."

"Mother-fucker," she muttered.

"Better," I agree. "Shorter, at least. But if you must curse, try something original. You're a pretty girl. Use it. Be feminine. Be mysterious. Say something most people don't understand, like 'mother-befuddler.' That's a new one."

She looked as if I had gone out of my head, but after I explained it, she was happy to use it. Her anger was dissipated by laughter.

This is a technique that no teachers' college has ever advocated. Somewhere along the boring academic line, most professors have missed the obvious—that kids really like to laugh; so do most people, only they never are taught to see the joke.

Mrs. Rosen was concerned when she came into my office to tell me that Constance and Anna were threatening to get her.

"What happened?" I asked.

"Well," she explained, "yesterday I was on the same subway train with them and they were really misbehaving."

"Like what?"

"Well, they were shoving people and threatening to break light bulbs. I didn't know what to do. I tried to ignore it—if they saw me—I was hoping they wouldn't and I didn't want to get up and leave. I didn't know what they would do."

"They expected you to tell them to stop," I told her.

"I thought as much," she answered, "but I didn't know them well, and I didn't know if I could handle them on the subway."

She was right. She was a new teacher, and rather than start something on the subway that she might not be able to carry off, it was better to ignore it.

"But now, they're after me all day. Constance says she's going to get me because I was spying on them."

Mrs. Rosen was really concerned. I could understand it; Constance and Anna came on strong. It wasn't always easy to see the babies they really were.

I called them both to the office, mainly to reassure Mrs. Rosen that their threats were mere words.

I asked them to stand in front of my desk, while Mrs. Rosen and I sat opposite them. Usually, girls sit—not now.

"How dare you?" I scolded. "How dare you say Mrs. Rosen was spying on you?"

"She was—" Constance started.

"She was not," I interrupted. "It was after three, wasn't it? It was after school. Do you think Mrs. Rosen would be a spy after school, when she's not getting paid for it? Don't be stupid."

Mrs. Rosen looked startled, but it made very good sense to the girls.

They left, apologizing.

"It's as simple as that?" Mrs. Rosen asked.

"Sure," I answered, "they expected you to stop them; and when you didn't, they were angry at your lack of concern."

"But how did you know that would work?" she asked.

"I didn't," I said, "but if I were Constance, that would make very good sense to me."

"How funny!" Mrs. Rosen laughed.

Mrs. Rosen felt free to come to me with her problems. That's how I first knew she would be a superb teacher. A teacher with an ego of her own can afford to ask me for help. She is not afraid of seeming weak. A poor teacher, who has no inner strength, is fearful of asking for help for fear she will expose her weakness.

Miss Hack also was strong. She too could ask for help. She called me into the yard when a fight was brewing. Roseabelle and Joy were facing each other.

"Get offa my back," Roseabelle warned.

"I'm not on your back," Joy answered.

"You're gettin on my nerves."

"You're on my father's nerves."

"I'm not on your father's nerves."

"Your mother—"

War was declared during lunch.

Everyone was silent for a second, the combatants, the observers. It was going to be a close one.

"Did anyone stop to think that shit spelled backwards is 'tihs'?" I suddenly asked.

Everyone laughed uproariously.

"What's all the fuss about?" I asked—and made certain I stepped between Roseabelle and Joy.

They all started screaming.

"Hold it!" I yelled louder than the rest. "Hold it—in another minute, somebody is going to say 'fuck' or 'shit' or 'mother-fucker,' or 'shut the fuck up,' or something stupid like that, and everybody will be fighting and I'll have to separate you and I'm too tired for that."

"Dr. Rothman!!!!" They gasped in horror.

"Don't like it when I say it? Well, that's how it sounds. I can assume that there is a basic disagreement between two people. There are two distinct points of view. I think perhaps we should discuss it. How about a conference in my office?" I was very high-toned. Everybody loved that.

"Get her?" someone laughed, but Joy was already on her way up to my office. So was Roseabelle.

"Ladies," I said when they were both settled, "I do like to communicate on a higher level, and not with the subterranean passages of your mind."

They didn't understand all of it, but they liked the way it sounded. We went on to discuss the difficulty. I deliberately used very high-toned words.

As she left, Joy asked for a dictionary, and not to be outdone, Roseabelle repeated the request.

I had enjoyed myself thoroughly. So had they.

"But it's so unprofessional to laugh," said Miss Feldman, a new teacher at Livingston, coming into the office with the tale of Bethel and Constance facing each other in the art room, each with nails aimed at the other's face, each taunting, "Hit me, shit, I dare you," and each backing up until they practically were at different ends of the room. Miss Feldman had restrained her mirth at the irony of it all.

"Look," I told her, "don't be afraid of laughter; if something is funny, laugh. They'll join in."

"But what if it's not funny to them?"

"You'll know it, Miss Feldman, and how you'll know it! But then you'll learn. Anyway, trust your instincts."

"That's the trouble," she said, "my instincts are sometimes wrong. When I get angry at a girl, I want to push her away. I think, *Who are you, you miserable thing, you, don't tell me what to do, I'm the teacher,* and I want to push her out of my awareness. And that's wrong."

That's when I was certain she was going to find her way and that she would eventually belong.

"Sure, it's wrong," I answered, "but you know it, so you'll change and you won't push her out. And after a while you won't feel like pushing her out, you'll keep her within your consciousness and your instincts will be right."

Miss Feldman smiled. "I'm learning."

She was.

"Good teachers are like trapeze artists," I told her. "We fly, but we always come down unharmed. We have to go where the girl is going; if she's silly like Constance, we can be silly like Constance; if she carries a baby python in her coat pocket to school like Abby, we accept the python—along with a slight case of heart palpitation—but don't be afraid to laugh."

Joy's laugh emanated from Mrs. Gray's office like a gaseous outburst.

"Don't tangle with Mrs. Gray," she said to Theodora. "She might have you on the critical list."

Theodora snorted at the idea. "C'mon, Mrs. Gray, let me go home. I have to go to the doctor."

"You're just not telling the truth, Theodora," Mrs. Gray insisted. "You've told me that tired tale a thousand times before about having a doctor's appointment and then you go off somewhere."

"She's not lyin," Joy interceded, "honest she isn't, Mrs. Gray."

"Well, I don't know how you would know that, Joy—" Mrs. Gray said.

"Call my mother, if you don't believe me," Theodora cried. "My mother is at home."

This time the story had the sound of truth. Usually, when Theodora told Mrs. Gray to confirm an appointment, no one was at home. Mrs. Gray called, and Theodora was telling the truth.

Theodora thoroughly enjoyed Mrs. Gray's apology. I came in to Mrs. Gray's office when Theodora was accepting it magnanimously.

"Well, how do you like that, Mrs. Gray?" I asked. "Here you are, saying you're sorry to Theodora, when only a few days ago Theodora told me that she never said she was sorry to anybody in her life."

"That's right," Theodora agreed. "It's a word I never say. Why should I say I am sorry? Why should I give anybody the satisfaction?"

"So how come you can't say you're sorry, but Mrs. Gray can?" I asked her.

"Certainly," Mrs. Gray, "I can say I'm sorry if I'm wrong. I'm sorry that Theodora can't, because she's bright enough to know when she's wrong."

"Well," I answered, "maybe she's never wrong. Theodora must have been born with a label that said perfect child."

Theodora laughed. She got the message. Now that Mrs. Gray has set the model, she can do no less.

Unfortunately, teachers are never taught in education courses to say they are sorry. It becomes a threat to their authority. Of course, if they had any real sense of authority, they couldn't be threatened so easily. These are the teachers, not always the very young teachers, who do not know or appreciate their own adult status. Many teachers who are chronologically adult not only seem to be aware of their own identities as adults, but, in fact, seem constantly to be in revolt against adulthood and, specifically, against those persons who represent the authority of adulthood. To the teacher who hates authority and is always willing to fight it the enemy is the principal. Such teachers are often chronic latecomers, or irresponsible in handing in reports. Everything routine that is asked of them, and certainly there are many routines, not all meaningless, appears to be resented and resisted. It is as if these teachers have never resolved their own conflicts with authority. Many would-be mature people still act out their hatred of authority figures, much as if they were still adolescents, subconsciously and consciously defying their parents.

"Miss W., why didn't you hand in your attendance sheet?" I asked.

"Bureaucracy!" she snapped. "I can't stand it."

Bureaucracy or not, the fact remains that we simply have to know daily who is in school so that parents of absent girls can be notified. But Miss W. saw every request from the principal as a part of the superstructure, the establishment, and the establishment must be toppled.

Miss W. talked constantly to me of "total fulfillment." With the girls, she supported the cause of "doing your own thing" beyond the limits of good sense or even kindness to the girls. She could not face the fact that a girl did not have the right to remain in the building during a fire drill, just because "it was her own thing" she was doing.

Neither could she face the fact that a teacher at our school who rebels against all forms of society, on every level, without differentiation, really is no different from the rebellious girls she is teaching. What can she teach them?

Like Miss B., she is using the girls, but in a different way. Through them, she is vicariously releasing her own inhibitions. Their aggression gives her considerable catharsis. Our girls don't need her.

The anti-authority child-teachers are self-deceptive when they convince themselves that they are dedicated to the girls. Miss N. didn't tell me that a girl had defecated outside her classroom. Instead, Miss N. shoveled it up and deposited it unceremoniously on my desk, smell and all.

Miss N. didn't mind saying why. She wanted me to see what "a nasty, dirty" thing it was. She didn't have to take this from the girls, she said, so she was giving it to me. Obviously, this was a teacher who was as sick as the girl who had tried in this fashion to insult her. The girl's problem became her problem. Miss N. simply passed the insult along to me, her authority figure.

Unfortunately, many teachers are drawn to our school not primarily because they are concerned with the girls, but because they are seeking resolutions to their own severe internal conflicts. Any center of therapy, whether it is a hospital or a school, attracts many people on staff who are essentially seeking therapy for themselves. They, of course, cannot remain.

But who does? Those teachers who have found through introspection and self-analysis their professional "raison d'être" for being in this school. Age doesn't matter. Race doesn't matter, or economic or social class. Sex doesn't matter—a young man, an older woman, a young girl, it really doesn't matter. Girls look beyond age and sex and race and see the person. They don't, however, look beyond clothes. Appearance is tremendously important.

If teachers dress in hippie style, it becomes an obstacle. The girls begin to relate to the appearance, rather than to the person.

Our girls make demands of the teachers. They look for an image, and the image is respectability, middle-class style. Our girls don't want their teachers to be like the boys or girls next door. They are the ones they couldn't get along with anyway. But beginning teachers often think that the way to form relationships is to dress in whatever is the teenage vogue.

Gloria was very angry at a visiting teacher who was seeking an appointment to the school.

"Who she think she be, that old hag trying to look like a chick?"

Gloria was right. The "old hag" was no more than forty, but if she wanted to look sixteen, she had identity problems of her own. How, then, could she help any girl mature?

Miss D. prided herself that she wore no bra and no girdle, and she often told the girls so.

"It makes them less inhibited," she told me. "Girls should move freely, not be restrained by garments."

"Miss D.," I told her, "our girls are too uninhibited, that's exactly their problem. They need some restraint. That's exactly why they're here. Being totally uninhibited does not necessarily lead to happiness. It creates anxiety. At what point do your impulses carry you away? At what point do you stop? Drugs? Murder—?"

She thought I might be right.

"Look, Miss D.," I said, "it's the upper- and middle-class students, shirking middle-classness and the bounds of their parents' values, who relate to the hippie teacher. They want a way out of their society. Our girls have never really been in society in any meaningful way, and we have to help get them there, and get them into jobs and professions. They have to play the middle-class role, they have to look the part."

She agreed. She wore undergarments.

The question of the teacher's civil rights, of course, becomes involved in the issue. Do we have a right to say to a teacher *No, you can't wear a dress ten inches above your knees,* or *No, you can't wear slacks?* The teachers and I conferred, and we all felt we were right to establish criteria of dress. We would expect and require a surgeon to wear a sterilized gown in surgery Teaching is no less a delicate operation. A teacher wearing no bra or undergarment, greeted with "Didn't you get it last night, teach, lookin' for it now?" can't possibly form a relationship with a girl. Well, she can—but certainly not the kind of relationship we consider healthy. If this is an infringement on a teacher's rights, then I suppose it is. But it is an infringement that I am willing to make.

Who is successful in this school? Those teachers who can relate to others. If they can't do it themselves, they can't teach it. They have to relate well to everyone and be perceptive of everyone's feelings. If they can relate, they can show others how to. If they can't relate, they will lose direction and succumb to frustration and depression. What's worse, they will make girls suffer.

The teachers I want cannot be afraid of emotions, or the expression of emotions. They cannot be fearful of agression. In fact, they must enjoy it. Their own aggression is, in fact, expressed by their own manipulation of behavior. They have strong superegos. They can stand up to abuse, relish it, deploy it, and feel strong for the girls to lean on. They are givers, not takers. And while they cannot be fearful of their emotions, they cannot themselves react with emotion. They must be dramatic, no doubt about it, to hold a girl's interest—a girl who has always hated school. They must be flamboyant in the class-room.

And having found their professional identity at Livingston, they must constantly question themselves, their insights, their techniques. This is salutary. It becomes damaging, however, when the questioning becomes self-paralytic.

"What am I doing in this oasis-school, teaching one girl not to bang doors every time she's angry, another girl how to read, and another not to fight, when there is so much more to learn and to teach in other classrooms?" Miss Miller asked.

The answer, of course, is simple. If we can't sweep the world, at least we can sweep one speck of dirt in one corner of a room. We can be concerned about the world, but we cannot become immobilized by infinity. Helping one girl find her role in society is one millimeter closer to a cosmos that approaches a state of sanity.

If it is a philosophy that sounds like a religion—it is.

The best part of this religion is that we don't have to wait for heaven for our goodies.

"Go to hell," Inez yelled at me when she couldn't convince me that she needed an extra subway token.

"Go to hell? Me?" I asked in mock surprise. "Me—your friend?"

Her voice became soft and low, a gentle thing in a woman.

"I didn't tell you to go alone," she said. "Me and Marie, we'll go with you."

chapter four

The Orientation Class

Most of the new girls who arrive at Livingston are escorted only by their mothers; rarely, both parents or a father will come. They sit stiffly on the leather couches and chairs squared off in the area of my office that I euphemistically call conference. On coffee tables and bookshelves nearby are plants, magazines, books, and toys. Generally, there is a purse or a scarf or a coat draped on a chair where a girl has left it in my custody. A fish tank for tropical fish is in one corner of the room. It is never maintained properly, because I don't have the time to devote to it, and the girls who like to care for fish feed them to death. There is always a cup of coffee on my desk, because I am a chronic coffee drinker. My office is not formal. Neither is it sloppy; sometimes it just seems that way.

The girls are usually impeccably groomed and generally frightened into immobility. They sit and stare at me, looking like the silent ladies of the fashion magazines. I know that they both fear me and hate me. In their minds and in the minds of their parents, I am the upholder of the suspension laws,

113

dispenser of punishment, and supreme authority in school. I am the last of the line of principals who have put each girl out of school. I therefore do not exist as an individual. I am the stereotype.

I try to break that mold.

I offer coffee and cookies to the parents and juice and cookies to the girls. Almost everybody refuses, at first, the parents usually from embarrassment, the girls from trying to appear ethereally ladylike. Eating is just too vulgar for them. They clutch their loose-leaf notebooks crammed full with clean paper. They seem eager to plunk all the wisdom of the school into their new notebooks already sectioned into English, Mathematics, and Social Studies. They are excessively ready for school, excessively polite. I know that neither the readiness nor the politeness will last, and that's a good thing, because excessive politeness presents the same barriers to communication as excessive cursing. It is a fence to be broken down.

This is the first meeting at which the girls and their parents meet me, Mrs. Gray, and the teacher of the orientation class. Orientation is the first class the girls will be in. It is the testing ground. I explain that the word "orientation" means learning about oneself in relation to a new environment and that in the orientation class, which lasts several weeks, each girl will learn about the school and how she fits into it. At the same time we will learn about her, which subjects she likes, which subjects she doesn't like. I set the stage immediately that at Livingston, learning by both teachers and girls is a mutual and a sharing process.

After a half-hour or so of official greetings from Mrs. Gray and me, the girls, still silent, go off with their teacher to their classroom, which is across the lounge from my office. Sometimes the teacher is just as nervous as the girls, particularly when the teacher is new at Livingston. I like to assign a new teacher to the orientation class, because like the girls, the teacher has a lot to unlearn and relearn.

I ask the parents to remain with Mrs. Landsman and me after the girls leave. I want to point out to them that we must give the girls time before we can begin to see change, that in fact, the behavior of some girls often seems to get worse before it gets better.

"Each girl is going to test to see how much she can get away with," I generally say. "She may be truant in order to see if we will notify you that she's absent. We always do. Never worry about that, or she may come home at nine o'clock at night and tell you she went on a trip with her teacher. I can tell you right now, we never take a girl on a trip unless we've notified you personally beforehand. But these are the things some girls will try to do to test you and to test us."

"Excuse me, Dr. Rothman," Mrs. S. interrupted, "but what you say is true. I suppose it's not a nice thing to say about your own daughter, but I have to say it because it's true, she has hell on her behind, that girl."

Bethel's mother seemed shocked.

"My daughter really doesn't cause any trouble at home," she said, "it's only at school that she gets into trouble. She does everything I tell her. Well, yes, she's high-strung, that's all, but at school—I just don't know what the problem is. They used to call me every day, it seemed."

"I know what you mean," Phyllis's mother was sarcastic. "I was over at that school so much, I told the principal I was going to bring in my cot."

"Well, I'm tired of going to school for Leila." Mrs. D. drew her fur collar closer around her. "I feel like I'm the student, I was there so much, and it didn't do any good. I just told Leila that I was not coming to school any more, that she was on her own, and I mean it, I'm not coming to any school any more."

What they really were saying was, "Please let me alone, I have borne all I can bear, now it's up to you."

But it can't be only up to me. The struggle is never over. They have to know it.

"I'm afraid that I will have to ask you to come in if I feel it's necessary," I told them. "When anything happens that I feel you should know about, I wouldn't be helping your daughter if I didn't tell you about it."

I could sense their unhappiness. They wanted to continue doing what they had done in the past—first, blame their own children for their troubles, then blame the entire school system. It is a seesaw game, alternating between rejecting their children and then overprotecting them. It is a game of personal guilts. Rejection—overprotection, it really is the same axis. I won't accept it. I can accept only one condition—a working active partnership and relationship between the parents and us.

I pressed for that relationship.

"And what's more," I went on, "if your daughter does something wrong and I stop her, the way I know you would want me to stop her, she might go home and tell you I'm prejudiced."

There was sudden silence and acute discomfort.

"If it's a white girl, she may say I prefer the black girls. If she's black, she may say I hate black people. I want you to be prepared for it, because it sometimes happens."

I didn't tell them how often. It is only recently that I even make reference to prejudice. I used to believe that some things were better left unsaid. I now know better. It is a fact of current life that accusations of prejudice are weapons that girls have seized, and like all weapons, they can be used destructively or constructively. With girls who are eager for a show of strength, the weapon is dangerous. I want their parents to understand this before it happens.

I could see the discomfort in their bodies and faces. Leila's mother arose hurriedly to leave.

Bethel's mother said, "Well, in my home we teach our children to judge all people on how they behave to you, not on the color of their skin."

"That's exactly it," I told her. "The girls will say that it's the way that I behave that is prejudiced, and that's because I do not permit them to behave in a harmful way. Only they won't see it as harmful. They would rather accuse me of being prejudiced than admit they are doing something wrong."

"Yes, of course," Bethel's mother answered, but it was a tight little answer, and it did not mean agreement.

"Well, I must be going now," Phyllis's mother announced to the room at large. They all got up to leave.

Tallageda's father, who was an old man, muttered, "I don't put up with none of that stuff," but he didn't look at me.

I wondered. There is always that question in their minds, especially before they know me. "Is she prejudiced?" I could not escape it. Nor should I. They have a right to ask it—so do the girls. The onus is definitely on me.

I used to think, rather stupidly, that all I had to do was send for a black teacher when a parent was hostile, when I knew the parent was thinking "white bitch." But, of course, it is not so; the same parent also thinks, "Uncle Tom." We have to prove ourselves by our actions, not by our color.

With this particular orientation class I had to prove myself almost immediately.

"I ain't comin here," Phyllis announced that same afternoon to her teacher.

"Me neither," Bethel agreed.

"Yeah, no Jew teacher is goin to tell me what to do," Jessie agreed.

"They'll tell you good," Leila laughed at her. "You ain't no better than nobody else."

Phyllis became hysterical with laughter. "Look at big titty there," she pointed to Leila.

Everybody became hysterical with laughter, except Leila.

"Who ya talkin to?" Leila asked.

"You, fat bitch, she talkin to you," answered Jessie.

"You black whore, you," Leila screamed at Jessie, "black and blue whore," she repeated, "black spasm."

Jessie became enraged, "I'll pull out your pussy if you say that again."

I hurried over to the classroom when I heard the uproar and brought them back to my office. The teacher told me hurriedly what had happened as we walked across the lounge. To put it mildly, she had been unable to stop them.

"Let's get this straight," I told the girls, once they were inside my office. "We don't have to put up with fighting for any reason. You want to fight? There's the door. Leave. We only help girls who want to help themselves. There's hope for them. If you want to go on the way you are—goodbye."

"Sure," screamed Bethel. "Get rid of us, but we have to go to school."

"Not to this school you don't," I said. "We take girls for whom there's hope."

Everyone was silent, except Tallageda.

"Tell it to the judge."

"Shut up," I snapped.

"Don't tell us shut up," screamed Tallegeda. "My mother don't say that to me."

"Yeah," Bethel agreed, "what kind of principal are you? You're supposed to talk nice to kids. You're supposed to set us an example. My mother didn't send me here for no principal to say shut up."

Everyone looked at me to see what I would do. They didn't expect deliberate silence.

"Oh, you all bore me," I finally answered. "And you're acting so stupid, it's just boring."

"We're not stupid," exclaimed Bethel.

"Mostly boring," I answered, "but you're right, I did say you were acting stupid, too. Anybody who insults anyone's race is acting stupid. I don't know what you would call it, but anyone who calls somebody black and blue is stupid, especially when that person is black, too."

There was mild laughter. I followed it up.

"I think it was black and blue whore," I said. "Of course, I don't know what that means, any more than I know what a black spasm is—"

"Think she smart," Tallageda muttered.

I did not let her get away with it.

"You bet," I answered, "and the sooner you learn it, the better. You really can't put anything over on me. You may for a while, and you may even get away with it for a while, but in the end—"

I didn't finish the sentence. They knew the rest.

"We're not stupid," Lelia yelled. "You think all colored kids are stupid—"

"If I thought all colored people were stupid," I answered, "I assure you I wouldn't be here. Why would I want to spend my life being with stupid people? Besides, I didn't say you were stupid, I said you were acting stupid, and there's a big difference between acting stupid and being stupid. I'm telling you right now, you're all acting stupid. If you really were stupid, do you think I'd bother explaining this to you? You wouldn't understand what I was saying. If you were stupid, you'd be in a school for retarded girls. We're a school for girls of intelligence who act stupid. And right now you are acting stupid."

Bethel shifted from foot to foot. She began to suck her thumb.

"Can we go now?" she asked.

"Sure," I answered, "provided the stupidity, which means the name-calling, has stopped."

"We'll be good," Bethel said pleasantly.

Leila was still angry. "It's stopped, it's stopped," she said. "Who wants to listen to you all day?"

"Shut up, Leila," Jessie warned her, completely forgetting that only minutes before, they had been fighting with each other. "You'll get into trouble."

I knew that Jessie and Leila were now establishing a tangential relationship. Within minutes they would be best friends for the day. Tomorrow, they might become enemies again. Strong, stable friendships are rare at Livingston, and so are strong, stable enmities. Relationships are not holding because the emotions of the girls are too volatile. In a sense, this is good, because out girls do not become involved with gangs. Gang membership demands constancy.

"Well?" Bethel demanded. I realized I had been studying the group and that they were waiting for my answer.

"I think you're ready to go back," I told them. They were. The first collective show of strength was over. There was no doubt about who had won.

I knew that they would almost immediately want to talk it over with Mrs. Landsman. They trusted her. Not me. Not yet. I also knew that the most intensive kind of group counseling would take place. Mrs. Landsman would help them sort out their feelings, she would explore with them what had happened, why each girl had said what she had said, why they had almost fought. She would let them relive the experience and gain a new understanding of it.

After an explosive moment with a teacher, the girls often come to Mrs. Gray or to me, but after an explosive moment with either Mrs. Gray or me, they go to the guidance couselor to work through feelings to the point of insight and relief from anger. The guidance counselor, after all, must be seen by the girls as the all-receptive all-understanding person in school. Mrs. Landsman is.

Later, she came into the office to tell me about it. As we were speaking, Tallageda poked her head into the open doorway and beckoned to me to go with her. I left my desk to meet her.

Tallageda wanted to know if she could leave early.

I told her I would call her mother and see if it was all right.

Tallageda left smiling. "You and me is gonna be friends," she said.

I laughed when I returned to my desk, to tell Mrs. Landsman what Tallageda had wanted.

"And stupid me," I continued, "the girl calls and I get out of my seat to go to her. Why didn't I make her come to me? She's not as tired."

But of course I knew the answer even before Mrs. Landsman supplied it with a question of her own.

"Did you ever get the feeling that we're all privates and the students are all generals?" she asked.

There was no doubt she was right, particularly when, on the next day, Jessie came storming into my office, waving a transistor radio in her hand. The radio was blaring.

"What kind of fuckin school is this?" she yelled. "Why won't that fuckin flat-behinded white-assed teacher let me play my god-damned radio?"

"Because you were told not to bring your own radio to school," I told her. "Each teacher has a radio, and if she wants to play it, she can. She apparently does not want you to play yours. Turn it off."

"God damn it, I won't—" Jessie raged.

"Turn it off," I ordered.

"Okay," Jessie cried out, "all you damned ofays stick together, shit on your fuckin school, that sign you have outside, that sign that says you have a friend at Livingston, you have shit at Livingston."

She flung the radio on the floor. It was still blaring. Tears were pouring down her face, and her arms went flailing in all directions. She brought her hand down on the coffee table and a vase with flowers in it went crashing to the floor.

I could almost feel the blood rushing to my head. I did not really know Jessie as an individual, although I certainly knew about her. My first impression of her was that she was one of the most primitive girls I had ever seen. She had just been released from the Training School and clung so ferociously to freedom that she saw any demands that were made on her as an infringement on her rights. I also knew she had assaulted her mother. This was extremely unusual. Most girls don't. She might not stop at me; I did not know. I could not be sure. Slowly, I got up from behind my desk and walked over to the door. I really was trying to put myself out of the realm of attack, but I did not want to let her know I was doing it.

"Let me get somebody to sweep that up," I said.

She was trembling. So was I, only she didn't know it.

"Look," I said, "you're upset. But nothing terrible happened. I never did like that vase, anyway."

I went and stood at the doorway, watching Jessie all the time. She picked up the radio and turned it off.

"Feel better?" I came into the room again and sat on the couch, next to where she was standing.

"Yeah."

"Sit down, Jessie," I said. "I want to talk to you."

She sat down opposite me.

"You sure can get angry," I said. "You really have a bad temper, don't you?"

"Yeah—"

"I'll tell you what, Jessie," I said, "I'll make a bargain with you, now that I know you. If you really have to do something, I mean you really have to do it, and you can't keep yourself from doing it, and a teacher won't let you do it, like play the radio, come to my office and I'll let you do it, whatever it is. Okay? But you must try to control your temper."

"You mean it?" Her voice rose in surprise.

"Sure," I answered, "I don't say things I don't mean."

"Why not?" she asked. "Everybody else does."

"Not everybody," I answered, "maybe just some of the people you knew. You'll just have to learn I mean what I say, and I keep my word. I never lie to kids."

"Okay."

"Want to play the radio now?" I asked her. "It seemed so important to you, before."

"No, that's okay. I just don't like anyone to tell me I can't do somethin," she answered.

"That's the way it is, though, you're going to have to learn to take it. You can't always have things your way."

"Yeah, I guess so."

We both sat for a while with our own thoughts.

"Tell me, Jessie," I asked, "why did you call me ofay? What does it mean?"

"Oh, that—" She was obviously embarrassed. There was a faint smile on her lips. "You know."

"But I don't. I never heard it before, and I thought I had been called everything."

"Well, that's a bad word for white people."

I didn't get any more out of her, but later I learned it was pig Latin for foe.

"Jessie," I said, "why were you so mad at me, because I was white, or because I didn't let you play your radio?"

She thought a while. "Both, I guess."

"What if I were black and didn't let you play the radio? What would you have called me then?"

Without thinking she answered.

"Nigger."

"You really are prejudiced," I told her.

"Me?" She was startled.

"Sure, you," I told her, "you hate both black and white people. You're really prejudiced against people."

"I don't like nobody," she muttered.

"That's the trouble," I told her, "not even yourself."

And, of course, that was the trouble. But she was too new for me to go into it with her. She was not ready just then for self-exploration.

We have more racial name-calling in orientation than in any other class, for just that reason. The girls are new and don't really know each other or the staff. More important, of course, they have not yet learned to know themselves.

Whether they are black or white, personal self-hatred becomes racial self-hatred. There are many white girls who openly deny their whiteness, just as there are many black girls who deny their blackness.

Very often, it is the white girls who have the most difficult time adjusting to the school. Not only are they often the sickest, but for the first time, they are in the minority. Some black girls make it particularly difficult for them. They don't want intruders in the school. The school is for them—the blacks!

For some black girls it comes as a surprise that white girls get into trouble. They can't quite absorb the idea that they are not the lowest of low, that white girls have problems, too, that white girls do not live in the never-never land of white perfection.

"What she doin here?" asked Esther and Olivia of Joan as Joan came to Miss Miller's room.

"Why?" asked Miss Miller. "Don't you think white girls get into trouble?"

They hadn't. It was a brand-new thought, and it was a thought of compassion. They had found the bridge to equality.

Once a girl establishes herself as a person, whether she is black or white, the other girls accept her for what she is. They become remarkably free from prejudice. This does not mean they do not use the words of prejudice; they do. And when they become angry, they even fight physically over the words, but unlike any other groups of people I have seen, the girls at Livingston are ready to evaluate each other on the basis of humanness and not color.

"Chile," Joanne came striding into my office with her friend Judy behind her, "you talk foolish. Dr. Rothman, you know that, you talk foolish?"

"Why?" I asked.

"Tellin them orientation girls that a rule of the school is they gotta be happy."

"What's wrong with that?" I asked. "I told them that a rule of the school is that they have got to learn how to try to be happy. There's a difference."

"Yeah, yeah, sure," Joanne continued, "all them words, mixin them up with all them words, you know what?"

She flung herself into a chair, Judy beside her.

"You've changed a lot. I used to hate you, Dr. Rothman, when I was in orientation, I used to hate you, but you've changed a lot." She shook her head sagely.

"Maybe it's you who've changed, Joanne," I offered, "not me. You just didn't see me clearly, or yourself, for that matter."

"I see you now," she answered, "and you know somethin, your skin's darker."

Judy, who had listened intently, asked, "Did you go to Africa this summer?"

"No," I answered, "and my skin isn't really darker. You're just seeing below the color of the skin, and you're seeing me as a person who's close to you, so you think my skin is darker. Wouldn't it be nice if no one had skin and we could all see below the surface?" I asked.

"I told you," Joanne turned to Judy and made a circular motion of her hand to her head, "she's gettin simple."

Judy agreed most pleasantly. I remembered back to Judy's own orientation days only six months earlier. She had seemed to be capable of muttering only obscenities. I had first come to know her when she had burst in on me, screaming at the top of voice.

"Fuck you, Dr. Rothman, fuck, you fuckin fuck and your fuckin teachers and the fuckin girls I'm gonna get that fuckin fucked-up fuck, I'm gonna kick her square in the fuckin behind."

She dashed to the doorway. I barred the way. She was a small girl. I knew I could stop her from "hurting anyone."

"Sit down, you're not going to get anybody," I told her.

"Fuck you, you up-fucked fuck," she screamed the words over and over again.

I could not get her to stop, nor could I get her to tell me what was bothering her, and obviously she wanted to be stopped or she wouldn't have come to me in the first place. She would merely have done what she was threatening to do, attack another girl.

"Judy, will you stop?" I asked almost in exasperation.

"You fuck," she cried, "fuck, you fuck."

Again, she went on and on. I listened to her with admiration. I had absolutely never heard the word used in so many different grammatical patterns and with such frequency. I decided Judy had a way with figures of speech. I also decided to try one of my own. It was a risk, but it was worth taking. I had absolutely no other way of stopping her.

I raised my voice to a shout.

"Well, somebody at least may want to fuck me, Judy—but you—look at you now—you're absolutely unfuckable."

It stopped her cold. The fact is that girls in orientation want to be stopped. They want to know the limits of their behavior because, knowing it, they can begin, through my strength and the strength of the teachers, to feel their own.

The process does not endear me to them—not while they are in orientation, it doesn't.

"You the principal?" Melanie asked during lunch one day, even though she had just been admitted earlier that day and knew who I was.

"Yes."

"Your name Dr. Girl-hater?" she asked in true innocence.

I laughed. "Who says?"

"The girls." Her manner was sweet. She was truly inquiring.

"Well," I answered, "you're new. Right?"

She smiled in agreement.

"To tell you the truth," I continued, "that's not a bad name for me."

I leaned over her table and put my arms around her shoulder. "I'll tell you a secret." I bent and whispered, "I hate all kids under thirty-five. I never speak to anyone under thirty-five. I even belong to a secret club in which no one speaks to any child under thirty-five."

For a second she didn't respond. She wasn't sure whether I was joking or not. Then, a soft smile played on her lips.

"Aw shoo, you're foolin, you're not so tough."

But many times I am. I have to be, particularly with orientation girls. They need to learn reality, and I have to show it to them. Upholding reality makes me the enemy.

I received a call from the police. They were bringing Phyllis and Leila to my office for causing a disturbance inside a vocational high school for boys that was only six blocks away from us. The girls were brought into my office, shoving each other and giggling. Two policemen escorted them in.

"It's not funny," I told them. "Only a few hours in this school, and you decided to go to a boys' high school. In ten years no girl in this school has ever done that before!" I was not acting. I was astounded at the sheer audacity of their behavior.

They began to deny it vociferously. They were never inside the building, everyone was picking on them.

"We picked you up inside the building, when the principal called us," the policeman interrupted. He then called me aside and explained that there had been four girls inside the building, but that the other two had run away. He also explained that the policemen had been assigned to the boys' high school because there had been a serious assault there the day before, and when the principal saw the girls, he was both furious and panic-stricken. He didn't know whether there was a connection or not between my girls and his assault, because the assault had been over a girl, and one of the boys was critically hurt.

My girls were, of course, completely innocent. They knew nothing of what had happened. They were just interested in seeing boys, a not unnatural interest, and when they learned that there was an all-boys school so close, they could not resist temptation.

I told the police I would handle it as a school matter. I sent the girls home after they had identified the other two girls. Then I called all four parents of the girls involved and asked them to come to school again the next day. To each I explained that this was the kind of situation to which I had referred. We must work together.

"But I really don't see why I have to come," Leila's mother complained. "I was just there yesterday."

"Because now she has done something wrong, and we must help her so she doesn't do it again," I answered.

"But she told me all about it," she said.

Nevertheless, I insisted that she come. She was a beautiful woman, totally unlike her daughter, who was stout and sloppy, with a foul body odor. I could not get Leila to react in any way as I sat there and accused her of going into the other school building. Her hostile imperturbability infuriated her mother.

"See, nobody believes me," Mrs. D. cried, in front of Leila. "She's a vicious monster."

Leila just looked at her, without saying a word.

"I'm an orphan," her mother continued. "I was raised in a home, and then when I was sixteen I had my oldest daughter, and later Leila. I have had to fight for everything I ever had, and I'm not going to throw it away on Leila. I give Leila everything."

"You give me nothin but shit," Leila cried.

Mrs. D. sat back almost in satisfaction that Leila had proved her point. She turned toward me.

"See, see, what did I tell you? Has she appreciated it? I didn't even have a mother—"

The bitterness poured out all over her. It was obvious Mrs. D. wanted gratitude from Leila for giving to Leila what was Leila's by natural right. Love.

How much could Leila take, sitting there so angry, and except for that one outburst, so silent, so bottled-up? Why should Leila have to be appreciative for being born? It hurt to think the question, particularly when it was my own daughter's birthday that day. Amy was almost Leila's age.

But I became even sterner. Leila could not be permitted to use her unhappiness as an excuse for misbehavior.

I turned to Leila.

"What did you do that was wrong?"

"Nothin."

"You went into another high school, that's what," I told her, "and you know you can't do that, especially an all-boys school."

"I did not—"

"Don't lie to me," I reprimanded. "You did so."

"I did not," she insisted.

"Okay," I finally told her after we had repeated the same question and answer several times, "so if you can't admit you were there when it is obvious you were, I'll sign you out of this school. That means you can't come here. If you made a mistake and did something you shouldn't have, admit it. Everybody is entitled to a mistake, but if you can't admit it, if you think you're not allowed to make a mistake, then go on lying, but you can't come here."

She was silent.

"Which will it be?" I asked her. "Tell the truth and say you made a mistake, or lie and you'll have to leave."

I was bluffing. I had no intention of letting Leila go. One thing I learned being principal—how to be a good actress. Leila's eyes began to well with tears.

I knew I was going to reach her.

"Tell me, what did you do that was wrong?" I asked again.

"I went to the boys' school," she started low.

"Right," I said.

"But I didn't know it was a boys' school," she spoke louder.

"Lies again, I won't listen," I interrupted.

"I didn't know," she insisted, "I didn't know there was a boys' school here until Bethel told me. I didn't know it when I came here."

"Okay, that's probably true," I answered. "Go on."

Little by little the story unfolded. Bethel had suggested it. Leila had gone along for kicks with the other three girls. She hadn't expected to be caught.

"Will it happen again?" I asked her.

"No—"

I let her go back to class. Leila's mother suddenly beamed at me.

"I wouldn't have believed it," she said admiringly, "I wouldn't have believed it, that girl hasn't cried since she was three."

I didn't feel admired. I felt like crying for her. Leila had not cried since she was three. Why not?

The next day Mrs. D. called me on the phone. "I told you she's a vicious monster," she said. "Leila wouldn't come to school today because I wouldn't buy her a raincoat. She's absent today. I couldn't get her to come."

"Doesn't she have a raincoat?" I asked.

"Of course she has, but she won't wear it in the rain. It's

new, and she's afraid the rain will spoil it, so she wants me to buy her another raincoat."

"Are you going to?" I asked.

"No." Her words were staccato. "She wanted that coat. She drove me crazy until I bought it for her, fifty-five dollars. Fifty-five dollars for a raincoat? And now she wants another coat? I can't afford it. I wanted her to buy a cheaper coat, and then maybe she could have had another coat, but it had to be that raincoat, no other would do. Well, I'm no millionaire."

"Well, don't let her bribe you, then," I told her. "She has to come to school without a bribe."

The last thing in the world Leila expected was for me to call her on the phone. I could hear the television blaring.

"Leila?" I asked.

"Huh?"

"Get your coat on and get over to school immediately," I ordered. "How dare you tell your mother you can't come because you want another raincoat?"

For a moment, she was silent; I knew I had taken her completely by surprise.

"You tell my mother to get me a raincoat and I'll come," she said.

"You have your nerve," I answered. "You get here, and you get here now. You're not going to use school as a weapon against your mother. You get here now."

I hung up before she could answer. Within an hour she was there, raincoat and all.

"You have your nerve!" I repeated.

"You hung up on me!" her tone was incredulous.

"Of course I did," I told her. "I told your mother not to buy you another raincoat. No blackmail. Understand?"

Surprisingly, she smiled. It was a very sweet smile. I was

touched, because she was a completely different girl—the baby who had not cried since she was three.

Leila was not absent again. A few days later, she came over to me in the lunchroom.

"Hi!"

"Hi, Leila," I put my arm around her waist. "You look especially pretty today."

Her smile was expansively beautiful. I felt good.

Leila had begun to find her own strength. She knew I would not permit her to be unreasonable, because being unreasonable would ultimately destroy her. Now that she knew the boundaries of her behavior, she could begin to control the large expanse that lay between those boundaries.

Something good had happened for Leila, but sometimes I need to talk things over with a former student like Agnes before I can fully begin to understand exactly what has happened to her.

"Girls in orientation hate you," Agnes explained. "When they curse you, it's because half the time they want you to yell at them and half the time they want you to love them."

"I always thought it was you who changed," Agnes continued, "but I guess it's me who changed, not you. You was always the same, I just didn't see it."

Agnes was right. When she had been in orientation, she could not accept compassion from me, therefore I could not fully give it. I had to hold back. It was only after she had been in school for several months that she was able to type this note and drop it on my desk.

Dear Dr. Rothman
I want to thank you for not being like other principals.
As you know I like it now in this school.

And i guess i want to stay in school i guess.
Thank you.

She was ready for my affection and the affection of others.

After all, feet ache the most after the tight shoes have been removed, after relaxation sets in. So, with the girls. In orientation we have to allow time for the negativism and aggression to be expressed, and we have to allow time for the pain of relaxation to be felt. Then our work really begins.

chapter five

Requiem for a Curriculum —
Board of Education Style

The curriculum at Livingston is an acting-out one character-ized by loudness, laughter, eating, talking, and room for lots of rough elbows. It is a physical place of open spaces in an old building where the ceilings are high and the rooms large, totally unlike the tight little structures that are called schools today.

It is an emotional place of open feelings, openly expressed through art, music, beauty culture, dressmaking, drama, and cooking. These areas are exploitive of the self and are definitely the prime focus of the school. These are the subjects that seduce the girls into coming to school. On our top floor, the fourth, the sound from pianos, clarinets, and singing groups bursts forth at you. The air there is usually permeated with delicious odors coming from the cooking classroom where hot biscuits or a chicken are likely to be in the oven. And across the hall, in the dressmaking classes, girls are truly absorbed by designing and sewing their own clothes.

The third floor is not generally as noisy, but just as active—the library with its many audio-visual machines, the drama class, the academic laboratory, two beauty culture rooms, a secretarial-practices room, and a busy art room.

We don't rely on words as the main method of communication between students and staff. Other schools do. They are verbal strongholds. If students are not proficient in words, they fail. Only the verbally fluent survive.

What a disaster!

At Livingston the process of education is what the Latin root of the word professes it to be, a "leading outward" of the individual, an emphasis on self-expression. It is a de-escalation of the war of reading, writing, and arithmetic as practiced in the regular schools. The girls have been defeated in the past by words and the academic subjects. Why continue to stress the defeats?

At Livingston, we don't. We are not bound to words. We are not confined to or circumscribed by verbal facility. We know that learning can also take place without words and that words, after all, are too often unreliable vehicles for transmitting thought. The words "mother," "apartment," "death," may set up one image in the mind of the person saying the word and a completely different image in the mind of the person hearing the word. How can the image be communicated by words, particularly by girls who are unskilled in and therefore inhibited by language?

"Hey, Dr. Rothman," Theodora said, "this is the now generation. Old ears gotta hear what the new ears hear."

"And what do you hear, Theodora?" I asked.

"Music."

Theodora was right. All young people respond to music. It is an emotional experience. Yet educators do everything they can to sterilize the emotion by scheduling students periodically for some inane exercise in pretended listening. They call it music appreciation.

"But why," I asked a visiting music teacher from a well-known high school in New York City, "why do you play Tchaikovsky's *1812 Overture,* when it bores the kids so they fight in the back rows and fall asleep in the front?"

"Because," she explained, "the chairman of the music department picked it as a good example of nationalism in music."

"Maybe," I said, "for students in the Soviet Union, but our children from the slums of New York City often have trouble differentiating between New York State and New York City, and you give them Russia!"

She shrugged.

"If you want to teach about nationalism expressed through music, what about Woody Guthrie's music, or Bob Dylan's? What about folk singing and folk rock and Richie Havens and Buffy Saint-Marie singing about her people, the American Indians?"

She had never heard of them.

Yet she talked of meeting the needs and interests of her students. How could she, when she didn't know the interests of her students, and she wasn't really ready to learn? Learning meant upsetting the musical applecart at her school. It was easier for her to upset her students.

Our girls, however, have been put upon enough. They love rock and roll. We may not, but that's our problem, not theirs. We teach it because it's what the girls want to learn. And every girl who comes to Livingston is taught to play the piano! No other school in the city does this. We are able to do it because we have broken a myth—the myth that learning has to be sequential, that learning progresses from the simple to the complex.

What nonsense! Some children walk without ever crawling. Some children speak in full sentences before one single word is uttered.

It is time for all educators to bury the concept that learning must be presented sequentially. This is why young adults drop out of school. They are presented with easy material that holds no interest for them; yet they cannot be given harder material until they learn the easy. It is wholesale incompetence on the part of educators who refuse to change their theory, because changing might imply that they have been wrong all these years. They refuse to learn from the children.

At Livingston, a girl bakes an apple pie before she learns the temperature of boiling water. She just may not be interested in how hot boiling water is.

A girl learns how to sew a slack suit before she sews an apron, and she learns to read the words "vampire" or "romance" before she recognizes "and."

And at Livingston a girl learns to play rock and roll before she can identify a single note by name.

Mr. Phipps, the music teacher, has evolved a unique method of teaching. Not only does he start with a rock and roll song which is unique in itself, but he discards musical notes. He substitutes letters. All a girl needs to do to play a song is to read the letters on her musical sheet and match them to the keyboard, which has been lettered.

Mr. Phipps, being an accomplished musician, arranges the harmonic structure of each popular song in such a way that the beat, which is the main structure of rock and roll, is played in chords with the right hand. Single notes are played with the left hand. For most people who, after all, favor their right hand, this system is easier to manage than playing chords with the left hand, which is the traditional system of song arrangements. Each girl learns to play each hand separately and then to put two hands together. Within one hour, most girls are able to play rock and roll without having to face the turmoil and the pain of learning the very complex symbolic system of musical notations.

Mr. Phipps does not stop at rock and roll, however. He goes on to teach classical music to those girls who are particularly interested, and he also teaches clarinet.

He taught Laverne to read music. Eventually she was playing a Beethoven sonata. Laverne was so gifted musically she could also play Beethoven by ear. Laverne, however, never believed in herself or in her own talent. Although she also sang on true pitch and had an exquisite voice, she refused to perform for others. She never felt she was good enough. We tried to get a scholarship for Laverne for a summer musical workshop. We hoped that we could save her from the summer streets if she were accepted, but she wasn't—not because she wasn't gifted—but because she asked to play for her audition, instead of sing. The judges, however, were adamant. Although they admitted that their program was not specifically for singers, they felt rules were rules, and they had made a rule that said everyone had to sing.

It did not make any sense to Mr. Phipps or to me, but we could not budge them. How stupid could they be? Very. They were working with children with problems, and therefore presumably had to be flexible, yet they wouldn't make an exception because they wouldn't make an exception, the rationale of most rigid adults.

Laverne was not accepted for their program, and she should have been. She returned in September to tell us she had slept the summer away, drinking and partying at night, recuperating during the day. She had been hurt.

We did not want to turn Laverne into a professional performer. If that were to happen, it would be wonderful, of course, but it was not our goal.

Our goal is not to turn out professional musicians. Our goal is personal enjoyment. Our goal is catharsis. Our goal is to offer an area of immediate success. Instant music is instant success. When girl feel they are achieving, they begin to feel better about themselves. When they feel better, they act better. When they act better, they feel better and when they feel better, they achieve even more. The therapeutic cycle has begun. Another word for the cycle is happiness.

It is odd, and sometimes I feel, tragic, that the word "happiness" is rarely used in education, psychiatry, or psychology. Yet our country was supposedly founded in pursuit of it.

It's a word we use often at Livingston.

"Come on, Joanne," I said, "get that scowl off your face. A rule of the school is to be happy."

"Nothin can make me happy," she glowered.

"Why not?" I asked. "What class can you go to that will make you happy?"

"Music," she muttered.

"So go to music," I told her.

"I can't. Mr. Phipps is filled up."

"Well, that is a problem," I told her. "Did he tell you what time to go back upstairs?"

"In fifteen minutes."

"Well, then, that's not so bad," I answered.

"No?" she grumbled. "How would you like to wait fifteen minutes before you could go to music?"

"I don't think fifteen minutes is too long to wait for happiness," I told her.

"Oh, no?" she asked.

It was hard for Joanne to wait that fifteen minutes, because being able to play the piano was one of the main reasons Joanne came to school every day.

It was also the reason Lydia and Emily came, particularly when they were extremely unhappy. Lydia played weird discordant notes. Emily, with rigid fingers, played as though she was evoking thunder. Afterward, both girls seemed less angry and less tense. They had found emotional release. Olivia, however, never needed the release. She played the piano lovingly. Her fingers were soft and pliable; sometimes she struck a wrong note deliberately and giggled. The wrong notes were truly Olivia; she was playing games.

But for quite a while music had its problems, mainly that of time. Mr. Phipps simply did not have the time to teach pano and clarinet and also teach singing. Yet the girls clamored to sing. The answer was obvious. We needed to expand our music program. Anita Mae taught me how. She burst into my office at a time when I was too busy with a parent to see her. It was obvious she was angry.

"Anita Mae," I said, walking her to the lounge, "can you wait outside until I can see you?"

She nodded, not happily.

"What can you do," I asked her, "to get rid of your anger without getting into trouble?"

She didn't know.

"Well, think," I told her. As I turned away, I remembered to ask, "Who are you mad at, anyway?"

She didn't answer then, but within the half-hour I found out. Anita Mae had written her Song of Hostility while she waited.

> Mr. M's breath I must say
> I have to stay
> Far far away
>
> I'm glad I don't have to stay
> With him all day

He Huffs and Puffs
enough is enough

the same for G. too
He smells like my shoes

Teachers don't smell too hot
they smell like a fart

so stay away.

We didn't talk about her anger. We didn't have to. Her song had dissipated it, except it wasn't a song yet.

"I'm going to sing it," she announced.

"To what music?" I asked.

"I don't know."

"Maybe you can play it to a song you already know," I suggested, "or write your own music."

"Yeah, I'll ask Mr. Phipps," she said.

I asked Mr. Phipps, too. He told me that it wouldn't be possible for him to teach girls how to write original music, but girls certainly could hum original tunes or improvise tunes and he could write down their melodies so they could play them.

The idea for a new curriculum area began to take shape—songwriting.

I thought very seriously about it. It was not an entirely new thought. Somewhere all during the years I had been teaching, particularly on the junior-high and high-school levels, girls had been buying song sheets. They always knew every popular song. They seemed to have memorized hundreds of lyrics. Many of these girls who loved to read lyrics would read nothing else. Mr. Rabkin, one of our remedial reading teachers, had used lyrics for years as motivation toward reading, but that's all it was—motivation. We needed a new emphasis, the study of phonetics to a rhythmic beat and a melodic line. I needed a music teacher who could teach reading through the study of lyrics and songwriting.

I interviewed teachers for several months before I found Mrs. Amino, whose license was in music and who had taught singing and piano but who had never taught reading. Mrs. Amino liked the idea of songwriting, even though she wasn't certain how she would approach it.

Neither was I.

"But what will I really be teaching?" she asked, "Singing, songwriting, what?"

"Reading," I answered, "through the study of singing. They can listen to popular records, sing, hum their own tunes which you will write down, study phonetics and song structure, and as I said, they will sing, sing, sing."

"Glee club?" she asked, her eyes twinkling.

I smiled back.

"They'd kill you." Then I added, "So would I."

We needed music that bridged the gap between student and teacher, not widened it. Songwriting and music bridge that gap. Nobody stays away from instrumental music or songwriting. The sounds of clarinet often intermingle, not always harmoniously, with the sounds of groups of girls singing along with records or singing by themselves. Five girls may be practicing five different songs on five different grand pianos placed strategically on the floor so that they rebound off each other as little as possible.

In addition, we have the Wurlitzer musical laboratory, which consists of six electronic student pianos and a teacher's console. The use of earphones permits girls to hear only themselves and their teacher.

All the girls, whether they are playing on the electronic

piano or on the grand pianos, are almost oblivious to the
sounds about them. So are the girls who are writing their lyrics.
While Theodora, fortissimo, accompanied the Rolling Stones
on record, Olivia wrote her "Song About a Winter's Night":

> The night is bright
> The stars shine so bright and far
> The sweet smelling air that smells
>   like blossoms so fair
> The calling of the cold air
>   makes me feel free
> And a bright spark from the star above
> Makes me know I am free.

Olivia's song was sugar-coated reading. So was Constance's.

> The music is light and gay
> By just hearing the musicians play
> So why work today
> When this is the time to play.
>
> Girls I don't have to hear you say
> That this is the time to play
> Your eyes are sparkling away
> And telling your heart is gay.

And Beverly's:

> Music is a poem of love
> That makes me free to see
> All the love that is in the air
> Music, music is all I hear.
> In the fall I love to hear
> All the songs from far and near.
> Country long, city short,
> Music is what I thought.

Not one of those three girls felt that she was going to a reading class when she wrote her song.

No girl who practices piano or clarinet or drums feels that she is helping herself to become a better reader. But she is.

I firmly believe that children who are well coordinated physically are generally better readers than children who are not. All modern research in psychology points in this direction. I therefore also believe that teaching children skills that will make them better coordinated teaches them to be better readers.

Playing a musical instrument requires coordination. When Joanne placed her fingers on the keyboard, she had to inhibit random finger movements, she had to exert body control, so that her fingers did what she required of them. Even just sitting at the piano can be an exercise in coordination, in body control, and in developing inner inhibitions. Oral, for instance, when she first started to play, had to stand at the piano.

It was not only negativism that made her refuse to sit, it was a physical inability to control random movements. Gradually, as she gained physical control, she sat on the bench. The force with which she hit the keys decreased. The rigidity and tension of her muscles slackened, and she not only sat, she played more softly. We noticed changes in her behavior, too. She was able to tolerate more instruction, to relate better to teachers. The finger control she developed in music helped her in typing. Most important of all, she began to read better.

As far as reading is concerned, we never ask a girl to go to reading, or to the library, or to any class that requires reading, for that matter. All we require of each girl is that she take a reading test when she is first admitted to school so that we know the status of her reading achievement. Miss Miller, one of our reading teachers, administers the test and later discusses with the girl the specific areas she needs help in. We are not interested just in grade scores; if we were, all we would have to do is look at the girls' record cards. Most girls are retarded four years or more when we admit them. But this does not tell us very much. In addition, we need to know how well a girl is coordinated physically and whether she has visual difficulties. By this I don't mean whether or not she needs glasses. Certainly glasses may be important but the visual competence needed for reading cannot be measured by the Snellen eye test. For this, children stand twenty feet away from a chart and read letters with one eye at a time. This may be satisfactory for determining visual efficiency for distance, but children *do not* read twenty feet away from the page, using one eye at a time.

I simply cannot get this message across to the Board of Education.

For years, I have appealed to them to administer vision tests that would test a child's ability to focus upon a page at normal reading distance, using two eyes at a time. Such tests do exist. They have been developed primarily by optometrists, rather than by medical doctors, but the word "optometry" seems to be anathema to the medical staff at the Board who are almost as sacrosanct as curriculum-makers. They do not like being advised by optometrists. They seem to resist any idea that the visual ability to look at a written symbol, focus upon it, and integrate it into the total neurological and physical complex of a human being is not tested by Snellen alone.

At Livingston, we ignore Snellen and concentrate upon determining the visual efficiency of every student. Our testing consistently indicates that over two-thirds of our girls have difficulties in perceiving written symbols correctly and are in need of visual and perceptual training. It is not that they need glasses necessarily; some do, many do not. Their need is to learn how to use their eyes correctly. Correct perception just does not come naturally and automatically with age. Eyes often have to be trained.

With the help of several optometrists whom I consulted, Mr. Rabkin and Miss Miller learned how to do this training. Reading became not only a matter of looking at the written word, it became exercises in visual focusing and visual-motor coordination. Reading became crawling on the floor, threading beads for jewelry, playing games of blindfold, and fitting the pieces of a jigsaw puzzle together. It became tactual and visual training. For some girls, headaches were the result of such training. They had to be consoled, comforted, and rewarded. But for most girls, reading was usually fun. Often it was a game.

Olivia played her usual game of hatred with me by writing a play in which she played me, and Phyllis played Olivia's mother. The Board would have been proud of me because it was a classical lesson, containing the elements of writing, speaking, listening, and reading. The problem was that the vocabulary was not exactly in the heroic style.

Telephone Dialogue Between:
Olivia as Dr. Rothman
and
Phyllis as Mrs. P.

Telephone rings.
Mrs. P: Hello?
Dr. Rothman: Hello, Mrs. P?
Mrs. P: Yes it is.
Dr. R: This is Dr. Rothman of Livingston High School.
Mrs. P: Oh, yes.
Dr. R: I'm calling about your daughter, Olivia.
Mrs. P: What has that child done now?

Dr. R: She is a very rude child, going around cursing teachers, breaking doors.

Mrs. P: Well, excuse me. I know my daughter's bad, but I don't think she is that bad.

Dr. R: Well, Mrs. P. she goes around cursing, quoting "Hell with you Mr. Turner, you lobby-headed bastard," and all that.

Mr. P: Oh please. Don't use . . . You're supposed to be a principal. You can explain yourself more clear without using those foul language words. Oh please, I cannot stand it. I'm tired of you. Every time my daughter do the least little thing, you call me on the phone and you tell me this and you tell me that. And my daughter has told me so much about you. She has told me you only take time when you want to. But really, a principal? Oh, I just can't understand it. If you want to send my daughter home, please send her home.

Dr. R: Well, that's just what I'm going to do, Mrs. P, 'cause I am sick of her 'cause she is a pain in the neck.

Mrs. P: Excuse me, but you are a pain in the rear.

Dr. R: Mrs. P. I can see who your daughter takes after. You're just as fresh as she is.

Mrs. P: Listen honey, I'll come to that school and drag your behind like white on rice.

Dr. R: Don't bother. But I don't want your daughter back in this school. She is a disgrace.

Mrs. P: Honey, just because your school have all them privilege, please don't get nasty with me.

Dr. R: I'm not being nasty. But please I ask you to keep her home tomorrow until I call you back.

Mrs. P: Excuse me, but you supposed to be a doctor, if you really want to know, and this supposed to be a school where they learn and you don't even want to take time with them. What kind of principal or psychiatrist are you?

Dr. R: I don't have time to take care of children that act like your daughter does.

Mrs. P: Well, excuse me, but I say . . .
(Mrs. P hangs up the phone).

I cherished my little Livingston drama, particularly because I had just witnessed a lesson in oral communication only a week earlier in a regular school. I remembered how it went.

"How are you this morning?" the teacher asked.

The child answered, "Fine."

This was unacceptable.

The teacher repeated, "How are you this morning?"

The child understood the unspoken reprimand, "I am fine."

It was still unacceptable.

The teacher said, "When I ask, 'How are you this morning?' you must say, 'I am fine, thank you.' "

The teacher then went on to ask her question again.

At this point, the child was not so fine.

I could have wept for that six-year-old who was supposedly being made "ready" for reading. I have never forgotten what it was like to be six years old and left back in first grade because I had not learned to read. No one had bothered to find out why. They had assumed I was not "ready." Good Lord, I had been ready since the age of four, but I simply could not move my eyes from left to right across the page. I always wanted to go from right to left. Maybe that's why I became so proficient in reading Hebrew. I was physiologically prepared for it. But no one was interested, or perhaps they did not know enough then.

There is no excuse, today, for lack of knowledge. Unfortunately, I don't really believe it is a lack of knowledge that prevents progress. It's apathy. Nobody wants to change policy, because nobody wants to change. For years I have been suggesting a reading program of visual and perceptual training for nursery school and kindergarten children. I always present evidence to the effect that many children are having trouble learning to read, not because they do not want to, not because they are not motivated, but because they need to learn to perceive correctly. The Board's answer is always the same. Having eyes is enough.

I simply cannot communicate semantically with the powers that be. Perhaps, I should try code. It is a favored way at school. Instead of saying, "Go with me," a girl says 143. Instead of saying, "It's quits between us," a girl intones 225. The code for marriage is 117 and 666 means FYIYHTEM. No girl will tell me what FYIYHTEM means, which suggests either that the thought is so reprehensible, it can only be represented in abstracted, truncated form, or that no one knows what it means. In the latter case, the process of abstraction has decommunicated the communication.

The secret about teaching reading successfully is generally not listening to the so-called experts. I have learned instead to listen to the girls. "Experts," for instance, claim that poor readers like to read soft-cover pocket books because hard-cover books are too threatening. What nonsense! Girls enjoy carrying hard-cover books with them—the more, the better; the heavier, the better. They feel important. It is a communication to the world that they are readers.

Our library, therefore, is a place with many more hard-cover books than soft-cover ones. It is a restorative place, for contemplation, relaxing, brooding if desired, getting over hurt feelings, enjoyment, and, of course, reading. Mrs. Greenthal, who was formerly a psychiatric nurse, is the perfect person to run a place of reading. Reading should be comfort, solace, enjoyment, pleasure, and she provides in the setting of books whatever emotional climate a girl may need. What better place than a library to get over cramps, nurse a headache, enjoy a quiet birthday, think? Mrs. Greenthal's husband, Bill, practically built our library single-handed. During the teachers' strike, when we all took turns sleeping in the building, he built private study areas or carrels. Each carrel is sheltered from the rest of the room by a half-partition. One carrel has a lounge chair where a girl may plug in earphones to a phonograph and listen to a dramatic reading. Another carrel has a miniature projector screen and reading slides. A third carrel is supplied with a typewriter. Everybody enjoys literature in some way, through tapes, through films, through phonographs, through books.

Girls make remarkable progress in reading as a result of our casual reading program in which we don't shove it down their throats.

No one tells girls that they have to learn to read because reading is a source of knowledge for the future or because a good job is dependent upon reading well. Girls will not settle for what is good for them in the future, particularly when what is prescribed for them does not come from within themselves. Educators mistakenly still talk of motivating children in terms of future goals. Young people often insist that there is no future, and if they want to learn it is because learning is pleasurable, not useful, and pleasurable *now*! Our girls do not feel pressured to learn, and as a result, they do.

As girls develop the self-image of themselves as students, they become what they self-idealize—students. We seem to go through cycles of girls wanting to look like students in that they decide that they want to wear glasses. Glasses become a sign of scholarship, and we go along with it. We often send girls to optometrists for non-corrective lenses, not because they need them visually, but because they need them emotionally.

Almost every girl who has ever been admitted to Livingston

has improved in reading. It is a startling fact. This is not to say
we bring every girl up to grade level before she leaves; we do
not. Some girls are practically non-readers when they are
admitted, some leave too soon to make up the discrepancy—
but on the average, most of the girls increase two years in
reading within the period of one school year.

Most girls attain their true potential; some far surpass their
own expectations. Laverne, for instance, gained over four years
in one year, and painlessly. She didn't even know she was
learning.

"They don't teach you nothin in this school," she once
griped.

"So don't come," I answered.

"But it's a fun school," she cried and dashed out of my office.

She doesn't realize it, but she is learning.

Part of our job is to make her realize that she is progressing,
make her know that she is not stupid. Thus, we make no bones
about reading or mathematics grade scores. We tell girls what
their performance is on standardized tests, and then we show
them on retests how they improve. At first some teachers were
skeptical about telling girls their scores. They felt it was facing
the girl with her own failure; but keeping the failure from the
child is lying to her. Each girl knows her own limitations, and
giving her the opportunity to share her limitations with a
teacher who will help her overcome them is the most therapeutic approach we can take with her.

I remembered Seon at Bellevue greeting a new child in my
classroom, "You better not be a good reader. Teach only likes
bad ones."

It wasn't quite true; I liked good readers, also, but there
were so many more bad readers than good ones that I had
more to like.

And though we don't force it the way other schools do, we

are reading-oriented at Livingston. That's because our society is. Yet one basic question needs to be answered: why should we consider reading as the sole source of receiving information?

We are so concerned wth reading that we completely blind ourselves to the possibility that reading as a means of obtaining information need not be the only source of information, that reading as a skill could possibly be phased out in the years to come and children still could be well educated. Why not? Cannot an individual think as logically, clearly, and definitively with information obtained through listening, as well as with information obtained visually? Why do we assume, when all psychological research contra-indicates the hypothesis, that all individuals learn best by reading? This is simply not true. There are different styles of learning behavior. Some people learn best by hearing and listening, others by visual images, not necessarily words. Still others learn by a combination of the two. We have not really begun to use sound as a prime means of learning, and yet what better way to appreciate literature, learn science, study mankind, than through sound? The time will assuredly come in the future when the prime method of learning will not be through reading, when perhaps we will need to develop new methods of listening as a means toward learning. Who knows, fifty years from now, speed-listening may be as much in vogue as speed-reading is now?

It is now a cruel hoax perpetrated by educators that reading is essential to the mastery of ideas or knowledge. Reading should certainly be a part of that body of knowledge, but not its entirety. Yet colleges, universities, and even good high schools screen out some top-rate students, because they are not top-rate readers. This is no accident. It eliminates from education, and therefore from a participant voice in society, the ghetto and poor youth of this country.

Doesn't Anita Mae's song indicate she is capable of absorb-

ing a college education? Yet her skills at receiving information
through reading are notably poor.

> I want to die
> I say to myself
> lock me up
> Put me on a shelf
> People say
> I'm here to stay
> Put me away
> I don't want to live another day
> I live in gloom
> I stay in my Room
> In the Streets
> The people I meet
> Are kind and sweet
> I stare at my feet
> Wanting to die
> this is no lie
> so let me die
> on the street
> staring at my feet.

"Anita Mae," I said, calling her into the office. "That's so
sad. Were you thinking of something special?"

"No . . ."

"You always feel like that?" I prodded gently.

"Sometimes," she answered.

"When?"

"Dr. Rothman, they left him there to die . . ."

"Who, Anita Mae? Who left whom to die?"

"My brother. They left Archie in the park, he was stoned,
but he didn't know what he was doin, they shot him up for free,

but he didn't know and then, they got scared cause he fell out
so they got ice and put it on his private, you know, but it split
his insides and the cops come and take him to the hospital and
call my mother it was Saturday—"

I interrupted her.

"How old is Archie, Anita?"

"Eleven."

My God—eleven. I was almost afraid to ask.

"Is he all right now?"

"I guess so, the cops say he lucky."

"I guess he is," I answered.

"But he din't know what he doin, they do it to him, shootin
him up—"

"With heroin, you mean?" I asked.

"Yeah."

"Why did they put ice on him?"

"They scared. He pass out and they think ice bring you to,
you know."

I didn't know. I was glad I didn't have to know. But how to
help Anita Mae?

She supplied the answer herself.

"I like to write me songs," she said. "It makes me feel good."

"Write another," I said.

Within five minutes, sitting there in my office, she did.

> Send me away
> I don't want to live this way
> Put me on earth to stay
> God blessed me
> the birds and bees
> Oh send me away
> I survived to this day

Please send me away
Sometimes I'm gay
But still send me away
let me die
I tell no lie
when I say
send me away
God send me away

Anita Mae

Anita Mae exploded with creative expession. In her case, her creativity was also artistic. She was a truly gifted girl musically, with words, and in art. Her art work was displayed throughout the building.

Our girls soon learn that dirty pictures and dirty words do not shock teachers. The result is that they don't bother to decorate the walls with the usual word or picture obscenities that most schools harbor. Not usually, that is. Neither do they destroy the art work on display, as happens in many schools. They respect the work of others, and if a girl in extreme, uncontrollable rage begins to pull things down from walls and tear up pictures or charts, it's usually her own work she destroys. The one she is generally angriest at is herself.

Art work is everywhere, from six-foot papier-mâché bananas, five-foot papier-mâché fish, and twelve-foot paper men, to delicate pastels, clay masks, original oils, crayon coloring, tracing from coloring books, and ceramics of all kinds. Very often, we start a girl's career in art with tracing and coloring from stencils. Most art educators abhor the idea. How awful, they say, to stifle a girl's creativity.

We are not stifling it; we are releasing it. How frightening for most young adults who cannot innately paint or draw well, to be confronted with a blank piece of paper and a pencil and to be told they must create! They cannot. Young children can. They do not compare their own drawings with reality. A tree is experienced as red. It is only when they are told that trees are green that they become fearful of putting on paper their own realities. The critics have taken over. Our girls are fearful of that blank paper. The critic within each girl determines her limitations. If she cannot draw what her eyes see, she becomes frustrated. If her artistic skills do not measure up to her artistic vision, she gives up.

We therefore generally start with someone else's dream, and the finished production meets a standard of beauty. It is an art production she can be proud of. The art experience becomes less frightening, and with help from Mr. Garber and Miss Feldman, the art teachers, she can begin to paint from inner experience.

Even in art we can help with reading. Tracing, coloring within lines, requires fine body and finger coordination. It is thus a further reinforcement for the state of physical being that is a prerequisite for the reading our society still demands for belonging.

Reading, of course, is often, but not always, a prerequisite for drama. Our girls are to the drama born. The put-on, at which our girls are expert, is, after all, drama.

"You gonna drink that coffee?" Maxine asked me.

I was going to, but I stopped—cup midway to my lips.

"I shouldn't?" I asked.

"Well, go ahead."

As I raised the cup again, she quickly intercepted with, "But I wouldn't."

I put it down quickly. "Why not?"

She whispered and pointed to Dolores, who had brought the coffee to me. "She spit in it."

It's not often my stomach communicates to me so quickly—but it did then. Although I had not touched the coffee, my stomach reacted as if I had. I left my desk and my office in a hurry. When I returned, somewhat relieved, Maxine was still sitting there, the cup empty in front of her.

I suddenly understood.

"You wanted that coffee, Maxine," I accused her.

"I missed breakfast," was her unashamed explanation.

"It would have been simple just to ask," I told her, but I didn't press the point. After all, it was the most dramatic way of getting a cup of coffee I had ever witnessed. It was easily understandable when I remembered that Maxine used to be tied to a bed when she was a baby so that she couldn't reach for cake when her mother was entertaining. Maxine had learned to be a clown just to be fed.

And Cecilia had learned to be a clown just to be noticed.

With hands on her hips, her hips undulating, Cecilia came deliberately swishing past Mr. Phipps and me, as we were talking outside his room.

"Stop showing off, Cecilia," I ordered, "and take your hands down from your hips. You've got nothing there to put your hands on, anyhow."

"I know it," she answered, "and you know it, but Mr. Phipps is looking, ain't he?"

"She's so dramatic." I deliberately addressed myself to Mr. Phipps and ignored her. "I bet she could be a very good actress."

"Oh, yes," Mr. Phipps agreed. "And she could be a very good musician if she practiced."

Cecilia rolled her eyes and curled her lip. We ignored her.

"She's angry now," Mr. Phipps continued, "because Laverne plays better than she does. What she doesn't realize is that Laverne is playing a lot longer and Laverne practices all the time, but Cecilia could be one of the best pianists in the school, if she worked at it."

"You both get on my nerves," she muttered, and sped away. I let her go. I knew she needed time to think over what Mr. Phipps had said.

I was right. Later that morning I found this composition from her on my desk.

I am Cecilia at times, but when I talk back to People the way I shouldn't I am not Cecilia R. its like my mind is on the other side of the world when I talk back to teachers. I don't really mean it and I hope they realize that. I can be good when I want to I guess. I don't like to get in trouble but I do just the same. I will try to improve i know I can sometimes. I could try to be very good but it will never work out. I don't like mean teachers you know I would have still been in my other school but no I had to be the clown of the school. Sometimes I was nice and sometimes i wasn't, only thing is that I will always wind up in a argument or a Fight. I think It is time for me to grow up.

"Cecilia," I said, "there seem to be two of you. One is always sorry for the way the other one behaves. You seem to be looking at yourself all the time as if the bad one of you were on a stage and the good one of you were in the audience."

It was an interesting idea. She seemed to like it.

"Let's reverse it," I told her.

"Huh?"

"Let's do the opposite. Let's put the good Cecilia on the stage and when the bad Cecilia sees how good the good Cecilia can be, and when the good Cecilia gets lots of praise, there'll be only one Cecilia left, the good one. The bad one will have given up."

"Can I go to Miss Hack?" she asked suddenly.

"Why not?" I answered. "Miss Hack is teaching girls how actresses can make themselves cry real tears."

For a second time that day, she turned and ran away from me, this time happily. She was off to drama class.

Drama was really inevitable. It grew as our whole curriculum had—out of the interests of the girls. Girls love to act; it was as simple as that, yet none of the girls had ever acted before because most schools except those that prepare students for the theater do not offer acting or drama as a regular school subject. It is relegated to the nether regions of the extracurricular.

It is very curricular with us. When girls go to drama, they go to express their particular viewpoints of the world that day.

Champagne, for instance, recorded an account of her subway trip to school:

See, this lady got on the train at seventy second street where everybody happens. That's somethin else. Well see, we got on at forty-second and this lady was sittin on there with her two children. I was comin and we saw these three seats extra. Well, I was standin there with a umbrella hangin on the pole, you know, and the lady swear I'm gonna hit her, and I had the umbrella like that. You know that little mother fucker hussy got up and hit me and I bopped her right over her fuckin head with the umbrella. Hello, what to do with that fuckin umbrella? Now, that goes for anybody that gonna hit me with my hand. I ain't even botherin the lady. I was sittin there mindin my business with the umbrella. The lady gets up. I said: I'm not gonna eat you. And I'm sittin there mindin my own business. That lady gets me smackin in my arm with the umbrella. Boy when I got finished with her my umbrella was broke.

Drama is indeed a lively class. Girls may simulate a job interview, a telephone conversation, or a fight. They may practice modeling, improvise upon a television script, or read scenes from Broadway plays. They may write, direct, and produce their own plays or their own movies. They may walk about the school or their neighborhood, camera in hand, taking snapshots of the interesting and dynamic moments of daily living. Photographs they have taken and photographs of the girls that teachers have taken are everywhere. Girls are honest photographers. Their pictures are reflective of how they see the world about them. Most of the time it is an angry world.

Rose took to the camera eagerly. She decided to make a study of me, and for several days she followed me around the school wherever I went. At first, she always seemed to snap my picture when I was at my sternest. Then my pictures began to change. I seemed to become prettier, and when she followed me into the yard when I was called to separate Phyllis and Theodora in a near-fight, she caught Phyllis and Theodora ominously facing each other, but she ignored me. As she did so, both Phyllis and Theodora saw her and the fight was over. Screeches of "take our picture" won out, and Rose snapped Phyllis and Theodora flanking me on both sides—all of us smiling. When Rose brought the picture to me several days later, I pointed out the differences between her early pictures of me and her later ones. She smiled and said nothing, but to Miss Grant, the teacher who was teaching her photography, she said, "I used to hate her—but she's only doing her job."

She learned more than photographic skill. She learned self-expression, and that's what we aim at in drama. But we also aim at more. Our focus is not only on emotional expression, it is also on expressive speech, on both vocabulary and articulation. Undoubtedly, one of the main reasons for girls remaining in poor-paying jobs is poor speech. Ghetto speech and ghetto language unfortunately keep them rooted to the ghetto, and often other competences go unnoticed.

We tackle speech everywhere, in English, social studies, and mathematics. These areas are particularly difficult to teach. They present many problems.

We found more solutions to teaching Mathematics than to teaching English and social studies. While girls do not like mathematics, and while they are notably poorer in it than in reading or English, they are not as threatened by it, either. Mathematics is a safe subject; no one can argue with it. Right is right, and wrong is wrong, and there is little room for discussion. A girl can come to class, do some arithmetic problems, and always come out with a good grade. The secret of teaching it, of course, is knowing the mathematics level of each girl and giving her work that is in keeping with her abilites but challenging enough so that her skills can increase.

Would it were as easy with English and social studies! While most girls have gone to social studies classes all their lives, they often don't know what it is. Teachers, too, I have found, often have hazy ideas—a little bit of history, a smattering of geography, and lots of repetition. They call it a spiral curriculum. Supposedly, the same material is taught at different grade levels with the idea that each higher grade level will present the concept in greater depth. In the fourth grade, for instance, children learn the New World Conquest. Somehow, when they got to the seventh grade, they learn it all over again, and lo and behold, when they get to world history in high school, there it is again. The trouble is, there generally isn't much depth.

Depth or not, it is usually boring. In college I learned that Napoleon suffered from severe constipation. When I first learned about Napoleon in the sixth grade, we weren't told this interesting fact. I really didn't care much in either case, depth or not.

This is generally what is wrong with social studies in all our schools. The way the subject is taught, no one cares.

We tried many approaches to social studies. We combined it with English; we left it alone. We combined it with journalism and anthropology and human relations. We taught about American history, current crises, international events, air pollution, genetics, racial heritage, war, murder, nationalism, world history, prehistoric man, cultural evolution, and foods. Elaborate lessons were often planned and just as often aborted.

"Is it true a baby can be born that's a hundred years old?" Goodbye lesson.

Richard Turner tackled the problem. He is a gifted writer and teacher, and he experimented with his own materials to see if he could captivate the girls into classroom discussions that centered on something even mildly or wildly resembling social studies. He did. He captured their lives, and he published the Livingston-Turner Series, booklets that centered on the self, living in New York, employment, family, communication on all levels, with the self, with friends, with parents, with teachers, with agencies, with the outer world.

The girls loved the series. So did all teenagers who read them. The Board of Education didn't. They wouldn't put the series on the accepted book list for several years and only did so after the books had received national acclaim. They objected, it seemed, to a story about drugs and to one line in one of his stories that read, "and he took her in his arms and kissed her tenderly." The Board doesn't approve of teenagers kissing.

Social studies certainly had its headaches. Not only did we have to meet the pressures of a Board of Education which states that social studies must be offered as part of the curriculum, but the increasing need for Black Studies made itself felt on our consciences. We went to ridiculous extremes in our thinking. Black, black, yes, yes, maybe we should serve only black coffee. And was serving only vanilla ice cream white chauvinism? How blind can one get? Very!

People under pressure succumb, and often they succumb without any direction. I was determined we were not going to do that. We were not going to run scared because some of us were white, including me, the head of the school.

It was hard not to be defensive when a black salesman strode into my office and asked to see the head of the social studies department.

Mrs. Gray, my assistant principal, and I looked at each other, almost in amusement. We had no chairman of any department. We were a very small school. I explained that we had only twenty-three teachers on the staff and that we were a special school.

"You do teach black studies?" It wasn't a question. It was an accusation. It was clear he was not interested in what kind of school we were. I felt my anger rise. I knew without looking at her that Mrs. Gray was just as angry.

"We are not your enemy," I thought, "we are not," but I knew I could never convince him of that. I was the white principal who couldn't understand; Mrs. Gray was the Negro who had sold out.

Nevertheless, we tried to explain to him that we did not have a chairman of social studies. We had a teacher of what we thought was social studies, but we weren't even certain what social studies was. We tried to be honest. Our emphasis, we said, was on human identity, of which social and racial identity is a part. The way an individual begins to feel self-pride, we told him, is through success and accomplishment and relationships with people who believe in the worth of human beings. Our entire curriculum is dedicated to this concept. Approach girls on the level of black nationalism alone, and it becomes words again—words without meaning.

Girls need to know about their own racial heritage, of course, but it cannot be just a single course of study in a school. It needs to permeate the curriculum. It's also hard for me to understand why the national heritage of black people should be taught only to black children. It would seem to me that it is the white people who need it the most. But at Livingston we don't deal with black children or white children, we deal with human beings. We try to teach each girl to appreciate herself for self-appreciation is a prerequisite for appreciation of others. In our social studies program, no matter how we do it, we always try to deal with the roots of prejudice, and we find, as we have found so often, that words have little meaning. Some words are "bad" almost without reference to their original meaning.

"You pug-nose grandpoppa old nigger," screamed Constance at a white teacher. She was certainly angry, and she spoke the first words that came to her head. The words themselves made no sense, although, of course, "old nigger" was hatred, directed inward. The truth is that Constance does hate herself, not because she is a black girl, but because she is Constance. If she were white, she would hate herself just as much. Constance is incapable of making an identification of herself as a girl. She is also therefore incapable of really seeing other girls as individuals.

She came rushing into my office.

"Tell them girls to stop lying on me—"

"Who?"

"Them white girls."

THE ANGEL INSIDE WENT SOUR

"Who?" I asked again.

She named them.

Everyone she named was black.

Words, again, of hate—white, nigger—all the time stemming from her own lack of human identity.

Jews come in for their share of the words—not because the girls feel anti-Jewish particularly, but because, again, it's a dirty word, without reference to its meaning.

"I'm going to that Jew store," Joanne said to me.

"Jew store," I repeated. "You mean Italian store, don't you? Those people who sell the hero sandwiches are Italian."

Beverly laughed. "She means juice store," she said.

But Joanne wouldn't be defended. "I said Jew store and I mean Jew store. Come on, Dr. Rothman knows what I said."

"Yes," I answered, "but they're Italian."

Joanne laughed, too. "I know, it's only a habit I got me."

"Why Jew?" asked her.

But of course I knew why. It was a stereotype. All Jews owned stores. All Jews were rich.

"My mother works for this Jew," Joanne continued, "and they give her a fur coat for Christmas. They give her boss things."

"You mean all Jews are rich?" I asked.

"Yeah," she answered.

"And the ladies never work. They sit home and buy clothes and never do anything," I said.

"Yeah," said Joanne in surprise. "Howdya know?"

"Well," I answered, "I'm Jewish, but I'm not rich."

"You are so," she insisted.

"Honey," I replied, "if I were rich, do you think I'd be working here, having to get to school by eight o'clock every morning?"

She didn't know the answer was yes.

"Oh." She thought a minute. "Nope. I guess you'd be at home with somebody to clean your house."

She didn't learn not to hate Jews. She just learned that at least one Jew wasn't what she thought all Jews were.

If this is social studies, we teach it all the time.

Miss Hack very sternly brought Veronica to the office.

"Dr. Rothman, I don't like the way this young lady is behaving. She just threw milk out the window."

Veronica was surly, but ready to explain. She wouldn't look at Miss Hack.

"What happened, Veronica?" I asked.

"Nothin, that's what happened. I was lookin out the window, you know, and this thing comes out the window, I guess it was milk, well, Miss Hack says it was milk, and she blames me. How could I throwed it if I was lookin out the window?"

"Wait a minute," I said. "I don't understand. You were in your room, and where was Miss Hack?"

Miss Hack explained that she was in the street, coming into the building, when something made her look up to the second floor. As she did, she saw Veronica throwing the milk container out of the window.

"I don't think she was throwing it at me," said Miss Hack. "She was just having fun and was as surprised to see me as I was to see her. It missed me, because I sidestepped, but I saw her do it."

"You didn't," cried Veronica, now really angry. "I was lookin out the window 'cause I saw it comin from upstairs."

"Veronica," I said. "That's impossible. Nobody is upstairs. All the girls are at lunch."

"She knows that," said Miss Hack, "she's trying to get out of it."

"You shut up," screamed Veronica. "You have nothin to say to me, you short white bitch."

That did it.

"Veronica," I said, "you may be very angry, but now you're making me angry. Call her white—that she is; call her bitch—that she isn't; but short? Do you think she can help being short? Is it nice to call her short? Don't you think short people like Miss Hack and me want to be as tall as you? Did we choose our height? Is everybody in the world who is tall going to discriminate against us because we're short? There's a word for it—it's called prejudice. Are you prejudiced, Veronica?" I asked.

For a moment, she was startled at the deliberate intensity of my speech. Then she looked at Miss Hack, who, drama teacher or no drama teacher, was having trouble keeping a straight face.

Veronica started to laugh. So did I. So did Miss Hack.

"What about the milk?" I asked her after we finished.

"I didn't mean to throw it," she said.

"So, do me a favor and don't lie next time," I said. "Accidents happen. You were just fooling around, that's all, so when you do something wrong, don't defend youself by making racial remarks against somebody else."

She smiled and turned her face away. She was ashamed.

"Okay."

"And remember," I said as she was leaving, "I can't help being short any more than you can being tall—besides, some of my best friends are tall."

"Oh, you—" she cried, and began to laugh some more.

The truth is, the school is a proving ground. We try to live social studies, whatever it is, not teach it.

Girls feel they have a voice in what they want to study. They feel they, as students, have a voice in what is important for them to learn, and what is important for one girl is not necessarily important to another.

"Oh," said Sandra, "I don't want to hear none of your mouth, Laura, about religion."

"It says so in the Bible, it does," said Laura. "There are ghosts."

"You have no mind, child," said Sandra. "Go to your church and find out."

"My church, nothin," said Laura. "If there are no ghosts, how come when this lady died, her son seen her the same night she was buried, standin over him, explain me that, and my mother seen it, too."

We ended the discussion with the thought that people's religions and beliefs were private, and that no one could argue with faith.

They were learning something. They were learning the right to be individuals and the right to disagree even with some of the established mores of society.

One of our greatest successes is teaching the concept that people have the right to petition against redress. Girls always have the right to petition against injustice in the school. They draw up petitions, circulate them, and present them to me.

Dear Dr. Rothman:

Mrs. S. is unfair. She says Gail called her a nigger. All Gail said was "If I get into trouble you had better take your ass to Jesus, you black bitch." She shouldn't have said it but she was mad. Mrs. S. says Gail wanted to leave the room. Gail wanted to go to the bathroom so Mrs. S. was lying.

> Signed
> Gain, Sandra, Jane
> Donna and Phyllis

I checked with the teacher.

It seemed Gail had told Mrs. S. that she was going to the bathroom and she was going to get the key from the teacher's aide.

Mrs. S. had told her that she would call the office and see if perhaps another girl had the key, which meant the bathroom was open and Gail wouldn't have to stop for the key. In calling down, Mrs. S. had said to me, trying to put it politely, "Gail wants to leave the room." Her words enraged Gail and the others. To them, Mrs. S. was lying. They didn't understand her euphemism. Gail didn't want to leave the room, she had to go to the bathroom; leaving the room to her meant going out without reason.

It was an interesting lesson for both Mrs. S. and me. To the girls, Mrs. S.'s euphemistic interpretation was false. The girls were more direct and honest. Mrs. S. and I both discussed the matter with the girls. Gail apologized to the teacher for her language, and Mrs. S. apologized for not understanding her. We all learned, and the matter of language was settled via petition.

Whether the petition is to me or to President Nixon to end the war or to the Mayor for an increase in welfare funds or to the Board of Education for a longer school day, they are written generally in the Academic Laboratory.

The Academic Laboratory is our solution, not only to social studies, but to the entire concept of relevancy in learning. As girls select the classes they go to, they can select the Academic Laboratory, where centers have been established for the sciences, mathematics, English, history, economics, human relations, genetics, biology, French, mythology, Spanish. If a girl names it, we'll teach it. Two teachers, Mrs. Maixner and Mr. Henwood, run the Laboratory jointly. Thus, it is never closed.

When one teacher is preparing materials or out of the room, the other is present. Some girls prefer to receive instruction from a man, some from a woman. They have a choice. Girls select not only their teacher, but also their subjects, and they run through cycles of preference and interest. And that is the way it should be.

Typing, like copying, tracing, piano-playing, or playing the clarinet is another area long unrecognized for the therapeutic value it holds for disturbed, uncontrolled girls who find that they cannot type unless they exercise body posture and control over their fingers. It is another area requiring inner control.

Because they feel so imperfect and because they view themselves as imperfect, many troubled girls tend to look and dress that way. They often seem to have a great need to be unattractive. In that way, of course, they can cushion themselves against the rejection they constantly feel. "They don't like me because I'm ugly" gives substance to their lives. It's an easier burden to bear than "They don't like me because I'm me." And because they cannot face the constant rejection they fear, they prefer ugliness. It gives a rationale to the defenses they have been building.

In view of this we started a beauty culture program with one shop ten years ago (we have two today). For the same reasons we began to emphasize dressmaking. This is all part of our curriculum centering on self and the development of the ego. Even cooking has a distinctly personal aspect and reason for being. Girls who go to our cooking classes see themselves not as cooks, but as chefs. We don't make oatmeal cookies, we made oatmeal cookies with almonds *à la chinoise*.

Girls in adolescence need to know that they are girls, and pretty at that. Many girls think so little of themselves that they find little virtue in their own appearance. So it is part of our curriculum to help them find their own inner and outer beauty.

We insist that all girls wear skirts and dresses. We do not permit girls to wear slacks. I am well aware that my ban of slacks is in direct violation of the ruling by the State Commissioner of Education that principals cannot standardize dress. While the commissioner is undeniably right that an individual's civil rights cannot be curtailed by a school authority imposing criteria for dress, we know that when a girl wears slacks to school she is preparing for a fight. The Commissioner, being a man, simply does not realize that a good fight cannot be fought in a dress.

I am willing to take the stand that requiring girls to wear dresses and skirts is therapeutic, while permitting them to wear pants is not, particularly when so many of our girls are experimenting with homosexuality; wearing boys' blue jeans and boys' clothing is a first step in letting other girls know they are assuming the masculine role. Ten years ago, they did not need blue jeans to communicate their homosexuality. They had a simple method of winding a black silk kerchief on the head and forehead and knotting it in front on the forehead. This was a direct statement that they were butch.

I did not permit girls to wear kerchiefs then, and I still don't, but for still another reason. Certainly, every girl who wore a kerchief was not homosexual. Girls wore kerchiefs to hide their natural hair that had not been straightened. The girls were ashamed of their natural hair. We did not permit them to use the kerchief as a symbol of shame. They could go to the beauty shop and style their hair, but hide it—no!

With the rise of black nationalism there is a great new pride in being black, and girls are wearing natural hair styles. The use of the kerchief either as a sexual communication or as a cover for shame has therefore become part of our educational history.

Betty Lou was not an ugly girl, by any means. Her skin was exceptionally white and she was extremely thin; her hair, long and straggly, was pulled back into a tight little knot behind her ears. Her lips were very pale, almost bluish. We immediately suspected a heart condition and referred her for a complete medical examination. The report, however, was completely negative. She was just constitutionally thin and pale, her thinness and paleness not helped by only three hours of sleep at night, with the rest of the night devoted to dating and drinking. She spoke warmly of her friends and apparently cherished their companionship. Yet she constantly complained that they made fun of her large blue lips, the upper one very lightly marred by a tiny mole.

She came to school only to go to the beauty culture class, where she spent hours setting and resetting her hair, always in the same style, and applying and reapplying her makeup, always with the same effect, her blue lips pronounced, her mole noticeable. Mrs. Schneider, the beauty culture teacher, offered Betty Lou help, but Betty Lou refused. She knew what she was doing, she said. Apparently she did, because when she finally weakened and permitted Mrs. Schneider to set her hair and apply her makeup, she became a new girl. She was transformed into luminescence. Her eyes were heightened by mascara and eye shadow, and her pink-tinged cheeks and light lipstick completely covered the mole and negated the natural blueness of her lips. Her hair—combed, recombed, and brushed—fell shining to the nape of her neck. She looked beautiful, and she couldn't bear it! Off came the lipstick, the powder, and the mascara; the hair got pulled back again. Betty Lou could face the world only as a reject. The transformation was too sudden. She couldn't cope with the image of herself as she faced herself in the mirror. It made her inner image a lie, and it was with this inner image that she had built her patterns of behavior. She could not tear it down. It left her whole previous life a lie. It left her defenseless.

We went too fast; giving her the pretty face was not the sole answer. It was too threatening for her to be catapulted into attractiveness. She needed more time. The inner self needed to keep pace with the outer one, and the inner self was not ready to feel attractive. On her sixteenth birthday, after months of truancy, Betty Lou was legally free to leave school officially. We had failed her.

Betty Lou's reaction was not unusual. Evelyn, too, could not tolerate her new image. Evelyn had had all her front teeth knocked out in a fight. Miss Service, our social worker, who worked very closely with Evelyn and her family, had arranged for extensive dental rehabilitation. Evelyn had all her teeth replaced. Evelyn, however, refused to wear her dental bridges. She made all kinds of excuses—that they hurt, didn't fit—but the simple truth was, Evelyn was not prepared to be more attractive. Betty Lou and Evelyn had started with the same feelings of nothingness. They had defended against the nothingness by constantly proving to themselves that they indeed were nothing. They were immunizing themselves against rejection.

We eventually succeeded with Evelyn. She felt attractive enough to get a boyfriend and become pregnant. She felt herself to be a woman. We failed with Betty Lou. Several years later, I learned she was prostituting. I refuse to believe that Betty Lou's fate was inevitable. Perhaps if we had ignored her obsession with her appearance, we would have helped more. I do not know. I do know that we cannot be bogged down by the debility of "might have beens." Nevertheless, I always want to remember our failures. Certainly, it is far more pleasant to dwell on our successes, but it wouldn't help a Betty Lou if she were to come our way again. And undoubtedly she will.

chapter six

The Myth of Discipline

Discipline has a very special meaning at Livingston, for we do not equate discipline with punishment. Yet, over and over, visitors ask, "How do you exert discipline?" or "What are your disciplinary measures?" What they really mean is: How do we punish the girls?

If they ask the question after visiting the school, speaking to the girls, to me, to the staff, the teachers, the counselors, the patrolman, the secretaries, the cooks, then they do not understand what the school is all about. Traditionally, discipline implies that someone imposes something on someone. Someone being disciplined has something done to her. Unfortunately, in most schools, discipline is like education. There is a doer and a recipient. Not at Livingston.

A patrolman is still at our school. He is not here for external discipline the way he was eleven years ago. His role has changed. He is here as a symbol of authority—a fair, just authority. He is here as an upholder of laws because any society must have laws. He is here as a friend who knows court

175

and police procedure and who can help girls and their families when they need such help. This is as it should be. Too often, the girls know the police only as "pigs." It is a new, wonderful experience to meet a patrolman who often teaches reading and who butters their toast at breakfast. They can learn from such a man.

No, at Livingston we don't exert discipline. The process of the program—the milieu of the school—*is* the discipline. Everything we do, the total school structure, the involvement of the girls in deciding for themselves what is right for them and what is wrong, is discipline internalized.

Discipline imposed is ineffective and wasteful of human spirit. It causes the generation gap we hear so much about. It causes aberration. It causes violence.

When girls learn that controls come from inner resources, they are being taught discipline. They are also being educated.

A visitor on any school day at Livingston might chance upon an atmosphere of quiet, of calm, of order, of every girl working, every teacher in a room. It might happen. Then again, it might not. There are days when visitors would see screaming girls having tantrums in the halls, and, in the lounge, impatient and obviously hostile parents waiting to see one of the teachers or me. There are days and there are days. We love every one because we have a feeling of what we are doing, and the feeling that there is an underlying structure to the school, that there is a basic sanity to our world. We help girls find and see the structure and the sanity at the very moments that they seem to be denying or defying it.

This does not mean we can solve every problem. We can't. Sometimes the problems of the girls are insoluble within the present structure of society. We grope for answers. We find some, and often we settle for less than the ideal because we can do no better.

Laura came to school obviously under the influence of some stimulant. She was giggly and laughing and falling over her feet. She was constantly talking, using her hands excitedly, moving with small jerky steps from one seat to another, gleefully announcing, "I'm learning me a word." Just a few minutes earlier, she had told the other girls that she had stopped off at a candy store in her neighborhood and had taken a few pills before coming to school. She said it loud enough for Mrs. Eisert, her teacher, to hear.

"What's wrong? What's everybody looking at me funny for?" She laughed in a loud voice.

"What did you take, Laura?" Mrs. Eisert asked solicitously.

"Me? Nothin. You believe these girls? They lie on you."

Mrs. Eisert sent for me. I sent for Mrs. Langness.

"What did you take, Laura?" I asked.

"Always think I take things, shit," she cried angrily. "Coca-Cola, that's what I take, Coca-Cola, doesn't everyone like Coca-Cola?"

She began to laugh.

The girls were silent—frightened.

As Laura became louder, the other girls became more upset. This had never happened in their class before.

"Come on, Laura, shut up," urged Henrietta.

Laura kept on laughing.

How pointless to handle Laura as an exercise in discipline! Laura needed help, and at a time like this we must first utilize the resources we have at school. The resources are the professional staff and the girls.

Mrs. Langness, Mrs. Gray, Mrs. Eisert, Laura's teacher, and Mr. Scarcella and I all conferred with each other. We caught each other on the run as Mrs. Eisert calmed the other girls in the class, trying to ease their anxieties and concerns over what was going to happen to Laura; as Mrs. Langness desperately tried to reach Laura's mother; as Mrs. Gray tried to keep other girls from trooping to the classroom to see what the excitement was all about; and as Mr. Scarcella tried to talk Laura into coming to sit in my office.

We had decided within seconds who was to do what. Mr. Scarcella was chosen to remain with Laura, because she sincerely loved him. "He's my father," she used to say to me, and then laugh with embarrassment.

Mrs. Langness finally reached Laura's mother. She did not seem particularly annoyed that we had called her, but she didn't seem particularly involved, either. She had to leave for her job. Besides, she was certain Laura hadn't taken any pills, because Laura was always silly like that. Maybe Laura was particularly silly, her mother said, because Laura's brother, Jaime, was home from the army on leave, before he went to Vietnam. Perhaps she would talk to him and call us back.

Mr. Scarcella had persuaded Laura to come into my office. He and Laura and I talked together as Laura sipped coffee. Laura's eyes began to appear extremely strange. She had trouble focusing. She wasn't laughing any more. The crying became more agitated. She wanted Mr. Scarcella to be physically close to her.

I knew that Laura should be seen by a doctor. I also knew, from sad, frustrating experiences, that no doctor would examine Laura without the permission and presence of her mother. I could tell them that Laura's mother had signed a written consent for Laura to be treated at a hospital in case of an emergency, but they would tell me that this was not an emergency. Loss of consciousness or a heart attack is an emergency. Being under the influence of a stimulant is not an emergency, particularly when Laura would deny that she had taken anything. "It's an emotional problem," the doctors would say.

Their reluctance to treat is based on their fears. Doctors do not want to be sued, and a parent has the right to sue for unauthorized medical treatment that is not for an emergency.

Just then Jaime arrived.

Laura's mother had sent him to school while she went on to her job. Laura began first to laugh, then to cry, when she saw Jaime. She was obviously very fond of her twenty-one-year-old brother. Jaime talked with me and told me he had seen enough drugs and pills back in the army and in his neighborhood to know that Laura was dangerously high.

Should we arrest her and ask that the court remand her to a psychiatric hospital? That was almost as hopeless as sending her to the hospital. It would start and end with me trying to convince the court I was looking for a psychiatric hospital and hospitalized treatment for Laura—not punishment—and the court would be reluctant to believe me. Who was I? The court would undoubtedly send Laura home, and I would be chastized because Laura had committed no offense for which she could be arrested and forced to accept help. How dare I? And how dare I suggest that Laura might attempt suicide after this episode? Was I presumptuous enough to predict behavior, just because I knew Laura and knew how depressed she could get?

Well, I could always suspend her for five days—a legal five-day suspense for behavior that was uncontrollable in school. After all, this was a matter of discipline. We would have five days of reprieve from Laura's problem, and Laura would have five days to destroy herself.

We decided with Jaime's approval to call an ambulance and at least have a doctor see her. We hoped they might see the need for hospitalization. But they only examined her superficially, said she appeared under the influence of some intoxicant, and sent her home.

The next day Laura telephoned. She was weeping. She was not coming to school, she was going to kill herself. Her sobbing on the phone made her words incoherent. All I could understand was that she wanted to die.

We spent the greater part of that morning telephoning her. When I didn't talk with her, telling her we would help her, we liked her, she could come back to school, we were expecting her, Mr. Scarcella spoke with her, telling her the same things. Mrs. Langness and I frantically tried to reach her mother at her job. At noon, we had succeeded for that day; Laura was calmed. She promised Mr. Scarcella she would not hurt herself; she would come to school tomorrow. She did, and we picked up the pieces that were Laura and went on with teaching her, offering therapeutic counseling daily, conferring with her mother almost daily, trying to work out a life for Laura in spite of not being able to get hospitalization for her. Several months later, Laura attempted suicide. Genuine help, not punitive action or so-called discipline, was called for here, but the community as it is organized let her down, because primarily it is set up to administer traditionally packaged discipline instead of offering genuine and innovative help to troubled adolescents.

Then there was Virginia, who came in with a bandaged wrist. She had cut herself the night before with a razor. She, too, disrupted her classes. She stood in the second-floor lounge outside her room and wouldn't move. She also wouldn't talk—not to Mrs. Landsman, not to Mrs. Eisert, not to Mrs. Gray, not to me. And yet we were all people she had liked and trusted. It is definitely a discipline problem when a girl refuses to move or speak except to say she will not move, even if she has to stay all night. There was no reason that we knew about for Virginia to be catapulted into an immobile state. But of course there was one.

And we proceeded to find out. I called Virginia's sister.

"Pay Virginia no mind," she said. "Virginia always talks about killing herself."

"Has she ever tried to?" I asked.

"Yeah—once or twice, she, you know, cut herself on the wrists. You know the way kids are these days, always wantin attention. Lots of girls do that—they just want attention."

"Well, if she wants attention so badly," I said, "then she must really need it, so don't you think we should give it to her?"

She understood what I was saying, although many professional people do not when I make the same point. They do not always see a desperate attention-getting device as a need for psychiatric intervention.

Virginia's sister wanted to talk to her mother first, before she agreed to psychiatric help. She promised to call her mother at work and then call me back. Virginia lived with her sister because her mother had lived as a sleep-in maid for fifteen years for the same family. Part of Virginia's difficulty, of course, was that she resented having no mother. While her own mother became a mother to the two children she took care of, Virginia was an orphan. Virginia's mother had even refused to come to school to sign the working papers when Virginia went into Upper School. We had always talked with Virginia's oldest sister because of her mother's refusal to be involved with Virginia in any way.

Virginia's sister eventually called back. Virginia was still mute and rigidly standing outside her classroom door. Her mother had said we should do anything we thought was right. I asked her sister to come to school immediately, although it meant a two-hour trip for her. Mrs. Landsman then called Virginia's probation officer and asked her to take Virginia to court as a person in need of emergency psychiatric help. The probation officer agreed that Virginia needed psychiatric treatment, but she also told us that the judge would not order such treatment without a psychiatrist's recommendation. My recommendation was not good enough. She also told Mrs. Landsman that the hospital would not admit Virginia without a court remand. Voluntary patients, particularly adolescents, are bad treatment risks, hospital administrators feel. They often leave against advice in the middle of treatment. Psychiatrists therefore prefer patients when they are remanded by court. They cannot leave.

I remembered a fifteen-year-old boy coming to the admissions office at Bellevue, pleading for admission, because he was hearing voices telling him to kill, and he didn't want to kill. The admitting officer referred him to an outpatient cinic. Only when the boy took out a knife and threatened to kill himself did they admit him. I remember that tragic child. I did not want the same thing to happen to Virginia.

I called our consulting psychiatrist, who was assigned only four hours a week to our school, and who had seen Virginia one week earlier. He had recommended treatment, and we had been trying to work out when, where, and with whom. In New York City it is not easy to be accepted for treatment. But we could wait no longer. On the basis of my description of her current behavior, he recommended emergency in-patient treatment. Mrs. Landsman immediately called the court to tell them of his recommendation. When I told Virginia that her sister was coming to school, that she and her sister were going to court with a letter from me, stating that Virginia needed to be in a hospital, she smiled for the first time. She was aware of the disorganizing impulses that were sweeping through her. She was receptive to the idea of help. It was a relatively happy

Virginia who left school to go to court to be sent to a hospital.

Virginia remained in treatment at the hospital with a diagnosis of agitated depression for almost seven months. When she returned to school, she was calmer and appeared to have settled many conflicts. Schooling and life continued.

Discipline case?

Are attempted suicides, active depressions, drugs, alcoholism, pregnancies, rape, assaults in the community matters for punitive action, for traditional discipline?

When our girls misbehave, if misbehave is the word, they are acting out their unhappiness—because unhappinesss really *is* the word—and we handle it clinically, not punitively.

To do this, we of course feel we are clinicians, not only by professional definition, but because we deliberately set up a total atmosphere for *accepting* feelings and behavior and then doing something about it. The clinicians include the teachers, the guidance counselors, the administrative staff, and a part-time social worker, Miss Service, assigned from the Bureau of Child Guidance.

Ten years ago, we started with a full-time clinical team from the Bureau, consisting of psychiatrist, psychologist, and social worker. During the course of the years, budgets have been slashed, and the team has dwindled to only Miss Service, two times a week.

I am outraged at this lack of concern. We simply do not have sufficient clinical help for the intensities of the problems we handle. Miss Service comes to school on Tuesday and Thursday, but if a girl whom she is treating is in dire trouble on Monday or Wednesday, what do we say—hold it until the day is right for us?

I have insisted consistently that it is incumbent upon the Board of Education to give more clinical service to New York

City's most aggressive adolescent girls. The Bureau of Child Guidance is very polite. They always agree with me, but agreement is not action. It is merely their way of avoiding a fight with me.

They claim budgetary helplessness. I claim they had better find a way. So far, I have not won. And I would like to. I feel that we need not only a full-time psychiatrist on staff, but also a consulting neurologist. What great research could come from Livingston, research that could help thousands of children elsewhere!

It is my firm belief, for instance, that not enough attention has been given psychologically, medically, and educationally to the relationship of impulsive acting-out behavior and physical impulsivity. What made Esther suddenly jump out of her seat and scream at her teacher, "You've dirtied my stockings. Here, wash them"? She began to strip them from her legs with such fury that she scratched herself severely without knowing it.

The intensity of her reaction was totally out of proportion to Mrs. Eisert's accidentally brushing her stocking with a pencil tip. Esther knows it, yet she could not help it. It was as if a physical force had been released in her. She went through a siege of frenzy, pulling at her clothes and throwing over typewriters. Nothing would appease her but that the teacher wash her stockings right in front of her, in a sink outside the classroom door. She would not permit the teacher to take them home, or offer to buy her a new pair. No—it was Esther's terms or nothing. Finally, of course, we appeased her, but when it was over, Esther could not explain it any more than we could.

The tantrum had come and gone involuntarily, almost like a seizure based in a physical disequilibrium. Why was it that a small speck of dirt could make exquisite Esther feel flawed and imperfect? Perhaps because she felt so flawed inwardly. Was it possible that Esther was somehow subconsciously aware of some internal disharmony, some internal imbalance, hormonal, neurological, which propelled her into behavior that is really psychologically alien to her? Esther literally could not help herself. Yet, we could find no specific cause, not without the neurological research that would be necessary. The whole field of delinquency, the reason why children often, without any real motivation, engage in impulsive, uncontrolled acts of delinquency, should be studied from this questioning point. Perhaps if we had some answers to the questions, we might be able to take corrective medical action and be a step closer to understanding and controlling delinquency.

But no help is coming from our Bureau of Child Guidance. They can't give me a pyschiatrist and a psychologist or a social worker full-time, and here I am asking for neurological research! The Bureau of Child Guidance is an inexplicable superstructure that exists on conferences. The inexplicability of it is that social workers seem to speak only to social workers, psychologists to psychologists, and psychiatrists to psychiatrists. They seem to need to group together to fight for power.

Whenever I think of the Bureau of Child Guidance, I remember my little nine-year-old boy in a so-called adjustment class in a regular school.

"Teach, do you have sex?"

Those were the days when I was a new teacher and I believed that little minds were inquiring minds, questions were purely innocent, children were wholly innocent. I was a dope!

"Well . . . uh . . . I'm married," I answered.

"Do you sleep with your husband?" he continued.

"Well . . . uh . . . " I continued, "married people sleep together . . . uh . . . you know."

"Do you sleep in one bed?" he asked.

"Well . . ." I went on, "uh . . . many married people sleep in one bed. . . well, uh . . . yes, we sleep in one bed."

"So who gets on top?" he asked.

That's when I called it finis. But the question is applicable to the Bureau.

I guess I will have to wait for my research on the correlation between delinquency and psychophysical malfunctioning.

Delinquent behavior is, of course, what most often brings a girl into court. If she is under sixteen, she goes to a family court. There is one in each borough of New York City. If she is over sixteen, she goes to adolescent court. A delinquent act is one that would be a crime if committed by an adult. If she is adjudged delinquent by the court, the onus for her behavior is definitely on her. If she is adjudged a person in need of supervision, she has not committed a delinquent act particularly, but she is beyond parental control. The onus is still on her. If she is termed "neglected," she may have committed a delinquent act and she may be beyond parental control, but the onus is on the parent. It often becomes a legalistic game of musical chairs in determining on which petition to bring a girl to court. To the girl it matters little; she may be sent to a training school operated by the State or to a treatment facility most often operated by a private agency, or she may be put on probation and remain at home.

I was idealistic when I first came to Livingston, or perhaps I was just stupid. I still have some ideals, I hope, despite the fact that I am less stupid; I have seen how often judges are incompetent, court personnel overworked and frustrated. The law may be valid, but the implementation of the law is flawed, not only because the machinery often breaks down, but also because judges are political appointees, not always suited by temperament, philosophy, or training to be the dispensers of justice in a family court, where the problems that come before the court are primarily social, emotional, and psychological, and only concomitantly legal. Judges should be versed in psychology and sociology, as well as in law. This is not now a requirement. It should be!

I have brought girls to court only a few times. Each time it was in the last desperate hope that I could get the help the girl needed. I have done it in the belief that if a girl needed psychiatric help in a hospital and we could not obtain it for her, the court could and would, almost with no questions asked, taking our word on good faith. I have done it in the belief that if a girl needed to be removed from a damaging home, we could ask the court to do it and it would be done. I have done it in the belief that her request would be honored if a girl herself asked to be taken away from her home. But the court is legalistic only, which is one aspect of what it should be, of course, but that is not enough. It is not often psychologically educated, and it should be—to deal with human beings.

When I had Glenda arrested for throwing a book at me, it was an arrest for technical assault. I wasn't hurt—the book had landed on my ankle—but I needed to make that arrest. It was the only way I had of making Glenda's mother accept psychiatric help. She had consistently refused to give us permission for Glenda to be given a psychiatric and neurological examination. We needed that examination to understand Glenda better; we could not determine the reasons for Glenda's sudden bursts of destructive behavior. Was there some organic brain damage that might require treatment? From everything we had observed about Glenda, there seemed to be such a possibility. I wanted the court to order a full psychiatric and neurological study; this meant hospitalization. I made my request, but the judge did not honor it. There was no evidence to support my suggestion. He could not, he said, remand every child who came before him for a full study.

He asked Glenda if she had thrown the book at me. She calmly admitted she had.

This seemed to please the judge. She had admitted her wrongdoing, and now she could reform. He placed her on probation and told her to go home with her mother, be a good girl, and return to school the next day.

School? That's when he lost me. Why on earth had I brought her to court? We were worse off than before. Glenda would return without receiving the help she needed, and it would be disastrous at school. The girls knew that no girl could return to school after assaulting a teacher. An arrest was a signal that there were limits to what we would tolerate. The girls also knew, as we did, that Glenda needed a lot more help than we could give her. The girls always understood need.

Not so the judges. The judge was still droning on when my mind returned to what he was saying.

Respect for the teachers, he was saying, Glenda should have respect for her teachers and her principal, respect for her mother and the court, respect for education, respect for the world. He became eloquent and suddenly remembered his boyhood. He had gone to school, too, he told Glenda, and he had always respected his teachers; when he was fresh to his teachers, his father had spanked him. Respect was the word. Respect.

Glenda listened stoically.

He finished. She spoke.

"Fuck you, judge."

I have never seen a face get so red so fast.

He screamed, "I am remanding you! Youth House! In all

my years on the bench, I have never had anyone speak that way to me. A hardened criminal wouldn't dare speak that way to me. I have sentenced men to ten years in prison, and they haven't spoken to me that way."

I could feel my smile spreading inwardly all over.

"Judge," I felt like saying, "you have never been a teacher."

"Remanded to Youth House until October 22," he repeated. He had seemed to pull himself together. His voice was lower. Then he picked up a pencil and spoke even lower, "Psychiatric examination ordered."

Glenda had come through for herself, after all. She knew what she needed, even if the judge didn't, and she had seen to it that she got it.

I was not happy about her being remanded to Youth House; I had hoped for Bellevue, but I shouldn't have worried. Glenda managed to get herself transferred within a few days. Good for Glenda, but what a tortuous way for a girl to get treatment. And the judge had been concerned with discipline!

I finally realized that I had to learn how to teach judges, so that when I was forced to use them as the last resource of hope, I could use them well.

There was Joan.

Joan needed treatment. She was sixteen. Her mother was mentally ill. So was Joan, and unlike many girls who have the amazing inner strength to live through what they do, Joan had succumbed. And again, unlike many girls who still cling to their mothers, still searching for love, Joan wanted out. A desperate out. Suicide. She tried it once, half-heartedly, by slashing her wrists, but her mother punished her.

So Joan came to school at eight-thirty in the morning, went to the school yard, took out a leather liquor flask, and deliberately drank from it in front of all the girls and a teacher. She

knew that without a doubt the teacher would bring her to the
office. It was a matter of discipline.

She was all bravado, stomping around my office, screaming
at the top of her voice, "Go ahead, arrest me, isn't that what
you do? Send me away. See if I care."

"Joan, try to calm down. I'm not having you arrested. Sit
down," I told her.

"Sit down?" she cried. "Is that all you care about? Sure,
Joan sit down, and everything is all right, sure, Joan, sit down
and everything is solved, is that all you know—bitch—sit
down? I won't sit down. Arrest me, see if I care, bitch, send
me away, isn't that what you do?" The screaming and pacing
went on.

"No, it's not what I do," I explained, "but why do you want
to be arrested?"

"Cause I'm crazy," Joan yelled. "She knows it, but she won't
let me go—I swear I'll kill myself if I have to stay with her."

I was slowly getting the message.

"Okay, Joan," I said, "you want to be arrested and get sent
away from home. I get it, and I'll help you. Is that why you
brought in a flask?"

She suddenly appeared happy and flopped into a chair, legs
sprawling, long hair flying, arms flailing. She seemed to be all
over the office.

"Yeah."

And I played a sudden hunch. "There wasn't any liquor in
the flask, was there?" I took the flask from my desk and turned
it upside down. It was absolutely dry and smelling stale.

"You didn't have to do this to get help, Joan," I told her.
"Why didn't you just talk to me, or to your teachers, or to Mrs.
Landsman?"

She became excited again and jumped up. "I did talk, talk,

talk, ask Mrs. Landsman, nothin but talk, but Mrs. Landsman can't do nothin, you can't do nothin, my mother won't listen to her, she won't listen to you, either."

Joan was right. Mrs. Landsman couldn't do anything to help Joan. Neither could I. Talking to Joan and her mother, trying to get them to understand each other, was hopeless. Joan needed hospitalization and treatment. So did her mother.

"So you pretend to be drunk," I said. "You had to do something like this to make someone listen. Is that it?"

Joan fell into a chair and began to sob, "I'll kill her. I'll kill myself. I'll never go home."

After a while, she calmed down, and Joan and I both sipped the Cokes I had sent for while she calmly repeated to both Mr. Scarcella and me that she wanted to die, that if I didn't send her away from her mother, she would kill herself—after she killed her mother.

"Joan," I promised, and I put my arms about her, "if it's not right for you to go home, you won't."

I told Joan that whatever I did, I must first get her mother's permission. I told her that if I couldn't get her mother's permission to send her for help, I would have to go to court and be a petitioner against the mother. I knew I would go through with it if I had to, but cringed at the thought. No doubt Joan's mother would get a lawyer to help her keep Joan at home. Joan's mother could be deceptively charming to people who did not see below the surface to the truth. I told Joan I would be willing to go to court—but before I did, I would like to try to talk to her mother on the telephone and see if I couldn't get her mother to agree to hospitalization.

Joan got excited again, but after much persuasion on my part permitted me to call.

I telephoned Joan's mother and told her Joan needed help

urgently and must go to a hospital where doctors could find out what was troubling her and help her, because Joan was very unhappy and if we didn't get help for her now, Joan might do something harmful to herself.

Joan's mother was unyielding. "There's nothing wrong with Joan, she's just stubborn. She refuses to do what she's told."

I repeated my points endlessly, but I was getting nowhere. So I decided to get adamant. "If Joan kills herself, Mrs. D., it will be on your conscience."

Joan began to grimace and laugh and yelled into the phone to her mother, "Bitch, bitch, bitch, bitch, bitch." She looked up at me. "See—what did I tell you?"

"She only wants attention, that girl," Mrs. D. shouted at me at the other end. "She's a pig, filth, slime, she won't bathe, I gotta make her take a bath—you ever hear of that, a fifteen-year-old girl who won't take a bath, I won't have filth in my house, I won't, she knows it too, that's why she does it." Her voice rose even more. "You know what she does, your precious Joan, she took the dirt from the toilet bowl and spread it over the living room, that's what she did." She was now hysterical, and in a sense I had her. I told her that she was right. I hadn't realized it before, but she was right. If Joan did that, she was dirty and should be sent out of the house. And of course, if she were in a hospital they'd find out why she did these things so that she wouldn't do them again.

Mrs. D. suddenly quieted down. "You're right," she said. Joan was sick. No daughter of hers coming from such a clean house would do such a disgusting thing as spreading feces all over the couch unless she needed help. She agreed that Joan should see a doctor in a hospital.

It was all finally arranged. I would arrest Joan for drinking in school, and I would ask for hospitalization. My concern was that Joan appeared extremely depressed and agitated. Depression and agitation are a combination that can lead to homicide or suicide. I felt Joan was quite capable of trying to kill herself, or her mother. So I was perfectly willing to use the drinking incident, which wasn't a drinking incident at all, to get Joan the help she needed—help that could be given only in a hospital where she would be protected from the disorganizing forces of her own thoughts and feelings.

The plan called for Joan's mother to come to court and agree to hospitalization. Under these circumstances the judge might order Joan to Bellevue, but of course I could not be certain. I told Joan that the possibility existed that the judge might just look at her pretty face and see only a girl who had never been in trouble before and send her home to her mother with an admonition to be good.

"What will you do then?" I asked. "What will you do if he says to go home?"

Joan laughed easily. "I'll tell him I won't."

"That won't do, Joan. You'll have to say it as if you mean it. You'll have to play it rough."

And then we practiced what she would say and what he would say. When she left, Joan was fully rehearsed for what she might have to do. She knew she would have to be dramatically unmannered.

Apparently judges don't fully understand that murderers and suicides can be very polite people.

Joan went off to court, a happy arrest. I felt a sense of relief; for the first time since Joan had come to school, we were really giving her the kind of help she wanted and needed. I didn't permit myself to be upset by Joan's mother, whose parting shot to me on the phone was "Oh, I can't come. I have to go shopping. But my husband will be there. It better be quick, though, you know how parking is."

Joan was diagnosed at the hospital as suffering from paranoid schizophrenia—acute depression. The treatment she began receiving eventually helped her to deal more effectively with the problems life had handed her.

Discipline? Punitive treatment? How would it have helped this girl?

Sometimes I wonder at the amount of maneuvering we must often go through to accomplish one single step forward in the girl's behalf. Courts and judges are not the only ones who often need a nudge to be moved; many times social agencies are equally impossible to work with. They rarely understand the structure and problems of our school, the fact that we are dealing with many girls and not just the child they are handling at the moment. Agencies are not always helpful, because they are most often socially unaggressive and don't reach out too vigorously. If a parent or a child stops coming for treatment, they close the case. Of course, there are exceptions of individual social workers who do reach out, but they are rare. Too often, the policy of an agency is defeatist. One agency, for instance, would not recommend residential treatment for a girl because there were no residences that would take her.

"But does she need a residence?" I persisted.

"Definitely."

"Well, recommend it," I urged, "put it in writing, tell it to the judge."

"Why bother? None are available. It's impractical," they said.

"So is denying the truth," I answered. "If reputable agencies don't set up a demand for services that are needed, then we just remain with the status quo. If we don't set up a clamor for what we need, how can we ever hope to get it?"

I might just as well have conserved my energy.

There are many times I feel this way—particularly when the agencies seem to operate outside the realm of reality.

"Well, Dr. Rothman, Lana's defecation on the floor is symbolic of her aggression," a psychiatrist from one of the agencies told me.

"Well, your therapy should teach her to express her aggression another way," I answered. "We can't keep girls in school who deliberately take a wastepaper basket, center it in the room, and deliberately defecate. We can't tolerate it."

I asked him for a medical suspense, which meant that Lana would not be permitted to come to school for thirty days.

"But she loves school," he told me, "she loves the teachers."

"Of course," I answered. "That's exactly the point. Loving the school means she will want to come and she will no longer do such things, once she understands we will not permit her to come under her terms."

"She loves you," he told me. I suppose he thought it would flatter me.

"I know that," I answered, "and that's exactly why she needs to be suspended now. I will tell her she can't come back for a month. When she does, she will no longer defecate in a classroom."

"Well, you suspend her," he answered.

"I will," I told him. "The girl will think it's from me. I will be the ogre, you can be the supportive therapist, but I need to be legally covered."

I went on to tell him the law. Legally, I can issue an administrative suspense for five days, after which the girl may return to school. Beyond five days, I need a medical suspense; if I don't get it from a doctor, I am breaking the compulsory education law. I don't want to break the law, but if the psychiatrist does not agree with me, I am left with no resource.

Lana's psychiatrist did not agree with me.

"She needs her education," he kept insisting.

"What kind of education can she get in a school where they

permit girls to defecate on the floor?" I countered. "What is she learning—that all forms of behavior are acceptable?"

He would not concede. It seems to me imperative that if child psychiatrists are really to help children, they should as part of their professional training serve an internship as classroom teachers. Then, and only then, can they understand how a child's functioning in a classroom group is different from the way the child may function elsewhere. Then, and only then, too, can they understand that what a psychiatric hospital can tolerate a school cannot.

Lana's psychiatrist put me in a bind. He would not issue the suspense because the problem was strictly a school one, not a psychiatric one. Lana, he felt, needed to be in school, particularly when she loved it so. He would not authorize a suspense. I did it anyway. I had no choice. I called in Lana's mother and explained exactly why I wanted her to keep Lana at home. I explained it to Lana also. I did not tell her mother I was committing an illegal act. Her mother understood; so did Lana, even though she left angry.

"You want me to go on my knees and beg you to stay," she said. "I won't beg you to stay, I ain't suckin no white teacher's ass to come to this school."

She ran out of the office, her mother, embarrassed, helplessly following her.

"Try it this way," I told her mother. "Don't be discouraged. It will work, you'll see."

Lana called me almost every day on the telephone. We had long conversations about acceptable and unacceptable behavior. I sent her homework by mail; she returned what I sent her, and more.

"Dear Dr. Rothman," she wrote (in a letter addressed to "Mrs. Dr. Rothman"),

Just these few line. to let you know I had a dream about you and it keep comeing to my mind. I dream that I was going to work. And I got in the school then it was your school and I saw you come out of the school and I call you. Please for give this word. And you look real old you was crying so I stop and think. So I told you that I was sorry and then I was asking you some questions and you said yes.

So frist I siad do you know how it feel to be in love with some one and you siad yes. And then I said well that the way love is because I fall in love with your school and you siad it happin to me before. So then I had to laver the school I siad good by. And then I saw your little gril and I siad to her you are a lucky gril because you have nice mother and she sure do know how to run a school. Any way I just wanting to tell you about the dream I had and to wish you a very happy thanks-giving.

Yours truly

Lana

Every time Lana called I was tempted to let her come back immediately, but I knew it would be wrong to permit my feelings toward her to overcome my judgment. Lana had to understand that I would keep my word. Her offense had been sickeningly serious. Besides, I really could not expect teachers or other girls to tolerate her behavior.

Lana returned in exactly one month. She never defecated on the floor again. It was not really too hard a lesson for Lana to learn. It was extremely hard for her psychiatrist.

Many professional people simply don't understand that our girls love school and that just depriving them of it is a form of internalizing discipline. Suspension can be therapeutic.

Long-term suspensions are infrequent. Much more frequent are one-, two-, and three-day suspensions during which girls are asked to stay at home, cool off, and think about their behavior. I do not generally tell them what they have done wrong; they have to tell me. And sometimes they have to tell me in writing. Only then can they return. Sometimes I determine the number of days they will stay out; sometimes they do it themselves. They may return when they have analyzed their own mistakes.

Constance was suspended for chronic fighting. Doris was suspended for chronically running out of the building to buy candy and cigarettes for other girls. Beverly was suspended for insisting upon wearing blue jeans every day and refusing to change into a skirt. She was always preparing for a fight with her enemy of the day. The suspension was meaningful to each girl. She understood it because she learned that school was something to earn, and that her discipline had to come from within herself if she were to stay.

The therapeutic-thinking-day suspensions are not authorized by the Board. In other words, they too are completely illegal. If I were to follow legal procedures I would have to send a formal letter of suspension to the parent and a copy of the letter to the Superintendent. I would have to preside at a formal hearing at which the child, her parent, teachers, social workers, and anyone interested in the child are present. It is a frightening procedure. It is the suspension procedure that each girl and her parent have gone through in the regular school before coming here. The result of that suspension was referral to Livingston.

If I were to follow the same rigid procedure of suspension, the implication would be that she has to go to another school, that we are referring her elsewhere, and that would be totally untrue. There is no other school to which we want to send her, and furthermore, this is not the intent of therapeutic suspension. The intent is just the opposite—to keep the girl at Livingston. Our suspensions are therefore not rigidly formalized, and that is exactly why we are so successful. Parents are not subjected to a hearing. They are consulted before I tell a girl to stay at home. Sometimes parents come in with a girl when she returns to school, sometimes they do not. It is a cooperative process between parent and school.

There are many intervening steps before suspension. The Principal's Task Force is one of them. It is one of our ways of letting discipline spring from the girls themselves. It consists of all the girls who are in our work programs. They mediate disagreements, fights, quarrels, and squabbles. They do a fantastic job of helping one another keep out of trouble. Sometimes one girl is a mediator, sometimes two. They sit in my office, the two opposing forces facing each other, the mediator or mediators, as the case may be, between them. First, I set the stage.

"Sandra," I said, after I called her from her class, "I'm sorry to interrupt your class, but I need a mediator. Can you do it, now?"

She smiled. "Okay."

I pointed to Audrey, "Audrey here is trying to stay out of a fight with Esther. Can you listen to her and Esther and see if you can settle it?"

Sandra immediately took over. "Send for Esther," she ordered.

I did.

Esther came sullenly into the office.

"Esther," I repeated, "we're trying to get this settled between you and Audrey. Sandra is going to mediate. But first, I want to hear from both of you that you're going to talk it out, not get mad and fight?"

"They'll talk," Sandra said, "you can leave it to me."

"Well, let's make sure," I insisted. "Audrey, can you talk it out?"

"I can if she can," she answered.

"Esther?"

She didn't answer.

"Do I have your word?" I asked. "Otherwise I won't ask Sandra to mediate. If you give me your word not to fight, but to talk, I know I can accept it."

"Yeah—" she begrudgingly agreed.

I went back to my desk.

"Okay." Sandra could barely wait to get started. She sat down. "Now, what happened?"

They both began to talk.

"Now, listen," she said, "I got me only two ears and I can't hear all that mess. You first." She pointed to Audrey.

She let Audrey tell her story.

"Now it's your turn," she told Esther. "Do you wanta fight her?"

"If she wanta fight me," Esther muttered.

"Now, that's stupid," Sandra replied. "She don't wanta fight you, that's why she came to Dr. Rothman for." And then she asked Esther to tell her side of it, giving running advice as Esther spoke at length.

Audrey finally concluded, "I think I oughta get my class changed."

The time came for me to intervene.

"Sandra," I asked, "is it settled?"

"I think so," she replied. "You gonna fight?" she asked Audrey.

"No."

"Listen," Sandra said, "I used to get into fights like that, but it just plain stupid. If you don't like nobody, stay away from them. If you like them, be friends. But don't fight."

They listened intently. Sandra turned to me.

"It's settled," she said.

"Can I get my class changed?" asked Audrey.

"Talk about it with Mrs. Gray," I said. "All right?"

They all left together. Later that morning, Sandra typed up her report on a form the girls had devised with Mr. McMahon's help.

NYC TASK FORCE

Livingston School

29 King Street

New York, New York 10014

Chief Mediator Dr. Esther P. Rothman

PARTIES INVOLVED

Esther

Audrey

REASON FOR DISPUTE

Two girls got involved with one another, they fight and talk about each other. Audrey asked if she could get her class changed.

RESOLUTION OF DISPUTE

I told them to stay way from each other, and I told them that fighting will not get them any where.

So just stay out of trouble!

I asked them to make friends and they did.

And it was settled.

Mediator   Sandra

Sandra felt very good about herself. It did not prevent her from getting into difficulty with Delores. She, however, did not want a mediator. She felt she could mediate herself by talking into a tape recorder and recording both sides of the argument. She did.

This is Sandra. I'm mediating myself of what happened today in class. Well it all started out in Reading, when Delores come in the class and then started annoying me by walking in and out of the room. And then I went to typing and she says to me, "I asked, who wrote on my paper," and nobody said anything. She got a attitude. And then she said she didn't do it. Rather she cursed at me and I said to her, "Well I don't think you should curse because I didn't curse at you." Then, it went on and on and on until I said she was starting to cry and she said she wasn't crying. And then she called me a black bitch, and I told her, "Don't call me no bitch." And I got up and I started towards her. Then she called my mother one and I was ready to kick her butt. And then she picked up a chair at me. Oh! She shouldn'ta picked up no chair 'cause I feel that chairs belong on the floor. And if she didn't want to fight me she shouldn'ta cursed and she shouldn't got big and bad about it. And that's the way I feel about it. That's all.

I feel Delores shouldn'ta took a attitude like she did towards me when I asked her a question. I feel that maybe I was in the wrong and maybe I wasn't in the wrong by asking a question. And I feel like this: that anytime you and a person can't get along, for you all just to stay away from each other, don't be around each other, go your opposite ways, so then there won't get in trouble. And, I feel that people shouldn't jump the gun too fast. They shouldn't say things too quickly without thinking about what they gonna say, and that's just how I feel about it for Delores and me.

Delores didn't need mediation. She worked out her problem with the help of Mrs. Langness. At any rate, a fight was averted. Audrey, Sandra, Esther were learning to avoid, to control, to talk through their problems.

When all else fails, we sometimes feign failure to help a girl get hold of herself.

"We can't go on this way," I told Joy. "Every day this week you've pushed a teacher on the lunch line, and today you threw Miss Miller's coffee on the floor."

"I didn't, she lies on me."

"You'll have to go," I said. "We have failed to help you here."

"Where will I go?" Joy asked frantically.

"Stay at home," I said. "That's up to you—"

"I gotta go to school, I need my education," she said.

"Not here, you don't," I answered. "If you insist upon shoving teachers, spilling coffee deliberately, then we have failed to teach you—you can stay at home."

"I was home." She began to lower her voice.

"That's right—I forgot," I said. "Two suspenses, and home instruction before you came here. How long?"

"Two years." Her voice was still lower.

"Then it's regular school for you," I replied. "That's the answer."

"Good," she exclaimed. Her voice rose. "That's what I want."

"Fine," I said. "We'll send you back to a regular school where nobody will notice you too much. There are just too many kids. And you won't be able to decide your own program."

"Oh, shit," she exclaimed.

"What?" I pretended to huff and puff with indignation. "In my office, an obscenity?"

"Okay," she grumbled, "I'm sorry."

"Yes?" I asked.

"And I'm stayin."

"And how will you behave?"

"Okay."

"All right," I capitulated, "it's a deal. No shoving teachers, right?"

"Yeah—"

"Boy," she muttered as she left, "this sure is a kooky school. You come here for being bad, and when you get here, if you're bad you get sent back to regular school. This school is really for good kids."

She understood perfectly. That is as it should be.

chapter seven

The Story of Dorothy

Dorothy, one of our few white girls, came into my office one day asking that I send her to the emergency clinic of a nearby hospital because she had a large sliver of shattered glass in the sole of her foot.

"How did you get glass in the sole of your foot?" I asked.

"I was dancing."

"And the glass cut through your shoe?"

"Oh, no."

"You were wearing slippers?"

"No-o."

"Well, how did you get glass in the sole of your foot?"

"I was dancing barefoot."

"How come the glass was on the dance floor?" I asked.

"Oh—the bottle broke."

"What bottle?"

"The bottle of bourbon my aunt threw at my uncle," she patiently explained. "But it wasn't full," she hurriedly amplified.

"Your aunt threw a bottle of liquor at your uncle while everyone was dancing?"

"What's the matter?" she asked impatiently. "Didn't you ever go to a wedding?"

Well, now I have.

It would not have helped Dorothy if I had laughed. It would not have helped her if, in fact, I had cried. I simply accepted—and saw that she got to the hospital. For one moment, she had come close enough to permit me to share an experience without critical comment. A few weeks later, she permitted me to share her feelings.

She sat in my office, hugging her arms around her body, rocking in her seat, and she wept.

"He peed on me, Dr. Rothman, he peed on me."

"Why, Dorothy, why would he pee on you?"

"I don't know," her breath came in loud gasps. "He was making fun of me, I guess, he was making fun of me."

She hid her face in her hands and sobbed without control.

"Don't cry, honey, please don't cry. Nobody would want to hurt you like that, nobody would do a thing like that."

I went over to her and put my arms about her and held her close.

"It'll be all right, Dorothy, don't cry."

"He did, he did, he did," she kept repeating the words. "He did, he peed on me."

I hated him, this despicably sick boy. He had to be sick to do a thing like that, but it didn't help, knowing it. This was my girl, Dorothy.

"Dorothy, can you tell me what happened?"

She shook her head no.

"It might make you feel better—"

It was one of the quietest times I remember in my office. It was one of the rare times my door was shut. The girls always respected that. Someone was in real trouble. They knew it.

"You won't tell my mother?" she gasped.

"No, I won't tell your mother," I promised.

"It was this dance," she began. "I went to this dance, and I knew him, he was nice, he lives near me, and when I was going home around twelve o'clock he said he was going home too and he said let's walk through this park and he said, let's stop. I didn't want to, cause it was getting late and my mother be mad, but anyway, we stopped on the bench and I thought—well, we were just—he just said we could—"

She was completely overcome.

I began to understand. It wasn't what I had thought.

"You had sex with him, Dorothy, is that it?" I asked it as gently as I could.

The word was wrenched from her. "Yes." There was a long period of weeping before she was able to continue. I could do nothing but watch.

"He laughed at me, he peed on me."

"No, Dorothy, no." I wanted to hold her even closer, but that alone wouldn't help.

"He wasn't peeing on you, honey. He wasn't laughing, he was loving you, Dorothy. That's what happens when a man and a woman make love," I went on to explain.

She listened—oh, how she listened—but the tears never stopped flowing.

"But what shall we do about it, Dorothy?" I asked. "You and me together, do you think we should tell somebody you trust, your aunt, maybe?"

"I trust you. You promised." It was an explosion of panic.

It was a mistake, my suggesting it. I quickly retracted it.

"Dorothy, I never break a promise. I'm not telling," I reassured her.

"Neither one of us will tell."

She sank back and breathed heavily.

"Are you all right?" I asked. "Do you feel all right?"

She nodded.

She was dabbing at her eyes. I knew she felt better just telling me, but I was worried. I couldn't impose my concern on Dorothy—she had just gone through enough.

"What do you want to do now?" I asked.

"Should I go back to class?" she asked.

"Do you feel you can?"

"No."

I knew she was still needing me.

"How about staying in the office? I've got loads of things you can do, these pencils forever need sharpening, my plants need watering, some cards need filing. Feel like it?"

She smiled.

"Okay," I told her, "but I can't stand girls with dirty faces working in my office. Wash your face and come back." It was an everyday kind of command.

As she turned to leave, I called out, "And later, before you go home, we'll talk some more."

She smiled again.

"Feel better?"

"Oh, yes."

She was ready to live again.

She left the office. It was going to be a torturous day, getting Dorothy through it. She would have her moments of relapse. She would need help and more help. God, I hoped she had not become pregnant. I deliberately turned to other things—a battleground where I knew the terrain.

I began filling out a library inventory for the Board. I had to indicate in triplicate how many books we had received this year, how many books we had on hand from last year, what their value was, how many were centralized in the school library, how many were in the classrooms. There was one question stuck in among the rest that had plagued me on these forms for years.

"Did you observe Arbor Day this year?"

I called in my secretary.

"Mrs. Magnus," I asked, "what would happen if I answered no?"

"Oh, you'd better not," she said.

"Why not?"

"Because we're supposed to answer yes."

"Let's be adventurous with the truth," I said. "Type in no."

"Okay," she said, "but you know the Board. You won't hear the end of it. Everybody in New York City answers yes."

"But why?" I asked.

"I don't know."

I was feeling brave. "Let's write in no."

"Okay."

"By the way," I asked as she was leaving, "when is Arbor Day?"

She was facetious. "I don't know. I don't even like trees."

I burst into laughter.

One learns to survive.

One thing I was certain of, Dorothy didn't need me broken up in little pieces. I would be of no use to her or anyone then. When I would return emotionally to Dorothy at the end of the day, I would be all hers to use again.

chapter eight

The Fourth R—Work

If I had my way, all children in school would work and be paid for the work they do. If the work of children is to learn, then children should be paid for learning. Money is a powerful motivator. I daresay that truancy might decrease and that more children would learn, even those children who have been relegated to the substratum of the non-achiever, if they were paid for services rendered. Someday, I would like a fund to pay girls for increasing their reading or arithmetic skills. Supposing I could say to a girl, "You increased your reading from fourth grade to fifth. You have earned five dollars." How great! If only we could do it. After all, teachers are paid additionally for supposedly increasing their skills via college courses. Increments are, in fact, often based on additional education. The same idea should be applicable to children.

At the moment, however, we are able only to pay for bona-fide work.

Work means money, and money is not only an antidote to poverty, but is also a generator of self-esteem. Girls who work feel good about themselves not only because they can buy what they want with the money they earn, but because someone thinks them important enough to pay them. Feeling important is the condition for learning. They are able to admit what they don't know, and willing to concentrate on learning. Their egos are not shattered by facing up to their academic needs. They are able to be challenged by failure. They are willing to cope with the challenge. It is not a straight line upward to success. There are a many slipbacks, many fears. The girls often cannot believe that an employer depends upon them, and is willing to pay them. They have difficulty in believing that they have meaning in someone else's life, that they are needed. They constantly test their own desirability.

Mrs. Burke, the dressmaking teacher, came to the second floor on her free hour. She was looking for me. The lounge was very quiet. Shirley was seated at the receptionist's desk, practicing her shorthand. She didn't look up.

"Shirley," Mrs. Burke asked, "do you know if Dr. Rothman is in her office?"

"Don't ask me." Shirley shrugged and continued her work.

"That's no way for a receptionist to speak," Mrs. Burke reprimanded. "When you are working you have to be polite, particularly when you are working as a receptionist. You can't hold a job and be this disrespectful. No one will hire you."

"Mind your own business." Shirley jumped up from the desk, grabbed her notebook, and ran.

Later, I discussed the incident with Shirley.

"It embarrasses me when you are rude," I explained, "because you represent me when you're my secretary. Do you understand that?"

"She could see you're in your office," she complained without too much rancor. "Why she gotta ask me? She can look for herself."

"Because that's a secretary's job," I answered. "And you're either working or you're not working. Which is it?"

"I'm working." She smiled.

"Good," I said, "because I need you." I then prescribed what I wanted her to do. "Understand?" I asked.

"Yeah," she answered.

"Secretaries say yes," I prompted.

"Yes." She laughingly uttered the word to the last distinct sound, and because Shirley, a deeply depressed girl, was actually laughing, I was lulled into inanity and I uttered one of those pompous phrases that every once in a while emerges from the educational wasteland of my training. It was totally irrelevant to our previous conversation.

"Where is your sense of responsibility?" I asked.

"Don't got none," she flung at me. "Where's yours?"

"Mine?" She took me by surprise.

"Yeah," she replied. "You have the responsibility to make sense, not me."

No wonder I loved Shirley. She had just done for me what I had done for her, and it spelled out accountability.

"Shirley," I asked, "what do you like best about being in Upper School?"

I wondered if she might say money. She didn't.

"I dunno." She thought a while. "I guess it's privileges."

"Like what?"

"Like being able to go out of the building for lunch and—"

"And what?" I prompted.

"I dunno, I just made it, I guess."

Indeed she had. So have all the thirty girls who are in the Upper School, for the Upper School consists of our work programs. Girls who go into Upper School have come a long emotional distance. They have gone to all their classes—well, almost all their classes. They have controlled their tempers all the time—well, most of the time. Moreover, they have each become fifteen. The criteria for admission to our work programs have been met. They are successes. Sometimes for the first time in their school lives they are achieving. Girls who were truants are no longer truants. Girls who hated school no longer hate school. Girls who were the disrupters no longer are. They are ready to return to the schools of their failures to display their personal victories.

The School to Employment Program (STEP) is the first level of the Upper School.

Girls in the STEP program work each morning (for a dollar an hour) and come to school each afternoon. They work in our school and in the schools of the regular school system, schools near their homes, or near us, although rarely at the schools from which they have been suspended. That would be too difficult, not necessarily for the girls, but for the teachers who had known them and might be resentful or fearful.

It is a heroic achievement for each girl who goes into Upper School. It is her conquest of self—her trip to the moon. Girls who have been the "discipline cases" of the school system are now returning to schools as secretaries to principals, assistants to teachers, aides to librarians. The defiers of authorities are now on the side of the authorities they once defied.

Unbelievable. Rewarding. Frightening.

"Me?" Yvonne yelled at Mrs. Landsman, who was counseling Yvonne and exploring with her her feelings about going into STEP.

"Why not you?" Mrs. Landsman answered.

"Because—because—" Yvonne struggled to find the words. "Because I'm me."

"You mean because you were once suspended for hitting a teacher?"

Yvonne didn't answer, but hung her head low.

"That's in the past," Mrs. Landsman continued, "and you're learning how to control yourself better, aren't you?"

Yvonne's yes was a very soft one.

"Well, you see," Mrs. Landsman went on, "the teachers have faith in you. Before we ask a girl to go into STEP, all the teachers meet and discuss each girl's behavior and work, and we all feel you're ready for STEP. Do you think you're ready?"

"Yeah."

But it was a pathetic affirmative. Yvonne could not believe that anyone in the whole world thought well enough of her to pay her money for doing anything.

We had debated a long time about putting Yvonne into STEP. Even though she had been with us for almost two years, since she was thirteen, she still seemed incapable of uttering one sentence that did not include a threat or an obscenity. If we did not put her in STEP, what then?

Without a goal in any direction, Yvonne would only deteriorate.

Yvonne's mother was an alcoholic who noticed Yvonne only when Yvonne stole the welfare check from the mailbox every month in order to buy food for her mother, her six-year-old brother, and herself. If she didn't steal it, there would be no food at all. Her mother, of course, invariably beat her up and then went out to get drunk on the money Yvonne had not spent.

Getting Yvonne's mother to come to sign the working papers

before Yvonne could be admitted to STEP required weeks of effort.

"She won't come," Yvonne kept telling us, and even as she said it, she would come running into my office two or three times a day asking, "Did my mother get here?"

The answer was always the same. She had not arrived.

We could not telephone, as there was no phone in the house. We sent telegrams asking her to come to school, but the telegrams were undelivered. Yvonne told us that her mother didn't like to receive telegrams, so she wouldn't accept them. Finally we sent a registered letter with a return receipt requested. We got back the signed receipt, but still her mother did not appear.

Yvonne's behavior became more abusive. She felt completely deserted and rejected. As far as Yvonne was concerned, her mother's refusal to come to school was undeniable proof that she didn't care at all about Yvonne.

I toyed with the idea of forging her mother's signature on the working papers.

"You can't do that," Mrs. Landsman objected.

"Why not?" I asked.

"Not because it's illegal," she explained. "I would say go ahead and do it if it would help Yvonne, but it wouldn't. It would make her feel worse. Every mother comes to school to sign the working papers, and if Yvonne's mother didn't, it would only make her feel more rejected than ever."

Mrs. Landsman was right.

Yvonne needed to know that there was one moment in her life when her mother could act like a mother and would come to school for her.

It was the promise of a ride in a taxi that did it. I told

Yvonne she could tell her mother to take a taxi to school and we would pay for it.

Her mother arrived, a shriveled woman, much smaller than Yvonne, huddled in a coat much too large for her. Yvonne presented her to me with pride. She had come through for Yvonne. She was not drunk, the way she had been for her initial interview with Mrs. Landsman when Yvonne was being admitted. She held out her hand to me in greeting. It was limp, clammy, without muscle tone. It felt dead. Instinctively, I almost withdrew mine in a moment of real physical repulsion, but of course I didn't. I offered her coffee.

She thanked me and then laughed with embarrassment. "I didn't have time for lunch," she said.

I immediately offered her lunch.

She began eating as soon as the lunch was brought up, meatballs and spaghetti, salad, roll and butter, fruit jello, and coffee. Mrs. Landsman and I sat and watched her. So did Yvonne, who generally was a compulsive eater but had nevertheless refused lunch. Mrs. C. ate voraciously, her head bowed low over her food, her mouth never inches away from the plate. It was painful to watch her complete absorption in the food. Suddenly, I realized how embarrassed Yvonne must be. I looked up at her. The muscles of her face were controlled, but she could not control the tears.

Almost impulsively, both at the same time, Mrs. Landsman and I, without speaking to each other, asked Yvonne to bring lunch upstairs for both of us. Even though we both had already eaten, we plunged into the food almost in the way Yvonne's mother had, and as we ate, we talked about Yvonne's progress and how well we felt she would do in our work program. Yvonne began to relax.

That was the day happiness started for Yvonne, because

work meant prestige. Even her mother's demands for money brought importance to her. Yvonne allotted her mother five dollars out of her paycheck. The rest she spent on clothing for herself and her brother. And on that little amount of money, she even managed to open a savings account. Then, because she began to see herself as a totally new person, she developed the strength to go on a diet. It was a tremendous achievement for her, because Yvonne, like so many girls with little gratification in their lives, had fed herself into obesity. Yvonne asked us for a referral to an obesity clinic, and she began losing weight remarkably, twenty-five pounds in two weeks. Then we found out why. Not only had we arranged for treatment at a clinic, but she had gone to her local hospital as well. Yvonne was taking double medication. She wanted her new look the way she wanted everything else—immediately.

Immediacy is our biggest problem. While it is undoubtedly true that girls work more for prestige and importance and significance than they work for money, money is nevertheless tremendously important.

"Theresa," I said, "you are in Upper School and you have committed yourself to working. That means you have to go to your job. The person you're working for depends on you."

She sneered in return, but didn't answer.

I was looking for a way to reach her, but I hadn't found it. "What's more," I said, "you need the money."

"A dollar an hour?" she asked contemptuously. "Honey, slavery went outa fashion long ago. It's been here and gone."

"Well, work hasn't gone out of fashion," I answered. "Not yet. Most of us have to work for our living, whether we like it not."

"For a dollar an hour?" she sneered.

"That's STEP," I answered, "but if you like, we can put you into Neighborhood Youth Corps."

"Big stuff," she answered. "They make a dollar and a half an hour."

I ignored her comment. "You haven't earned it, of course, you haven't gone to work every day, but we'll make the exception. Maybe you'll like it better. It's like a civil service job. You work in offices in city agencies. Would you like that?"

"For a dollar and a half an hour?" she asked again. "Are you kidding? I don't need me a job like that."

She didn't, not financially.

Theresa had been brought to school several times in a white Cadillac driven by her boyfriend.

The picture was clear in front of me. I decided to be abrupt.

"Theresa," I said, "how smart is that—where is it going to get you—letting your boyfriend buy you fifty-four-dollar boots and a fur coat? What do you have to give in return?"

Theresa snorted in derision. "Where did it get *you*—not giving anything? You had to marry a man before you could get any money from him."

She stopped me cold. I have never heard the word "marry" sound so derisive.

I ignored her question. "What happens when your boyfriend doesn't want to give you any more money?" I asked.

"Him?" she sniffed. "He ain't nothin to me, I can cut him loose any time."

"That's not what I asked," I answered. "What are you going to do when you need to work?"

She flung her head sideways and dismissed me with a move of her hand. She didn't bother to answer. I knew I could not persuade her to stay in STEP or stay in school. At seventeen, she had a right to leave school, and she did.

There was nothing we could have done to hold her. It was not that we had failed but that her mother had won.

"She's grown now." Mrs. W. was obviously very annoyed

with me for having insisted that she come to school. "She can do what she wants."

"But her education is important," I found myself pleading. "You don't want her to leave school."

"That girl, she don't listen to me nohow."

"You have to make her listen," I almost scolded. Quite irrationally, I suddenly felt like shaking her physically, as if by shaking her I could make happen what I wanted to happen. I wanted Theresa's mother to be a mother.

"I can't give her them expensive clothes she wants," Mrs. W. continued.

"That's not the important thing now," I explained. "Her education is important."

"Yes," she agreed very easily, "education is important, she should stay in school, but what can I do?"

I recognized her inadequacy. There was no point in pressuring her any more. She could not do any better. I tried again with Theresa.

"Your mother really wants you to stay in school," I told her.

She looked at me suspiciously.

"She tell you that?" she asked quizzically.

"Yes." I didn't tell her how weak I thought her mother was. I didn't know then I was wrong.

"I don't wanta hear none a that shit," she cried.

I began to understand. Her mother, weak? Never!

"She tell you one thing and me another. Where you think she got that color television set from? From that little job of hers? My friend got it for her, that's who, so what you tellin me, I don't wanta hear none a that." She clasped her hands over her ears and ran out of the room.

Theresa was right. I suddenly recognized that her mother wanted the money more than Theresa did. Theresa wanted her mother to love her, and she wanted status. She found them both in being the mistress of an older man.

"I like sex," Theodora announced, the day Theresa left, "but not like that, uh-uh, not like that."

"She think her butt smell like flowers," Jill said, "but when she be old like when she twenty or twenty-five, what she got then, huh?"

"Yeah," argued Dolores, "it make me sick," and then as usual, when they become angry or upset by another girl's behavior, they found a scapegoat—the school.

"It makes me sick," Dolores continued. "The trouble with this school is you have too many advantages. I'm not used to it."

Somehow, the irrelevancy of her statement seemed to sum it up for everyone. They were satisfied with what she said. I didn't understand why. I puzzled over it quite a while.

I finally asked Dolores what she had meant. She was embarrassed.

"Aw, you know."

"No, I don't," I assured her.

"Yes, you do," yelled Vanessa who had listened to our conversation. "You've got a weird bag, Dr. Rothman, makin out you don't know that privileges sometimes scare people, specially when you've never had them before."

Insight. For the first time I understood what she was telling me. It is not easy to learn how to accept opportunity, because accepting opportunity often means negating the past, denying the values of friends and sometimes even the values of parents. Accepting opportunity therefore is being a traitor to the past, while not accepting it is being a traitor to what the school stands for and to yourself.

It is a dilemma, and no matter which side the girl ultimately chooses, it always leads to some anxiety and sometimes to depression and self-imposed punishment.

Maxine, for instance, took herself to court and asked to be placed in a juvenile detention center before she did something bad. Maxine needed both punishment and protection from her own impulses. She had chosen to be in STEP, to work as a teacher's assistant in a third-grade class, and in choosing she had denied her former friends, who now scoffed at her. It was more than she could bear. We could not sustain her at school, nor did her job give her the strength she needed.

For almost all girls, though, the work experience itself is therapeutic. It is an experience in which for several hours a day one's own life can often be forgotten, and one can be absorbed in others. But even more important, often it is a way of filling in the emotional and experiential gaps in their own lives. As teachers to young children in nursery school, kindergarten, and the primary grades, some girls sing the songs and play the games of childhood that they themselves never learned, because for the most part they have had no real childhood. There are other values. Girls learn to look at the behavior of children, and in looking learn to see themselves and analyze their own behavior.

"They bad," Yvonne told Miss Grant, her teacher, "those kids are so mean, the way they curse and talk back to the teacher. They fresh."

"Yvonne," Miss Grant laughed, "you must be kidding. You curse almost more than anybody in this school."

"They need a good beating," she said, "they bad and mean."

"Little children aren't mean, Yvonne," Miss Grant told her. "They're acting in the only way they know how to act. You need to understand and help them, that's all, the way people need to understand you."

"People tell lies on me," she said. Miss Grant felt Yvonne's anger suddenly beginning to overtake her. "There he be," Yvonne pointed to a teacher passing by in the hall, "fuck him, old bald fat-headed faggot grumpy Jew, he came with his little words cursin in my face—"

"You're cursing right now, Yvonne," Miss Grant told her. "Should I beat you?" Miss Grant put her hand gently on Yvonne's arm, but immediately felt that it was a mistake.

"Take your fuckin hand off!"

She withdrew it.

"See, Yvonne, beating isn't the answer. You don't even like it when I touch you, do you?" Miss Grant asked gently.

She felt Yvonne's anger subside as quickly as it had risen.

"What do you think a teacher should do with children who curse?" asked Miss Grant.

"Talk to them," Yvonne said promptly, "like you're doin now."

Even if she had wanted to, Yvonne could not have given Miss Grant a better present.

Yvonne was really learning—not only about herself, but about children. Perhaps it would make a difference in her own life with her own children. The cycle of ignorance and neglect has to be interrupted somewhere.

Working with children is a good place to start that interruption. By observation of children in school, by working with the children and the teachers, girls have an opportunity to identify with both the child and the teacher. The experience provides insight into themselves and into the behavior of others.

Self-knowledge through work, or work as a process of therapy, is a concept that many people do not understand, even the experts in vocational guidance. In 1961, our school was of a small group that participated in a five-year study run by a vocational rehabilitation agency to provide work experience for fourteen-year-old girls. The idea was rehabilitation through work. The result was boredom, because the concept of work established by the experts was a factory assembly line. The girls objected.

The experts kept insisting that girls had to learn to do things they didn't like to do. I insisted that if girls didn't like the work assignment, they wouldn't work. The experts' answer was always the same. "They have to." The answer was simple. Girls didn't have to. They refused to work. I was unable to withdraw from the project because my participation had been approved by the Board of Education. I took the second best approach. I fought with them for five years.

The project ended a failure, and of course the school was blamed. We didn't provide the remedial reading teaching, they said, that would have totally rehabilitated the girls.

There it was, the convenient excuse for failure. Blame it on reading. But the fact is that work has to be exciting, work has to be challenging, work has to be invested with emotional meaning.

The success of STEP proved I was right. Girls loved their jobs because the jobs were meaningful. But we still had a problem—after STEP, what? Is it not part of the American dream that accomplishment needs to be rewarded?

Neighborhood Youth Corps (NYC), subsidized by the Federal Government, is our promotion. It is the second level of the Upper School, and the girls earn a dollar forty-five an hour, which means a forty-five-cent increase in hourly salary for them.

The girls who go from STEP to NYC feel that they have earned a promotion not only in terms of money, but also in terms of status, for they no longer work in the cloistered setting of a school, but move into the city agencies and the community. They work in offices at the departments of Health, Hospitals, Welfare, Police, and in community social agencies and settlement houses. What excitement to be aligned with the sources of power in the community, and to be on the giving side of service instead of being on the receiving side!

This does not mean there are no problems. There are many. Janet's mother, for instance, refused to admit that Janet was pregnant, although Janet told her teacher, Mrs. Eisert, that she was. It was Janet's second pregnancy; her son was now two years old, and her mother cared for him while Janet attended school and then went to work. We wanted Janet to go to a doctor for pre-natal care, but Janet refused because her mother might be angry. Her mother was afraid that if Janet's pregnancy was confirmed, we might not permit Janet to work.

Janet was a sickly girl, anemic and thin. She tired easily and was extremely listless. All her energies went into just getting to and from school and her job. Janet's fears of doctors, plus her fear of her mother, who would be angry at Janet for listening to us and going to a doctor, were enough to immobilize Janet. Certainly Janet needed the money she earned. Certainly, too, the only reason Janet could not work during pregnancy was that physically it was too much for her to travel to work, then attend school, then go home and help care for her baby.

We had hoped to get medical attention for Janet, keep her in school and in her job until the fifth or sixth month of her pregnancy, and then discharge her to a special school for pregnant girls where she could continue her academic education and continue to receive pre-natal care. Her mother, however, would not accept this plan. Her mother wanted Janet to work up until the time she had her baby. Her need for money was greater than her concern for Janet's health or the health of the baby. Nor did she understand how important it was for Janet to see a doctor. After all, clinics had not inspired her with the greatest confidence in their ability really to make a difference in anyone's life.

Only when Janet became very ill were we able to impress her mother with the urgency of accepting a referral to the School for Continuing Education, a rather dull and uninspiring name for the special schools maintained by the Board of Education for pregnant girls.

Money problems are acute, perhaps more so for the girls in Neighborhood Youth Corps than for the girls in STEP. NYC girls are older. Emotionally and socially, they are often more mature. Often, too, they have greater responsibities at home. As a group, therefore, their behavior is generally the most subdued of any group in school. They attend school each morning, work each afternoon. Like girls in STEP, they used to work three hours every day. At that time they were earning a dollar twenty-five an hour. Even at that wage, the raise over STEP was substantial. Unfortunately, when Federal budgets were curtailed, our girls were permitted to work only two hours a day. Their paychecks dropped from eighteen seventy-five to twelve dollars and fifty cents a week.

We tried to involve the girls in protesting the decrease, but after the first anger they became resigned to defeat. We suggested picketing. They declined. We suggested a letter campaign. They said yes, but no one wrote a letter. We suggested telegrams. They were disinterested.

Mrs. Eisert contacted their parents and tried to get them to protest. The parents, too, were reluctant. Money was important, but they were fearful of jeopardizing the program. They did not want to take the chance of losing it all. Of course, they were also apathetic. What was the use? They felt powerless.

The teachers and I were enraged. Repeatedly, Mrs. Eisert and I tried to see public officials. Repeatedly, they refused to see us. I wrote letters to the Human Resources Administration, the administrative agency responsible for the Neighborhood Youth Corps funds and program. I asked that our hours be reinstated to three hours a day per girl, fifteen hours a week. Their answer was always the same. No. They didn't have the money, they wrote. I told them it didn't require money. They wanted me to put fifteen girls in the program, each girl to work ten hours. I told them that I wanted only ten girls in the program, each girl to work fifteen hours. The money was the same. Ten times fifteen was the same as fifteen times ten. They didn't seem to understand that basic mathematical fact. I should have sent Mr. Friedland down there to teach them math. The answer was still no.

The more involved I got, the more I learned. I talked to a lot of people in the payroll division about why my request couldn't be granted, and some of their answers contradicted each other. Slowly, I began to recognize corruption when it hit me in the face.

I tried to bring my evidence to the attention of Mayor Lindsay, to the Human Resources Administrators—there were several—to the comptroller's office. No one would listen. No one. I wrote letters, sent telegrams, made telephone calls. All I got in return were polite little notes from his many assistants. For instance,

Jan 2, 1968

This is to acknowledge receipt of your telegram.
We refer you to all our previous correspondence.

It was signed by an assistant to the mayor.

In sheer desperation, I sent the mayor a telegram suggesting that he acknowledge his own telegrams. He did.

July 12,1968

Thank you for you telegram of today's date. I refer you to all of my
assistant's previous correspondence.

It was signed by the mayor.

When the New York City misappropriation of Neighborhood Youth Corps funds became a national scandal during that
summer, I felt a moment of hope for change. But the Battle of
the Hours continues.

This was one of the reasons we kept looking for another
work program. Mrs. Eisert finally found it, the cooperative
education program, one of the few good programs adminis-
tered by the Board. It is a program in which girls work one
week full-time and on alternate weeks come to school full-time.
As girls get paid directly by their employers, there are no
Government restrictions concerning how many hours a girl
may work a week or how much money she may earn. There are
no such cruel restrictions as the economic eligibility require-
ments that Neighborhood Youth Corps imposes by accepting
only girls from families whose *total* income is sixteen hundred
dollars a year or under. Any girl who is sixteen can work. We
pick our girls carefully. Betty, for instance, works in a civil
service position as a typist. She earns over seventy dollars a
week. It is not only the money, however, that is making her
proud. It is her tremendous achievement—the knowledge that
she is making it. The economists call it upward economic
mobility. Isn't this an important building block of democracy?

It is. And contemplating this further broadened my thinking.
We had worked out jobs that dealt with children, jobs that
dealt with social agencies and the community, but a large area
was still unexplored. Free enterprise—capitalism, if you will. It
is the economic basis of our society, but one from which

minority groups long have been excluded. The time had come for black and Puerto Rican girls to learn about business, to understand merchandising, to be able to enter the business world as entrepreneurs. They could not enter it alone; they are too unpredictable. What they needed was a business that could tolerate lateness, temper tantrums, fights, and insults to the boss. We also needed a business that could employ girls of thirteen and fourteen, who were too young to obtain working papers. Many of these girls were ready for work psychologically and needed the status of work emotionally.

"Next year, Audrey," said Mrs. Landsman, "next year, you'll be able to work. I know you're mature enough now, but I can't break the law, I really can't."

"Sure," Audrey grumbled, "next year I'll probably be dead and working for the devil."

It is infuriating to be fourteen and to be unable to work, when work means adult status. Certainly Audrey could earn money out of school, lots of money, if she wanted to. She could run errands for drugs-sellers and numbers men, and if she became desperate enough, she might. We had to compete—not with money, we don't have enough—but with self-concept. We had to provide status, but not status alone, status with glamour, status with femininity.

Our answer grew out of the fact that a brand-new, beautiful cash register had been delivered to me one day, unordered and unannounced.

Who ordered it?

I hadn't.

Who sent it?

Not me.

But there it was, several hundred dollars' worth, its price attached, already paid.

For two years, that cash register had stared me in the face; I felt it was trying to say something to me. But what? I asked Miss Miller if she would take it in her room.

"For reading?" she asked. I can still see the shock on her face.

I asked Mr. McMahon if he would like it in his room with all the business practice equipment.

"It's a damned nuisance," he explained. "You really can't teach anything with it. Anything that can be learned on it can be taught in five minutes. All the girls do is bang on it."

I asked Mr. Friedland if he would like it in his room.

"Well, I'll hold it for you," he said, "but you really can't teach math with it, you know."

He held it for me, and every time I went into his room, there it was, almost human, woebegone. It had no status.

In a way, Audrey and it belonged together.

The cash register belonged in a store.

So did Audrey.

A business of their very own. I presented the idea to the Board of Education, and because it was completely haphazard, unthought-out, and unplanned, they approved. So did the Federal Government, who provided the money to operate it. We were in business.

But what kind?

A boutique, of course. We opened a shop where we display and sell the art and clothing we make at school, from bead earrings to paper flowers to ceramic ashtrays and aprons, potholders, and highly stylized dresses and slacks. In addition, we buy novelty items and resell them at a profit. We alter clothing and sell original stories and poetry.

It is an all-encompassing shop—like our school.

What to call it? There was only one name possible. I realized that as soon as I began to deal with landlords, sales tax numbers, the Department of Real Estate, the Board of Education's Legal Department, the Department of Sanitation, the Board of Estimate, the New York State Department of Education. There was only one name truly descriptive—The Headache.

Tension Headache Number One: It was somebody's bright idea that the landlord be paid at the end of the month, instead of at the beginning. We were almost dispossessed before we opened.

Functional Headache Number Two: the Department of Sanitation objected to collecting garbage because we were a business, and as a business, we had to pay for private refuse removal. We now camouflage our garbage to look like the garbage of our neighbors.

Organic Headache Number Three: The Department of Education in New York State said we were defying some law or other because we were competing with private enterprise. I wrote them a long explanation. Macy's stopped worrying.

Pervasive Headache, encompassing headaches one, two, three, and four: Dealing with the Board of Estimate who do not recognize the Board of Education who do not accept the Board of Estimate who wonder what the Department of Real Estate has to do with it all.

Nevertheless, somehow, in some way, we finally opened. We were in business, *Square Business*, naturally. That's what the girls finally called it, after seven meetings and a few heated arguments.

The Square Business Boutique is located at 237 East 5th Street between Second Avenue and Third. Girls from both Lower and Upper School are assigned to work at the store at their own request.

Each girl's condition of work is suited especially to meet her own needs. Some girls work daily, some weekly. Each girl receives a salary, depending upon her work status, whether she is in STEP, NYC, or Lower School. Again, girls work not only for the money. The store is theirs. They work for the pride of ownership and with the knowledge that we will all share in the profits at the end of the year.

Emma looked concerned when a very young, shabbily dressed couple walked into our store one day and plunked down their infant, complete with milk bottle, on the counter.

"Don't you let that baby shit there," she snapped.

I knew then that we were off to a good start. Emma's pride, something she has little of, was showing! Pride—an essential personal ingredient. All the girls who work find it.

chapter nine

Decisions, Decisions—Learning to Make Them Is Learning

Stately, impulsive, distractable, seductive, Ophelia defied definition. A prominent neuropsychiatrist had diagnosed her as psychotic with brain-damage syndrome. An equally prominent psychologist had called her schizophrenic with hysterical features. Her mother called her high-strung, and every teacher in New York City through whose classroom she had floated called her unmanageable. Pudgy, growling, rambling, fighting, cloying, clinging, and destructive, Bethel was equally mysterious. Every time she went to the mental hygiene clinic for her therapeutic session, she brought with her sundry friends and such havoc that the psychiatrist could find no diagnosis that fitted except—help!

Bethel and Ophelia spent more time outside the classroom than inside, and this troubled me because the question I had to ask myself was obvious—why?

233

I know we have a staff who put heart into what they do. They continually search for interesting projects to engage the girls. Even a casual tour of the school indicates that.

Could Ophelia and Bethel find no interest anywhere, not even in the reading rooms on the second floor?

Of course they could. They are alert girls interested in everything from butterfly wings to chocolate pudding, but the problem is that their interests in a subject never seemed to coincide with the time when their class was scheduled to study that subject. When Ophelia's class was in English, she wanted to go to beauty culture. When Bethel's class was in the library, she wanted to sew.

Was is mere negativism on their part, or did it go much deeper? Should we just insist that they go where their class was scheduled, or were they really emotionally incapable of following a class schedule?

Berenice helped supply the answer. Girls had come running to the office crying that Berenice was standing outside the beauty culture room, banging with both fists on the door.

I ran up the stairs.

"Cut it out," I commanded. "You know better than that."

She stopped.

"You can't stand there all day, just banging on the door. Where are you supposed to be?" I asked.

"Nowhere."

"That's silly," I told her, "your class is scheduled somewhere."

"You asked where I'm supposed to be," she answered. "I told you—nowhere."

There was logic to what Berenice had said. My question had been a stupid one. Berenice did not and could not care where her class was supposed to be. She was an individual in her own right, and she was nowhere.

"Where would you like to be?" I asked her.

"In your office," she answered.

I took her by the arm and led her downstairs. "Why didn't you come and tell me that," I asked, "instead of making all that fuss?"

"Cause then you'd say I was cutting, and I don't want to cut." I saw her struggling with the words, "I'm trying to be good."

"I know you're trying, Berenice, but don't you see that banging on a door just gets you into trouble? You should just have come to the office and let me worry about your cutting class. I'll tell your teacher you're not."

Berenice's problem was solved that day, but what about the others? More and more it was beginning to seem to me that the girls needed independence from their classes. Was it because the school actually was better, that we were doing more for girls than we had ever done before, and were more responsive to their needs?

And was it time for our program to change radically?

Was Audrey telling us something when she poked her face in my doorway?

"You need any help?" she offered.

It was my clue, but I wasn't certain to what.

"Maybe," I answered cautiously, "but why aren't you in class?"

She ignored the fact that a parent was in my office and flung herself down on the couch. She didn't answer.

"Trouble?" I asked.

Her words spilled out with a sudden fury. "You can tell that Cookie if she don't stay outa my face, I'm goin kick her butt in."

"Okay," I answered. "Cool it. I guess you're trying to stay out of trouble, is that it?"

She shook her head yes.

I could not tell her to go. She was obviously controlling herself. She was practicing what we had been teaching, walking away from trouble. It was not easy for her to turn her back on a fight, especially when she knew that some girls would accuse her of being afraid.

"If I send you to another class, will you be able to stay away from Cookie?" I asked.

"I'll stay away from her," she answered, pointing her finger at me, which was always a dangerous sign of anger, "but if she keeps comin at me, I'm gonna hit her."

I couldn't take a chance.

"Well," I answered, "I think too much of you to let you get into trouble. How about doing a job for me until we can talk? Mrs. Magnus was just asking me for a girl to help her."

It was a grudging okay she gave me, and I called in Mrs. Magnus, my secretary, who had an absolute genius for spontaneous contrived assignments.

"I need someone to work on the adding machine," she said.

Audrey's face lit up.

I turned back to the parent, but in seconds the intercom in my office was buzzing.

"Audrey is cutting class," her teacher told me.

"No, she's not," I answered, "she's staying out of trouble, and if that's cutting, it's therapeutic cutting. She's using good judgment."

And she was. Hadn't she decided to choose that alternative path of behavior I was always talking about to the girls? She had looked at the situation clearly, hypothesied that she could either go to class and fight, or walk away from class and not fight; and she had decided to walk away. Decided. That was the key word. That one word bolted me into a whole new world of thinking. Decision-making.

I thought back to Berenice banging on the door. Hadn't she decided that she couldn't go to her class at that moment—and hadn't she been right?

I thought back to Priscilla bursting into my office, a huge leather apron tied around her waist, a large painting, still wet, held outstretched in her hands.

"Can I stay with Mr. Garber in the art room and finish my painting?"

"No," I answered. "it's the end of the period. Mr. Garber has another class coming in and you have another class to go to."

"Please," she begged.

"You can finish it when you go to art again," I told her.

"But that won't be until Thursday!"

"So, that's only two days away. You'll finish it on Thursday."

She became furious. "How do I know how I'll feel on Thursday?" she cried.

And she was right. How could an artistic expression stemming from the emotions be scheduled?

I gave her permission to finish it.

What about Esther, who was absent each day her class wasn't scheduled for dressmaking? If she could decide for herself to go to dressmaking every day, would she not come to school every day? If we made life as exciting inside school as it is outside, if we competed successfully with television, daytime drinking parties and sleeping late, perhaps Esther would come. We had to try.

Each of the girls in deciding what was right for her had broken a school rule. Each had deviated from a schedule. The question I, of course, had to ask myself came bursting into consciousness. Was the rule necessary? Did we have to have a schedule? What if the girls were permitted to make their own schedules, were able to decide for themselves what classes they would go to and what time they would go to them?

It was a heady idea. More and more I considered it seriously. The time had come, I was convinced, for another drastic and dramatic overhaul of our school structure. Bells, schedules, programmed classes were anachronistic. Girls needed to have a voice in scheduling their own learning. Their lives, disordered as they were, could not be made ordered by the imposition of forty-five-minute classroom periods; their thinking, distorted as it sometimes was, could not be made logical by mandate. Schedules and order and logic had to be internalized. Girls had to see a meaning to order, and they had to have a voice in creating it. How foolish to insist that they accept scheduled classes, that they be where they were told to be just because they were told!

Why should a girl have to wait until Tuesday and Thursday to type for a forty-five-minute period, when if she is motivated to learn to type she can learn the entire keyboard in one week if she devotes almost full time to it daily? And why not? Isn't that how people really learn? Students learn what they want to when they want to learn it, as a rule. Could changing classes at the sound of a bell be obsolete?

I thought back. Ten years ago we purposefully had discarded tradition and the stereotypes called education. We stopped organizing classes by grades, and we became nongraded. We individualized instruction completely.

Two years later we expanded our horizons by organizing a work program, which we call the Upper School. Girls in that program work part of the day and come to school part of the day.

We had made our school a place of solace, not punishment. The proof of our success was our inability to get girls to leave early when they were misbehaving. Remaining late was not detention. It was reward.

But now it was the new year of 1969, and the time for change again. Students throughout the world were becoming increasingly determined to have a voice in decisions that affected them. Our girls had to learn to be part of that world, whether they were ready or not. The world would not stand still for them. And being part of that world meant making decisions. We would not ask them to examine national or international politics, nor to become social critics if they did not want to, but we would teach them that within their power they had the right and the obligation to themselves to control their own destinies. In school this meant making decisions about learning. Outside of school, it could mean deciding not to join a drug society, or to finish going to school, or not to become pregnant.

Girls would learn not only to accept and react to their environments, but to react and shape those environments. They would learn to be involved with the world, and involvement meant a belief in their own power. The girls had to learn to believe in their own sources of strength because if they did not, the alternative is alienation. It is a disastrous alternative, for it is a concept that is rooted in weakness and defeat, and girls who feel weak, defeated, and powerless often retreat and withdraw into the world of drugs. Yes, we would definitely fight against those forces of alienation.

I began using every situation I could with the girls to bring up the idea of a decision-making curriculum.

"Joanne," I asked, "here you are in my office because your teacher reported you for cutting a class, and so you're in trouble. What if you never had to cut a class because there would be no scheduled periods and you could go to any subject you wanted to, would you like that?"

"Yeah," she beamed, "I'd like that."

"Where would you go?"

"Music, I'd go first to music and maybe beauty culture, and oh, I'd go to the yard."

"The whole day?"

"Yeah."

"Well, that's one day," I said, "but what if you had the choice of going where you wanted every day for a whole term or a whole year. Would you like that?"

I expected her to pounce on the idea gleefully but she didn't.

"Naw."

"Why not?"

"Cause I'd never learn nothin, that's why. I'd never do no readin or math or nothin."

"Why not?" I asked again.

"Cause I'd never go," she explained.

"Why not?" I insisted a third time.

"Well, you gonna make me?" she asked.

"No—"

"See?"

"Yeah, I see," I said, "if you didn't decide to go by yourself, no one would make you go, and you'd be stupid. Right?"

"I guess so," she agreed.

"So?" I asked. "What's wrong with that?"

"What's wrong with that?" she screeched. "Are you funny or somethin? Teachers are supposed to teach, that's what."

"And pupils are supposed to learn," I said, "only teachers shouldn't order you to learn, you should learn because you want to."

I was silent for a minute, then ordered, "Joanne, look down at your shoes."

She was startled, but she looked.

"What do you see?"

"My feet," she said with obvious annoyance.

"That's right," I answered. "Your feet are in your shoes. No one else's. Did someone else get in your shoes and make you walk away from class?"

"No—" She was loath to say it.

"So," I said, "if you want to be stupid, that's your own feet doing the walking. That's your business, isn't it?"

"Yeah, it's my business, I suppose," she said glumly.

"So, if you want to go to class and learn, you'll be smart, and if you don't want to go to class, you'll be stupid, and you'll have nobody to blame but yourself."

"That's right," she agreed heatedly, "and that's hard, too damned hard, I don't like it to make my own mind up, I'm not used to it and I won't know how to get used to it, and I don't like it."

Audrey put it another way, when she, Constance, Aletta, and Joanne came to the office all yelling at each other.

I knew they were coming. Miss Hack, the drama teacher, had sent them down because they had been pushing and shoving each other, with Miss Hack in the middle.

Aletta was angriest of all, but not the loudest.

"She oughta mind her own damned business."

"Who?" I asked.

"That teacher, she oughta mind her own damned business."

"You are her business, Aletta," I answered, "and why are you insulting yourself by calling yourself damned? Aren't you her business?"

She looked startled.

"I guess so," she agreed tentatively.

"So don't call yourself damned," I said. It silenced her because she was trying to figure out my reasoning. I admit it was hard.

"I wouldn't hit her," Audrey shouted, "I wouldn't, but see, see I wouldn't hit her, I wouldn't, but see, she had a piece of dirt on her head and I went to push it off and Joanne pushed my hand and—"

"I did not," Joanne cried at the top of her voice. "That's a lie."

The other three verbally pounced on her.

"I didn't mean it, shit on you, Joanne," Audrey finally yelled. "It's your fault."

"Oh, please," I begged, "please let's have a shitless day for once."

I had their immediate and silent attention.

"We might converse," I continued, "provided you are willing to do so in an atmosphere of quiet."

"What that mean?" Constance asked.

"It means keep your big mouth shut," I said.

"Talk some more like that, Dr. Rothman," laughed Audrey, "usin them big funny words."

"Certainly," I answered, "and there is no reason why each of you could not similarly converse if you had a mind to."

"I wanta talk like that," Audrey said.

"You might do so," I answered, "provided you went to classes and engaged in intellectual pursuits."

"Huh?" Constance asked.

I decided to make my point in language they could not mistake.

"Learn, baby," I said, "learn. Go to class and learn. You

were messing around in the halls, running off at the mouth, and your mouth was no prayerbook, right? If you had been in your classes, where you should have been, you would have been doing right. Right?"

"That's right," Aletta agreed.

"And Joanne wouldn'ta bit my hand," Audrey accused.

"Shit, I did not—" Joanne cried again. She threw her books down and ran out.

"See?" I said to the other three, and to keep their attention I became very erudite again, "That's unwillingness to accept responsibility for your own behavior. One has to look into oneself, one has to have insight, in order to know that one has to go to class to learn."

"Yeah," Audrey said.

"What she mean?" Constance asked again.

Audrey explained, "She mean you gotta dig yourself if you wanta make somethin of yourself. No messin around."

"That's right," I agreed. I found myself quoting Joanne, who had just run out, "That's hard."

"Square business, that's what," Audrey said solemnly.

Constance repeated it, "Square business."

"How about it?" I asked. "Suppose you were able to go to any class you wanted, suppose you were able to plan your own schedule, day by day, do you think you would assume enough responsibility to do it?"

"I could," said Audrey, "I'd go and learn me some big words."

"Me, too," said Aletta. And then she sat prim and proper and upright and pronounced each word with conviction.

"I don't want anything I said to incriminate me."

"Wow!" The voice was mine, and Aletta beamed.

We could do it, I knew we could do it. We could institute a

brand-new idea in a Board of Education school. That in itself was momentous.

Enthusiastically, I approached a Board of Education functionary with decision-making as a school way of life.

He was less than cautious. He was reluctant.

"Well now, Esther," he drawled, "you just can't come in with a new idea—"

"Why not?"

"You have to research it, see if it's been done before, spend some time in the library—"

"What difference will that make? Our kids are here and now. What do I care if it was done in Winnetka in 1939?"

"Now, Esther, you know better than that. We would have to set up a research design, involve research people, set up goals and procedures and build in some evaluation procedures."

I decided silence was the better part of valor. He decided that my silence was acquiescence.

"Tell you what, write up a research proposal and send it on to me," he said, which was one way of saying forget it.

I knew than that I would do what I had always done. I would go ahead with my plans and not tell anyone at the Board until it was a *fait accompli*. If I waited for permission, nothing would ever be attempted, much less achieved. I called the teachers together for a series of meetings to discuss decision-making as our new curriculum. I believed very strongly that the time had come to put into action what we say we believe in—self-determination and democracy.

We like to say that we control our own destinies, but generally we certainly don't. It's an American myth foisted upon us, for we do not decide whether or not we will go to war—we do not really decide our country's policies, although we clutch at the ballot box as a sign of our power. We make very few vital decisions that are really our own. Even the decisions that we like to believe are truly our own are really most often decisions based on chance. The choice of a marriage partner, or whether we marry at all, depends largely on whom we meet. The choice of a career depends largely on the family we were born into, finances, and the availability of colleges. As teachers, the schools we get into and the children we teach are often decided for us by others. Therefore, it is time we try to put into practice the concept that we can and must make decisions for ourselves that pertain peculiarly and particularly to our own lives. Let us begin to believe that we can control some things in our lives—not many, but some. And perhaps that will help us to grow toward many.

Let us teach young people that they do in some measure have a control over their destinies, not in matters of national war and peace, perhaps, although we should love it if it really were so, but certainly in matters of what they shall study tomorrow, what it is important for them to learn today. The most important thing we can teach is that each student has control over her own life to a large degree. Our teachers certainly were ready.

First, however, an important part of the program had to be considered—where would a girl go if she didn't feel like going to any class, or if the classes she went to were filled and she couldn't get in? We decided upon the outer school yard if she wanted a five-minute smoke break, or the second floor if she wanted to sit. Only there was no place to sit. I had long wanted to create a lounge on the second floor, as it is a very busy place. Girls were constantly intercepting each other going in and out of our offices, and they needed a place to wait. Now was the time.

We moved in some old maple furniture, fondly called Early

American. It no doubt was, too—circa 1875, the year our building went up. It bore marks of distinctive service—dirt. Later, I was able to requisition modern furniture in cheerfully colored imitation leather from the Board of Education, and at last we had a real lounge that even included an electric percolator, so we could offer refreshment to visitors and teachers.

Then we tried out our new decision-making program, first for one day at a time, later for a week at a time, then for several weeks, finally for a month, and then permanently. Between trials we reverted back to our old program. The girls understood what we were doing, but each time we went back to scheduled classes the uproar was heard loud and clear.

"I thought you trusted us," Joanne complained.

"I do," I answered.

"Sure, then how come you're goin back to treatin us like we got no minds of our own?"

Bethel definitely did have a mind of her own. She was very happy to let us know what was on it by keeping a diary of her first day of decision-making.

9:00-11:15 Beauty Culture
I had my hair did in Beauty Culture by Miss Schneider. My conduct was good! or you might say Excellent.

11:15-11:20 English
I worked on a eight grade Book. About urban blight and my sister Connie worked on it too! Only Constance and I were in English My Conduct and Work for a change was excellent.

11:20-12:00 I was with the great Dr. Rothman. We started to talk but were intorupited. So Hollywood and I didn't speak.

12:00-1:00 Now is Lunch time the lunch was terrible to me ! ! !

1:00-1:15 I was down in yard with me myself and I for a while than went to cooking

1:15-1:36 Cooking. I didn't do anything cause it was too late to Bake and I wanted to Bake.

1:36-2:00 Lounging on second floor for a while then got yelled at By Dr. Rothman for. awhile then Mrs. Gray for awhile! They all gave me Hell. Then I went to store to get Miss Magnus some candy and Mrs. Gray some candy & Because they Both saw my delicus chocolate [sic] candy! I Brought Dr. Esther P. Rothman a tomatoe! went home at 2:30.

Bethel loved the world that day. Not only was she calling me Hollywood, which was the epitome of flattery, but she promoted yesterday's enemy, Constance, into sisterhood. This from Bethel, who devoted her life to hating and abusing the world, was an astounding achievement for us.

Nevertheless, the teachers had some reservations.

"What if the girls waste a lot of time," they asked, "and don't go to a class?"

"So what?" I answered. "Do we spend each day entirely profitably? Aren't there days we all goof off? And don't teachers have unassigned periods, supposedly to prepare teaching materials, and aren't these periods away from the girls? The old cry, 'teaching is too hard, we need time away from the kids,' should be made applicable to our girls. Perhaps sometimes they need some time away from the teachers."

They agreed.

"But what if there are some classes no one will go to?" was a persistent question.

My answer was simple. We should begin to worry. We should begin to study ourselves, to look into ourselves before we began to talk of "them," their lack of motivation, their surliness, their problems. If girls do not come to class, the onus is on us. Is it possible we are failing them? It's a painful question to ask, even more painful to answer, but a necessary one if we are to do more than just collect our paychecks.

No teacher ever had to ask the question, because it never happened. And that's because the teachers are good, very good. And they care.

At first, of course, when we tried decision-making for a day at a time, we knew that many girls would not go to their academic classes, and we weren't too concerned. We did begin to worry, however, when we tried decision-making for an entire week, and found that again only a few girls went to English or Math. At the end of the week, however, we felt considerably better when we read Eva's evaluation.

I really liked this week but I stayed in the yard. I stayed with them because I was afiaid do say no and I wanted do know my friends better. If we had this prugram I would speak for mysely and follow my own schedule. I fell that I can learn more in my classrooms that I can by staying in the yard.

After the second consecutive week Eva, indeed, did not stay in the yard. She wrote:

When I finished my work, I didn't have to stay with the class till the period was over. I was able to walk away and go to the next class.

As Eva voluntarily spent more and more time in the library and with her reading teacher, her reading began to improve.

When Theodora wanted to do arithmetic, she did, provided there was room for her. If not, she had to make an appointment. How marvelous for girls who have resisted all academics to have to wait their turn to be admitted! It's like standing room at the theater. The show has got to be good. Everybody wants to get in. This does not mean all is peaceful in academia.

Theodora was learning geometry. She drew a square on the blackboard.

"What's that?" asked Esther.

"Your father," said Theodora.

"Funny," said Esther, only she didn't laugh. She went to the board and drew a circle. "That's your mother," she said.

This was too much for Theodora, although she had started it. She drew a semicircle and taunted, "You're a semicircle, your father didn't finish the job."

Mrs. Maixnor dampened the fireworks by complimenting them both on their knowledge of geometry. Besides, Esther didn't really want to fight since she was wearing a new dress she had made in the dressmaking class.

The enthusiasm of the teachers rose. So did the attendance. The girls began competing with each other to get to school not only every day, but also on time, because they wanted to get to classes before they were filled to capacity. Girls planned their programs daily with the help of their official teachers. If they went to a class and it was filled, they went to another class. If they felt the need for a break, they would go to the second-floor lounge or to the yard.

One rule applies: no girl can be disruptive. If she is, the teacher asks her to leave. There are no bells and no periods. Girls can enter and leave when they please. This, however, does not mean that they can leave the building during the school day.

When I saw Champagne, who was as effervescent as her name, holding a huge box containing a pizza that was still hot,

I knew she had broken the rule. Before I had a chance to speak, she held the box out to me.

"What some?"

"No, I don't want some," I answered crossly, "and who told you you could go out and buy it?"

"But I asked the teachers if they wanted some," she whined.

"And I'm sure none of them took it," I answered.

My unfortunate words were hardly spoken before Miss Feldman came into the lounge, a slice of pizza in her hand.

"And I'm certain Miss Feldman has no intention of eating that pizza," I continued.

The pizza was midway up to Miss Feldman's lips. It stayed there.

"How dare you leave the building," I scolded Champagne, "and then try to bribe teachers with pizza?"

"I wasn't bribing," Champagne wailed, "I just wanted pizza. I just left the building for a minute."

"Is that what you and your teacher planned for you to do?" I asked. "Is that a new curriculum offering, the eating of pizza?"

Champagne wailed more loudly than before. "I just decided to leave the building, we're allowed to decide."

"You're not allowed to decide to leave the building," I told her. "Some regulations are not open to decisions. There are regulations we all must abide by, like no smoking in a school building. It's a decision made for us for everybody's good."

Champagne merely looked glum.

"So," I continued, "you may have decided to buy the pizza, but I am deciding that you can't have it. It just cost you—" I took the box from her and looked at the price— "one dollar and ninety-eight cents. That's an expensive decision you made."

She stood there pizza-less.

Miss Feldman followed me into the office.

"I made the wrong decision," she said. "But I really didn't know what to do." Miss Feldman was a new teacher.

"We all have to learn," I told her. And we did. Everybody was not as cavalier as Champagne about making decisions, nor as uncertain as Miss Feldman.

Phyllis, for instance, was upset by her new responsibility. She asked to stay home during those first experimental days. She felt she would get into trouble if she came, that she would not be able to control herself, that she would run through the building aimlessly and not be able to decide what to study.

"Okay, Phyllis," I told her, "you can stay home, but you know what you're doing, don't you? You're deciding to stay out of trouble by staying away. That's a decision you're making, and it's a good one for now, but soon you'll be able to decide to come to school and still stay out of trouble. You tell me when you can do it."

And she did, a few days later. Phyllis decided to come to school, but because she was afraid of the new program, afraid she would waste all her time, she wrote out a weekly program, period by period, and followed it, just as if bells were rung. Far better for Phyllis to internalize her schedule than for us to force it upon her.

Phyllis was not alone in her fears. Although the teachers were truly excited about decision-making, most found that it was as hard for them to adjust as it was for some of the girls. Like the students, they, too, relied on periods and bells and being told what to do and when. Teachers, like most of society, are prone to follow the patterns of their pasts, and their own school lives had been regulated by periods, dismissals, home rooms, official and subject teachers. This new program meant greater freedom for them to work out their own programs. If a teacher needed to close his room for a period of time in order to write some reports, he simply posted his schedule on his door, but only after he cleared it with the office to see that every teacher had not closed at the same time. Decision-making was a two-way process for both teachers and girls.

Some teachers feared that decision-making might become just a laissez-faire approach—learn if you want to, don't learn if you don't want to, and do as you please. They weren't sure of their roles. What was a teacher?

We talked and talked, and out of it came our philosophy that a teacher guides. Teachers would not say to girls, "You don't have to go to class," or "You must go to class," but rather, "This and this is the consequence of your decision. If you go to a class, this will happen; if you don't go, something else will happen." Girls will learn to see the relationships between decisions, planning, and results. We realized how important it would be to the girls to learn that some decisions will have results that are not pleasant; in fact, some decisions might lead to some failures. Failure, however, is also learning. Failure and unpleasantness are part of the process of learning. Science could not progress without trial and error.

We no sooner solved a theoretical problem than a new question arose. If both the girls and the teachers were in a position to make decisions of equal importance, would not the teacher's authority be lessened? The answer was no. Girls learned that there are privileges and rights in any society. In a school society, a teacher has certain rights simply because she has attained the position of teacher. This is reality. Girls began to understand that we all have equal votes in society, but our positions and jobs give us privileges unique to each. For instance, my vote may be equal to the President's, but my authority simply is not. Teachers have certain authority, girls do not, even though both are respected as individuals. Decision-making emphasized the necessity of and for authority.

"Look, girls," I said to Bethel, Constance, and Audrey, "it may be your decision to come to my office and be noisy, but it's my decision to throw you out if you make too much noise. I have some phone calls to make, and I need quiet. I won't be able to hear."

"But we want to talk to you."

"Well, you'll have to wait," I answered. "If you can sit and wait about ten minutes and not be noisy, I'll be able to do my work and then talk to you. All right?"

They decided to wait with reasonable quiet. And they learned something; they learned that they have access to authority by coming anytime to a door that is never closed except in an emergency. By implication and extension of the practice, the doors of authority can be opened to them for redress of a grievance any place in the community. If this is a lie, then our whole concept of democracy is a lie. I prefer to believe it isn't.

At Livingston democracy starts in the morning when teachers and girls eat breakfast together in our lunchroom, which also doubles for a yard. As all the girls eat breakfast in the same large area, although at separate tables, it is relatively easy for girls to consult with teachers or teachers to consult with teachers to work out daily programs. Thus, if a teacher is too busy at a certain time, he tells the girl when she may come, either at another time that day or another day. Girls make appointments, as it were. Teachers post what they are teaching that day and the hour that they do not have classes. Thus, teachers can arrange for time without teaching in order to prepare lessons or plan material.

Breakfast is an important teaching and socializing time. We

can tell the tenor of the day by the way girls come in. We can see which girls are angry at girls, which girls are angry at teachers, which girls are angry at themselves. If many of the girls are wearing slacks, we're in for trouble. It is a quick overview of the coming day, and being alert to danger signals, we are able to direct and avert difficulties.

"Good morning, Sheila."

"Don't good morning me, nobody," Sheila thundered.

Could Sheila tell us any more distinctly that she was troubled?

I alerted Mrs. Landsman, the guidance counselor, so that she would make herself available for Sheila as soon as possible.

"And how are you this morning, Pat?" I asked.

Big smile. "Fine, you know what I did yesterday? I did five pages of homework."

Pat's depression is lifting. That's good news.

And we did not need to ask Alberta how she was this morning. It was easy to tell. Her wrinkled, dirty clothes looked as if she had slept in them. Her mother had probably locked her out again. I made a note to call her probation officer and see what we could do to help her.

And the day started.

Pat was feeling particularly good, so I asked her to evaluate the entire school as she saw it from the second floor. I asked her to pretend she was a teacher's aide, whose job it was to describe exactly what happened in the second-floor lounge. This is what she wrote:

OBSERVATION OF THE second FLOOR

Sandra goes out and plays handball.

2 girls play the game nok-hockie

A group of girls come down and take a smoke.

Sometimes the girls would play around with each other and get loud.
Mr. McMahn sits in his class typing and smoking at the same time.
Mr. Robbin in his room asking questions and giveing compliments to girls at the same time.
Teacher and student is walking out the hall discussing a problem.
Custodian and office lady, Guidance Counselor all walking around the hall being concerned.
Mr. Scarcella put the coffee pot back together.
Girl stops teacher to run off at the mouth.
One girl comes in late and teacher calls her and she keeps on walking.
Guidance Counselor walks in and out the office but really don't know where she wants to go finaly she decided to go to her own room.
Girls asks about her class.
The officer keeps on talking about coffee and speaking to a student.
A visitor signs the book.
A ball decided it would get up off its legs and come up the walls onto the second floor.
Mrs. Eisert is getting ready to leave the building.
A student and adults hold a convertsation.
Mr. McMahn wants coffee but Can't get it because it's not ready.
And here comes a girl shouting ass and every time I saw her today she was repeting herself.
Mrs. Gray walks through the hall asking about Mr. Turner.
Mr. Robbin walks and talks to me and walks into the walls.
Princeable discussed a problem with a girl.
I think all the teachers want coffee.
Miss Miller just walked out with a girl.
Sandra is playing ball and rolling it back and fourth through her legs.
Miss Grant came down and is taking pictures.
Deloris is walking and running around the hall like a nut.
Now the coffee is perking.

Education?
Education, yes.

On Moratorium Day, October 15th, I called the entire Upper School into the office to discuss the meaning of that day to the nation.

The Board of Education had just announced that both students and teachers could be excused from attending school that day if they wished to protest the war in Vietnam.

The teachers had met earlier in the day to discuss our position. We had decided, with only three exceptions, that while we were vehemently opposed to continuing the war, we would voice our protest after school hours, and we would keep school open so that our girls would not be forced to stay out and possibly get into trouble in their communities on a day when thousands of people were going to be in the streets.

I explained to the girls in my office that the decision was theirs to make, that they could stay out if they wanted to voice their protests in their communities, or they could come in and voice their protest with us in a letter-writing campaign to the President. I made it quite clear, however, that they could not just take a holiday.

They listened very intently and seriously. Every one of them felt deeply. Almost every one of them had a brother or a cousin or an uncle or a boyfriend in Vietnam. They wanted the war ended.

"Then, that's settled," I told them. "You make your decision yourself." I repeated the conditions.

"That's right," Vanessa said, "I'll stay home only if I have to take care of my little brother and sisters if they don't go to their school."

"Yes," I agreed, "you may have to do that, and that will be a good decision for you to make. Everybody has different things to consider."

They began to speak up, seriously considering their actions on the next day.

"Yeah, sure, sure," Sandra began to speak loudly, and then as if not a word had been said, she exploded with, "Why we gotta come to school? All the schools in my neighborhood are gonna close."

"Sandra," I explained, "we've been through all that. Shall we go over it again?"

Vanessa forgot that I had just complimented her. "That's right," she agreed with Sandra. "This school never closes. Why don't you close this school?" Her words began to race. "Sure, I know, you'll say you're doin it for us, we need our education and all that shit, you just wanta come to school."

Gail got into the act.

"Queen of Sheba, that's what she thinks she is, Dr. Rothman is Queen of Sheba, tellin us what to do, who she think she is, Queen of Sheba?"

"Oh, come on," I laughed, "we've just had an intelligent discussion. You know the score."

"Yeah," Vanessa agreed, "during the strike last year, all the schools closed in my neighborhood, but not here, never give us no day off."

"And we don't get time to play," Sandra interrupted.

"Queen of Sheba, Queen of Sheba," Gail intoned.

"Yeah," Brenda called out. "Why you keep this school open?"

"Queen of Sheba."

"No time to play handball," Pia screamed. "Why ain't we got time to play handball?"

"Why you never close the school?"

"Hold it!" I yelled. "Hold it. I'll tell you why we never close the school, and I'll tell you square."

They all stopped and listened.

I knew I had to go along with them. We had been serious, we had been concerned with war and peace. They were moved. Now it was time to play.

"I don't give a damn about kids learning."

"See," Vanessa said, "what did I tell you?"

"That's right," I agreed, "there's one word for it. Teachers come for only one reason—look it up. Masochism."

"Huh?"

I spelled it for them. "Look it up."

They scrambled to their rooms for their dictionaries. Gail grabbed at mine and fled.

The teachers and I began to laugh. But we laughed too soon. I had completely forgotten the analytic definition.

In minutes, Gail was back. "Here, I found it, I found it!"

Everybody listened while she read it aloud. "A form of sexual perversion in which one finds pleasure in abuse and cruelty from his or her associate."

The joke was on me.

chapter ten

Developing Self-Esteem: A Therapeutic Approach

To find her way to self-esteem each girl must fight two enemies, the enemy within and the enemy that is reality. Before she can fight either one, however, she must first learn to find them. This is not an easy task. We teach her how.

Reality—the enemy without—is usually easier to find, but harder to fight. Poverty, friends who are not really friends, parents who have died or deserted, or parents who are so destructive no child should be asked to live with them, are realities that no girl wants to face. Yet we force her to. And we teach her how to fight back. Sometimes fighting back means that a girl and I both go to court to petition against a destructive parent. Sometimes it means I find a decent apartment for a family to live in. We fight back when we can. We cannot always. We cannot fight death or desertion or poverty. But we try! How we try! Otherwise, how can a girl begin to believe in herself?

Each girl begins to find her own strengths when she begins to seek out and fight the enemy within—her own defenses—the things she does for which she is solely accountable—things that are destructive to herself, such as withdrawal into phantasy, alcoholism, running away from home, the use of drugs, acts of violence. These are defenses that defeat. They must be attacked, first by us, later by each girl herself. We attack directly. We say "No" and "Stop" and "Don't" and "You can't," and we offer alternative ways of behavior. Therapy at Livingston is definitely a collision course. We aim for non-violence in behavior, but of necessity, we have to arouse violence in feelings. This is as it should be. Without it, we cannot hope or plan for change. Conquering the enemy non-violently is not as simple as it sounds, for the two enemies, the enemy that is self-destructive and the enemy that is reality, feed upon and perpetuate each other. There is only one cure—confrontation. It is an incredibly painful process. For all of us.

"This is the way it is, Theodora," I said in language that I made certain she would understand. "You're a new girl, but you might just as well get it straight. You can't go around here feeling girls up. And you can't go around with your blouse unbuttoned. Nobody is interested in seeing what you've got."

"I didn't tell them to be interested," she yelled. "What you saying, that I'm a butch?"

"I don't care whether or not you are," I answered. "That's your business, not mine. It becomes my business when you make it my business. Look at you, why isn't your blouse buttoned?"

"Because the buttons just popped. That's why." She screamed again.

"All three of them?" I asked.

"Yeah, all three of them," she repeated. "I can't help that—"

"You must think I'm stupid if you expect me to believe that," I answered. "I'm not stupid, so please don't insult my intelligence by repeating that nonsense."

"You make me sick," she muttered.

"Too bad," I told her, "but sick or not, just cut it out. Wear clothes that button. If you're not butch, don't act like one. If you are, nobody is interested. The girls are pretty tired of your going after them."

She exploded in full wrath.

"They got nothin better to do then come baby mouthin to you? What kinda school you got? Everybody goin around mindin your business. Why don't you mind you own business?"

"You are my business," I answered with emphasis on each word. I say these very same words a hundred times a day, it seems.

"I'm nobody's business," Theodora cried angrily. "I wanta be in a big school where they don't snag you for every little thing. This school make me sick."

Like an electric feedback that charges itself, her words of anger were stimulating her to further anger. I decided to cut the circuit.

"Girl," I said sharply, "you've got nothing but mouth now. You could have something, because you've got brains, but right now, you've got nothing, because you're not using your brains. I'm telling you—stop the butch act. As long as I'm principal at this end of the desk, and you're a girl acting stupid, standing there at that end of the desk, I win, not you. That's it."

She came over to the desk, stood over me and thrust her face in front of mine, her mouth inches away.

"You braggin?" she asked.

I looked at her and stared her down. "Yes, I suppose I am," I answered. "And when you get to be principal, so can you."

Suddenly she laughed. The transformation was so sudden, she was a thirteen-year-old again.

"Okay," she stepped backward. "I was just askin."

I clinched it. "And I'm telling."

"Yeah."

She turned and left. We never discussed it again. We both understood. She had pushed and pushed hard to defy the social code in school, and she had met me. She had tested to see how far she could go, and she had found her limits. I was stronger than she. She would behave well now because I was demanding that she behave well, and this, after all, is what she desperately wants and needs to believe, that she can behave well. She does not want to be completely without controls and therefore hopeless and beyond help. She wants to believe in and respect herself. The process of building a new ego has begun.

She became a frequent visitor in my office. "I like to see what's goin on," she told me one day.

"You're like radar," I answered, "coming down to learn the gossip and spread it. Ever think of becoming a reporter?"

"No," she laughed, "just a snoop. I like to do what you do, figure out what kids are thinkin."

"You don't mean snoop," I said, "you mean spy."

"Yeah, that's right, I wanta be a mind spy."

A few days later she had her chance.

"Maybe you can help Judy, Theodora," I said. "Maybe you can help her better than I."

I pointed to Judy standing inside my office, hands clenched, leather jacket zipped up to her neck, tears swimming in her eyes.

Theodora peered at her.

"She mad?" she asked me.

"Yes," I answered. "I just told her she can't play butch. You know how it is, you've been through it yourself. Can you talk to her? Can you make her see she has to stop? No matter what the reason is she's acting this way, she has to stop."

"Okay."

"I'll leave you two alone in my office."

As I left the room, I saw Theodora sit down in the chair behind my desk.

A half-hour later, I saw her again, this time outside my office. Judy was still inside.

"Dr. Rothman, I think she'll be all right. You don't have to suspend her."

"I wasn't going to suspend her," I answered. "You know that."

She didn't hear me, she was so intent on her own thinking.

"She's really scared of the girls, and she thought if she'd act tough, they'd let her alone. She didn't know she's making it worse for herself." Suddenly her own words struck home. She started to laugh. Her smile was contagious. "Oh, you know."

"Thanks, sweetie," I told her. "I'm getting scared of you. You're soon going to take my job."

I could practically touch the glow that emanated from her. Through it, like a double exposure, I could almost see the report of the psychiatric examination that had just been sent to me. The psychiatrist had very poetically put into psychiatric jargon what I had told him prosaically in the first place. No recommendations or suggestions were made, just diagnosis, one that must have taken years of study to put into a psychiatric classification system, "Explosive personality, 301.38."

Thank you, Doctor, it certainly is helpful to catalogue people, like books, especially if all we ever plan to do is shelve them. But not for us! We are more vital.

With Theodora, confrontation had been an overt show of

strength with me, nothing more, and it had been relatively easy. The real work, the second phase—self-confrontation—had not yet begun.

It had with Adrienne. She was on the way to self-discovery. I looked at her, sitting there so huddled and small in that big seat. She seemed overpowered by it. It had taken Adrienne months to confide in me, months of building a relationship. Mostly, I had listened, to encourage her to feel comfortable about talking. I had given her time to believe in me, to believe in her ability to express her feelings, to believe that working together we could find a way out of her unhappiness. But now the time had come for her to face herself bombastically. Only through the process of confrontation would she be able to stop what she was doing to herself and substitute new patterns of behavior. Only through confrontation could she begin to face the reality of change, and value herself as she could be.

"This is the way things are, Adrienne," I said. "Your mother is dead, your grandmother is very old and drinks, and no one really cares for you, no one but your teachers and me. I don't even know how much you care for yourself."

She hung her head low as if my words crumbled her.

"Okay," I continued. "So things are tough, but tough or not, you do not have the right to shove other girls off subway platforms. That's hurting them. Why should they suffer because of you? Is that fair?"

Adrienne had a profound sense of fairness, as did most of the girls.

"No," she whispered.

"And is there any reason you can't wear a clean dress and do your hair? Must you be dirty and uncombed?"

My tone was not conciliatory, nor was it harsh. It simply was a statement of fact. If Adrienne was to do something constructive for herself, first she had to stop feeling so sorry for herself that she wallowed in self-destruction.

"My grandmother don't take care of me," she whispered.

"Oh, come off it." This time I was harsh. "How old are you? Fifteen. You can take care of your own things."

"But everybody needs somebody to love them," she sighed.

For a moment I thought, *my God, that's a song lyric*, but the pain of her longing shot through me, and for the first time I understood, really understood, why Adrienne spent a good part of every school day in my office, listening to music. Almost every song of longing was a summation of her life. She had literally nobody to love her. She had no idea who her father was. She lived with her alcoholic grandmother, who had produced Adrienne's mother, a fatality of an overdose of drugs at the age of twenty-three. Having failed her own daughter, what could she possible give to her daughter's daughter?

There was no point in saying any of this to Adrienne. She was going to have to learn that she and only she had to care enough about herself to overcome the realities of her life. What a hard, almost impossible, task I was setting for her. Yet I refused to believe it was impossible, and perhaps if I refused to accept the impossibility, so would she.

"Did you ever stop to think that when you shove girls off the subway platform you're not lovable?" I asked her. "When you stay out all night so your grandmother doesn't know where you are and she calls me to see if you came to school, you're not very lovable. So whose fault is that?"

"Mines," a low, low voice.

"Yours," I repeated.

"And maybe your grandmother loves you as much as she can love anybody, but she has hangups of her own. I don't know about your grandmother, but I do know that your unacceptable behavior must stop. You must come to school. You cannot stay out all night. You cannot get into trouble on the subway."

I ended up with steel in my voice. "Understand? I don't care what troubles you have, you're not going to do those things to other people and to yourself. I won't let you. I think too much of you to let you go down the drain."

She didn't move or answer. Her apathy was reaching out to me. I wanted to find someone all her own for her to love and to love her, but I could not permit myself to think along those lines. How would that help?

"Okay," I finally said, "I guess you don't want to go down the drain. You want to help yourself? Is that right?"

She nodded.

"So let's start. And I'll tell you what I want you to do. I want a clean dress on you tomorrow, and your hair done."

She began to whimper, "My clothes are in the cleaners."

"I didn't tell you to take your clothes out of the cleaners," I interrupted. "I only told you to wear clean clothes. If you don't have any, wash your blouse tonight and iron it. Press your skirt. Wash and set your hair. Come in tomorrow like the attractive young lady you are. Can you do that?"

She didn't move or answer. We sat silent for a few minutes. Finally, a very low yes.

"Are you going to do it?" I repeated.

"Yes," louder.

"Is that a promise?"

No answer.

"Okay, Adrienne," I said, "is it or is it not a promise?"

"I don't know."

"Why don't you know?"

"I don't want to promise and then not keep it," her voice was almost a moan.

"Feeling sorry for yourself again?" I raised my voice deliberately. "Go ahead, go out of here and run home and cry and stay out all night again, drinking. Your grandmother says that's what you do. Here you complain about your grandmother drinking, and you do exactly the same thing, except there's no excuse for you. Your grandmother is an old lady and she's had a rotten life, but you're giving up before you even try."

I permitted my voice to rise even more.

She became angry. "No wonder everybody hates you," she cried.

"You can hate me all you want to," I answered, "but I still won't let you behave in a way that will hurt you. So go ahead, get angry at me, get angry at me because I say you are better than you think you are and you can be more than you are trying to be. Get angry, if that makes you understand what I'm saying." I stopped and looked at her. "Do you understand what I'm saying?"

"Yes." I barely heard her. I knew she was thinking deeply, absorbing what I had said.

"What?" I prodded her.

"I heard you," she shouted.

"Tell me, then," I said.

"That I'm better than the way I'm acting and I should act better." She screamed it out.

"Right. And what are you going to do?"

"What?" she asked.

"Don't 'what' me," I answered. "You know damned well what I'm talking about. Are you going to wash your clothes and set your hair and come on time to school tomorrow looking like an attractive young lady and without getting into trouble on the subway?"

"Okay, okay," she agreed.

"To what?" I insisted.

"To everything," she yelled.

"Say it," I yelled back.

She spoke at the top of her voice. "I'll wash my blouse and iron my skirt and wash and set my hair and come to school on time and not get into any trouble on the subway and be good."

"Are you committing yourself?" I asked. "Are you making a statement about yourself that we both understand?"

"Yes!" she screamed.

"Say it again," I insisted. "Tell me again what your commitment is. Use the words 'I commit myself.' I want to hear it."

"I told you before," she hedged.

"Tell us both again."

"I promise—" she started.

"No," I interrupted "commit yourself to a course of action."

"I commit myself," she said loudly, but she was no longer screaming, "that I will wash and iron my blouse and skirt tonight and wash and set my hair and come to school tomorrow without getting into trouble on the subway. There!"

Push had come to shove again. Confrontation.

"Good." For the first time I smiled. "And that's only for tomorrow, but it won't end there. Little by little, I'm going to ask you to make other promises, not only to me, but to yourself, and you're going to keep them and you're going to be all you can be, which is an awful lot. Perhaps in a few days you can get into our work program, if you keep your part of the bargain. And then you won't have to worry about money for the cleaners."

She smiled in return. It was a beginning. She was fighting back—not destructively, at undifferentiated targets, as she had all her life, but with a new focus upon herself. She had recognized the enemy—herself. For a brief moment, she had tried to believe the enemy was I, and I had accepted the role. I had become the enemy until she found out who the real one was. It was not an easy lesson for her to learn, but it was essential that she learn it. Neither was it an easy role for me to play, yet I had to force myself to play it. I play it many times.

I play it to the point of commitment, to the point where a girl is able to put into her own words not only her promise to me, but mostly to herself.

Shirley came into my office high. I would not have known it, but Mrs. Greenthal, our library teacher, who had been a nurse, told me that Shirley was definitely drugged. Her pupils were pinpoints, and her pulse was irregular.

"What ya want?" she asked. The words were barely out of her mouth before she began to grimace and laugh and dance around the room.

"What did you take, Shirley?" I asked.

"I didn't take nothin." She was angry again.

"Shirley, you must have," I answered.

"I ain't no liar," she yelled. "I didn't take nothin."

I remembered my talk a few days ago with Charlie Devlin, an ex-addict and director of Daytop Village, a residential treatment center for addicts, who had recently visited the school at my invitation. I had asked him to come because I was concerned about the increasing number of girls who were being drawn to drugs.

"You have to make them admit the truth," he had told me. "They will never get off the stuff until you have got them to admit they're on it, or to admit they're experimenting, anyway."

I started again.

"What did you take, Shirley?" I asked.

"Nothin."

"You're lying."

"I'm not lying." She began to laugh.

"Of course you're lying," I said, "your eyes don't focus, you're laughing without reason."

"I've got a cold, that's why."

"Maybe—" As soon as I said it, I knew it was a mistake. I was ready to back down because I really wanted to believe Shirley. I wanted to believe Mrs. Greenthal was wrong, that I was wrong. How I wanted to believe that!

But this is what Mr. Devlin had warned me about. "Don't let a user con you. They're experts at it."

Mrs. Greenthal was too good a nurse to be wrong, and my own eyes did not deceive me. Shirley was high.

"Maybe you have a cold," I said, "maybe not, but you're still high. What did you take, Shirley? You took something."

For a moment, she had believed she had fooled me, and she had been pleasant, but now her pleasantness had turned to anger.

"Nothin," she screamed. "Nothin."

I was back full circle. I had to leave. I asked Mr. Scarcella and Mrs. Langness to stay with Shirley while I went into the general office and called Mr. Devlin for help. He was not in, but the woman who answered the phone offered her help. She was an ex-addict, too.

"Make her hurt," she told me. "Get to her with something that hurts her."

I knew where Shirley hurt, but how cruel it was going to be . . . I went back into my office. Shirley was talking with Mrs. Langness. She felt comfortable. She thought she had won.

"Shirley," I tried again, "what did you take on your way to school?"

"Nothin, I told you." Now she was more sullen and withdrawn than angry.

"You're destroying yourself," I continued. "Is that what your mother would want you to do?"

"Don't you talk about my mother. My mother is dead." It was a sudden outburst after the calm.

I followed my instructions. I knew that the only chance I had of reaching Shirley was by assaulting her with the pain of her mother's death. Shirley's mother had died only a few months earlier, and Shirley was deeply grieving.

I remembered Mrs. Landsman's telling me of Shirley's admission interview. Mrs. Landsman had never seen a girl more abusive to her mother. Shirley had mocked her mother, insulted her, defied her, treated her with disdain. The death of her mother had to have hurt Shirley deeply. It must have aroused all her guilt, because Shirley, in her fantasy, must have wished her mother to die. Undoubtedly, she now felt responsible for her death. No wonder Shirley was going to pieces.

Nevertheless, I took my stand.

"She died, Shirley, she died," I cried, "but she lives on in you. What are you doing to your dead mother, Shirley, your mother who lives on in you?"

"Stop it," she screamed, "I won't listen, stop it."

She ran to the door. I barred her way and grabbed her by the arm.

"People have children, Shirley, because they want to live on in their children. Your mother can live on in you, Shirley, but you're doing something to her. What are you doing to your dead mother, Shirley, is she going to die all over again, Shirley? What are you doing to your dead mother, Shirley?"

I was sweating. I could feel my words pierce through her, as they pierced through me. I forced her to look at me as I grabbed both her arms and held her tight.

"Shirley, what did you take this morning?"

"Nothin," she screamed.

"You're lying to your dead mother, Shirley," I cried. "Swear on your dead mother you didn't take anything. She wants you to live, Shirley. Swear you didn't take anything."

"No." She broke away from me.

I saw Mrs. Langness and Mr. Scarcella, who were in the office with me. Their faces were stricken. Was I right? I wouldn't let myself listen to my own question. I had to be right. This was the only way. Otherwise, what chance had she? To continue lying, to continue being high? Where could it lead?

"Shirley," I cried, "your dead mother loves you. She wants you to live. What did you take this morning on your way to school?"

She began to sob and fell on the chair.

"A reefer."

I was unyielding. "You're lying. No reefer makes you like this."

"I had two reefers," she whimpered.

"You're still lying. When are you going to stop lying to your dead mother? She's asking the question through me, she's asking it."

"I had three reefers," she cried, "and that's the truth." She began to sob hysterically.

I had gotten her to admit the truth. Where did we go from here?

I called up my unknown adviser at Daytop.

"Now what?" I asked.

"Now, get her to go for help."

They gave me a phone number for Shirley to call. "But she has to make the call herself, make the appointment for herself; don't make it for her."

"Shirley," I said, "now what are you going to do about it?"

"I don't know," she wailed.

"But I know," I told her. "I'm going to give you a telephone number. You're going to call them. You're going to tell them you need help. You're going to give them your name, and you're going to make an appointment."

"Can't you call?" she asked. Her face was all wet from tears.

"No." I was still unyielding.

"Here." I shoved the phone in her direction.

"You dial," she pleaded, "please. I'll talk, but you dial."

"No."

She sat down. I watched her move, slowly, deliberately. She took the phone and dialed. Then, in a very halting voice I heard her say, "My name is Shirley. I'm fifteen and I need help." There was a long pause. Then she answered. "Three reefers at once." Again, a pause. "Tomorrow? Okay."

She hung up. "I have to call them tomorrow at twelve," she said without any emotion in her voice.

I could understand that. She was numb. So was I. I was physically, mentally, and emotionally drained. But it was not over. I knew that. Tomorrow was a long way off. I was too tired to be furious that they had not seen her immediately, but that is the way it is in New York City.

"What about tonight, Shirley?" I asked. I didn't let her see how weary I was. "I want you to promise your dead mother that you won't take reefers, pills, or any drug in any form anytime today, tonight, or tomorrow, before I see you again. Promise?"

"I promise," she said softly.

"No, not good enough. Tell me in your words that you promise to your dead mother and to me—to both of us."

"No," she moaned.

"Yes," I demanded.

"I promise to my dead mother and to you that I won't use nothin tonight or tomorrow till I see you, no reefers, no goofballs, no nothin—I promise."

She began to weep.

I put my arms around her.

"I believe you, Shirley. You have made a commitment. I believe you."

I was right to believe her. Shirley kept her commitment to me, to her mother, to herself. She has kept it for a long time, and I hope it will be permanent. Shirley still mourns, but now occasionally she smiles, and she is beginning to face the anger inside her, the first step up for her.

Love is the only cure for self-anger. Shirley must be helped to believe that she is worthy of it. But first she must feel worthy unto herself. She can only feel it if someone loves her.

I summoned her into my office.

"You didn't tell me the truth, Shirley, you didn't go to the dentist yesterday. Where did you go?"

"I told you, I went to the dentist." Her lip curled upward on one side.

"Tell the truth, Shirley. Where did you go?"

"To the dentist," she persisted.

"You're lying, Shirley. I hoped that was where you would go when I gave you permission to leave school early, but you didn't. You're lying, Shirley! Where did you go?" I wanted some of that anger directed toward me. "You made a promise to me, to yourself, to your dead mother, to help yourself, and you're lying to all of us. Is that what your mother would want?"

She leaned over the desk toward me, her eyes blazing. Good. She was redirecting her inner fury outward.

"And I kept that promise. I never took nothin since I made that promise."

"I believe you," I answered. "Then why are you lying now? Where did you go when you didn't go to the dentist?"

Her voice suddenly became hushed. She seemed quieter.

"I wanta ask you something first, okay?"

"Okay."

"How did you know I didn't go to the dentist?"

"Because I care enough about you to call the dentist and check, that's how."

"Oh."

"And I care enough about you to keep after you. Where did you go?"

"Home," her voice was still hushed.

"Why did you go home?"

"Because I felt like it."

"That's not good enough. Why did you feel like it?" The respite was over. I needed to build up to a climax of anger again. Only then would I reach her.

"Because I felt like it."

"I won't let you give me that nonsense," I insisted. "I want a reason. I want to know where you go on school time. I want to know why you are so miserable and making yourself more miserable."

"You ain't got no right to know."

"I've got every right," I insisted. "I care about you. Your mother has died, your father is in Puerto Rico and you haven't seen him in years, and you live with an aunt who really doesn't care one way or another about you. She uses you as a maid, you do work for her, that's all she seems to care about, as far as you're concerned. Well, I do care! Get that through your head. I can't be your mother, but I'm what you have and you're what I have, and that's a fact."

"You got rights over me when I'm in school," she cried, "but not in the afternoon, not in the nights, oh no, you ain't my—"

She stopped and clamped her hands over her mouth.

"Go on, say it, Shirley," I commanded.

"No."

"Say it," I commanded again, this time louder. "You were going to say I'm not your mother."

"You're not, you're not my mother," she cried.

"No, I'm not," I answered, softly this time. "I can't ever be your own mother, but I can care about you. And I do care about you. I took the right to care about you."

"I didn't give the right to you," she yelled.

"Well, give it to me then," I yelled back.

I became soft again. I was taking her on an emotional roller coaster.

"Shirley, I am totally committed to you. Now, are you going to be committed to me or not? Are you going to let me care about you?"

She didn't answer.

"Tell me." I was firm again.

It was a small voice.

"Yes."

"Tell me in your words that I have the right to be concerned about you every day, during the day, every afternoon, during the afternoon, weekends, weekdays, all night because I care about you."

"You have the right to tell me what to do," she said, "because you like me."

"When?"

"All the time."

"When?" I shouted.

"Okay, okay," she was angry, "after school, during school, any time."

"Okay," I said. I was very matter-of-fact.

"Okay." She started to leave, but not completely. She hesitated at the doorway. I took my cue. I knew she needed something more from me. Reassurance.

"Shirley," I said, "You're my girl—right?"

She didn't look at me. "Yeah—if you still want me."

"I do."

She grumbled and left. I didn't listen to the grumble, because I saw the quiet smile.

And despite the fact that Shirley complains about me all the time, how I get on her nerves, how I should mind my own business, she finds time several times a day to come to my office, to scold me, to insult me, to bring me coffee, to bring me love. Without confrontation she could not have reached this far. Without confrontation she could not have begun to write her autobiography. The preface read:

"Any kind of person with any kind of problem shouldn't be lied to. Sometimes a person with any kind of problem like to be lied to. They are scared to face the true. Some people don't want a pretender. They wants help. We have to push them out of their make-believe world and put them in reality.

"So Be Careful. Don't lie to make a person with a problem feel good. Only true is good and you got to learn it sometime the hard way."

Confrontation is just that. The hard way.

chapter eleven

Learning to Live with the Board of Education

If I can't learn to face up to the enemy myself, then I can't teach it to girls. In my case that enemy is the morass of officialdom that calls itself Headquarters, or the Board of Education.

I used to have an image of the Board of Education. I used to believe that it was run by "they," those vague inchoate beings who reside in the building but who can never be located in time or space or body. One thing is certain. "They" set policy. "They" don't like changes, not even suggestions.

During the years I have been forced to search for "they" more closely, particularly when everything new I wanted to do required the approval of "they." I looked hard and long but I never found "they" because they spin their own hiding places and bury themselves deeper and deeper into their own automated droppings—red tape.

Then my image changed. The Board of Education wasn't "they." It was one huge supervisory totem pole. Everybody is climbing up. The foot of each and every climber is clamped squarely on the head of the person below him. The tongue of each and every climber licks the boot of every person above.

At various times and under varying conditions of the way the school was functioning and my own personal state of well-being, I have looked at my images and been depressed, frustrated, agitated, chagrined, or amused. Always, I have been angry.

My battles began six months after I came. After living through the program, the teachers, the problems of the girls, I finally had time to go over the building in detail and discovered that we needed many things. More important than the fact that the building was designed for primary grades and still had bannisters two feet from the floor, kindergarten furniture, and blackboards that couldn't retain an image was the fact that we prepared hot lunches; we had a cook and an assistant, but kitchen facilities consisted of an antique three-burner iron range as old as the building—1875!

In February, 1959, I began requesting through channels the installation of a new stove and oven.

July 1, 1960: From the Superintendent of Schools, in charge of Maintenance, to me: "Memorandum: Hazardous condition in school. Request installation of stove."

July 19, 1960: Letter from Director of School Lunches to Associate Superintendent in Division of Housing: "We fully concur in Dr. Rothman's request that adequate facilities and equipment for the preparation and service of lunches be provided in this school. The present equipment consists of a three-burner gas stove, an old sink and inadequate refrigeration. We have attempted to prepare and serve lunches with this wholly inadequate equipment. The Department of Health has rendered a very unsatisfactory report on this lunchroom. We cannot continue to serve lunches under these conditions.

September 5, 1960. Action: Call from a superintendent. "What are you doing? You're making such a fuss about the conditions being so hazardous that they're taking away hot lunches. You'll be getting peanut butter and jelly sandwiches from central kitchen."

Plea: "No, no, no. Our girls are deprived enough. They can't be given peanut butter and jelly sandwiches. We'll have a riot."

Magic word: Riot.

Plea granted: Stay of Execution. No central kitchen peanut butter and jelly sandwiches, not even apple jelly sandwiches. "But don't let it happen again, Rothman, stop asking for so much."

Hot Lunch program remains. So does 1875 oven.

September, 1960, Letter to Assistant Superintendent, Division of Housing, From Associate Superintendent of Schools.

"On July 19, 1960, H.A. wrote to Dr. M. concurring in the request of the Principal of Livingston School for Girls that standard kitchen facilities for on-premises food preparation be installed in her school.

"I visited the Livingston School the other day and found that they were doing their cooking on a three-burner gas stove. This is not the kind of school where either central kitchen lunches or cold lunches should be served."

1964: Success. Installation of an oven. Only, it is not a new oven, it is a very old oven that has been discarded by another school. We have accomplished one thing. We have substituted one antique for another.

1965: Explosion of same.

1965-1968: Frustration, relieved by periodic letters and threats to the Board of Education.

November, 1968: Telegram to Board of Education: "I have asked for a new oven since 1961. [I was being kind. It was really 1959.] This morning for the second time our oven exploded. I cannot believe that the city of New York cannot buy a new oven."

November 4, 1968: Eureka! Letter from Board of Education, Bureau of Supplies, to me. "Please be advised that we have requisitioned a new range."

So a requisition was made to Roper Company, Kalamazoo, for a new oven. Apparently it's cheaper than Macy's. It arrived via Chattanooga. Also cheaper than Macy's?

And in November of 1969: Arrival of oven at King Street via Chattanooga and maybe even Kalamazoo. Arrival of driver of truck. Discussion with custodian.

"No, sir, they didn't pay me to bring it into the school building. Sidewalk delivery only. That's what it says."

He was definitely hostile to the idea of taking three steps upward and into the building—with the stove, that is. However, he was not hostile to taking sixteen steps up to the phone in my office on the first floor to call his office, call his union, call his office again.

Quick consultations in large and small groups. Custodian, principal, odd assortment of teachers, truckman. "No, sir. They didn't pay us to carry ovens into the building from the sidewalk." Unanimous collectively and unanimous individually.

They were right, everyone except the truckman, that is, and although every teacher in the school and the custodian would have carried the stove in single-handedly, it became OUR CAUSE. The Board was going to do it right.

So, calls to Kalamazoo, calls to Chattanooga, calls to Livingston Street.

Oven went back to truckers.

November, 1969: Arrival of bill from trucking concern informing me that they were storing oven until disposition was made. Price of storage—$3.75 a day, billed to school.

"Are you crazy, you Board of Education people? I am going

to Macy's to buy an oven, have Macy's deliver it into the building, have Macy's install it, and bill you, you Board of Education people." That's what I said to everyone I could find at 110 Livingston Street.

Finally, in December, 1969, the original truck returned to school. As Mr. Phipps pounded out Beethoven's *Fifth* on the fourth floor, so that it thundered throughout the school, the driver and a helper stepped out with our stove and wrestled it up three tiny steps to the ground floor. Girls and teachers stood by, massed in silent wonder. A Christmas present for the school. Ten years in coming!

End of story? No. The oven is too small, suitable for family of four, but complain? Who—us?

Sometimes I feel schizophrenic. On one hand, I uphold standards of behavior, standards that the girls are ever ready to knock down. On the other hand, I am the renegade, assaulting educational scripture and Board of Education regulations that make no sense. I am therefore the upholder and the toppler, a member of the establishment and of the revolution. To say the least, it keeps me in balance, if not in friendship.

"Dr. Rothman, you cannot have the classrooms painted pink, orange, and yellow," complained the man from the Department of Maintenance.

"Why not?" I asked.

"Because standard regulations are gray or blue or blue-gray walls," he explained. "They wouldn't approve, you know."

"But physical environment is important," I argued. "Gray and blue-green are the colors of prisons, and I don't care about who doesn't approve."

"Blue and green last longer," he argued in return. "Regulations are not just arbitrary, you know, there are good economic reasons."

Economic reasons? That did it! I saw Mrs. C. in front of me, weeping, bludgeoned by economic reasons, economic reasons why she couldn't get a television set for her children, why Inez couldn't get leather boots like other girls, why Maria couldn't buy a pants suit. The last time I had seen Mrs. C. she was in her coffin.

"Look," I cried, "did you ever go to a funeral parlor in the slums?"

He looked at me startled.

"Go," I ordered. "Even in death, there is smallness and littleness and insignificance. Families buy ornate, expensive coffins for that last, final moment when their relatives can enjoy the splendor of a big room for the first time in their lives. Only it's not life, it's death, and even then, they don't have the room to themselves. There's not one coffin to a chapel the way it is everywhere else, but two or three, crowded to the last."

I may have been slightly incoherent, I didn't know, but my anger seemed to reach him. "Our girls," I continued, "shouldn't have to wait for that ornate coffin as a symbol of beauty. They should see school as a place of beauty. School should be beautiful, not just the program, but the building, big, wide, colorful, open space and beautiful." I stopped, short of breath, and threw a challenge. "So?"

The battle escalated from one word and the level of the Department of Maintenance to many words and the Superintendent.

But yellow and pink walls it became.

It was victory on one hand, but defeat on the other. Everybody at the Board, it seemed, wanted to know why I had written "no" to the question, "Did you observe Arbor Day this year?" In fact, I was ordered by a superintendent to explain my dereliction of duty to trees.

Before I answered him I decided to find out why my

uncelebration of Arbor Day threatened to topple the entire school system.

In my quest for information, I called the Division of Libraries first, because after all, the question was part of a library report. "Why," I asked, "did they feel it necessary to know if I celebrated Arbor Day?"

They didn't know why they wanted to know, they just knew they wanted to know. For the past ten years, they have wanted to know.

I called the Bureau of Research and Statistics next.

"Why," I asked, "did anyone care whether or not I observed Arbor Day? Why," I asked rather indignantly, "didn't anyone care whether or not I observed Flag Day?"

They did not know that I had not observed Arbor Day. "And when was Flag Day?" they asked.

Their attitude seemed highly immoral to me.

Lastly, I called the Public Relations Department. Trees were not a matter of public relations, they told me.

My answer to the Superintendent was therefore a simple one. Not knowing why it was important to the Board of Education for me to celebrate Arbor Day, I decided coolly, deliberately, and with no malice of forethought, to uncelebrate it. I based my decision on history.

For the past ten years, I have looked outside my office window at a hole in the asphalt that once nurtured a tree. I have asked for my tree. I have gone up and down and around and through procedural channels to get my tree. I have implored. The hole is still there—treeless.

I must live according to the code I teach—confrontation. Out of respect for the girls I can do no less. But with the Board of Education, as far as Arbor Day is concerned, confrontation has become stalemate. I have told them that when I get my tree, I shall observe Arbor Day. Until then, I refuse to celebrate other people's trees.

It sometimes is fun to play these war games with the Board. It is the pause that refreshes. If I did not have my Arbor Day, I would sometimes explode from the frustration of dealing with the educational bureaucracy.

For reasons I can never fathom, the Bureau of Supplies, which is the central warehouse for all the schools in the city, is always out of supplies.

I can accept their being out of stock on a sitar, perhaps, which after all is an exotic musical instrument not generally used in schools, but I cannot understand how they can be out of stock for two years on scotch tape, pencils, or paper.

When I called the Bureau of Supplies to tell them we were in the midst of an emergency, the school had been vandalized during the Christmas vacation and our typewriters had been stolen, I was told that they could not replace them, as typewriters were not kept in stock.

"Even if the Superintendent of Schools needed a typewriter," they said, "he would have to wait."

I believed them.

But three years?

This kind of inefficiency goes beyond the realm of mundane dull ineptitude. It requires real creativity.

Other departments are similarly gifted.

Three years ago I requested a budget just for breakfast. It was granted through a Federal subsidy. Then, because subsidies come and go, a year later ours went. Supposedly, we were to tell the girls that we could not serve breakfast any more. Of course, we refused. The teachers subsidized the breakfast program for one entire year. Serving juice, eggs, toast, and cocoa to a whole school is not inexpensive. We prayed for the return of our subsidy, and being good teachers, we got answers to our prayers, except that we apparently had not prayed hard enough. All the Government, via the Division of Lunches, could afford was one egg to a girl, two times a week.

The bargaining began.

"Two eggs per girl, every day," I insisted.

"Can't be done," the budgeteers answered.

"Besides," chanted the lunch division, "two eggs a day every day is very unhealthy. Too much protein. Bad dietary planning."

"What do you have for breakfast?" I asked.

The question was a mistake.

Fifty-seven cartons of cornflakes suddenly arrived.

"You must be kidding," I said. "The girls hate cornflakes. And if you are giving us cold cereal, why can't we have a choice of cold cereals, why only cornflakes?"

We bargained some more, and Government subsidy and all, we continued to pay for eggs for breakfast ourselves.

"Damn it," the teachers said, "if they can pay for cornflakes, they can pay for eggs."

"Look, the cornflakes are over two years old," the cook said. "See?" She was right, one of the cartons was dated.

"This is not breakfast," Mrs. Gray said angrily. "This is surplus."

It was a good line. I immediately telegraphed it to every city agency I could find that dealt with food.

"Okay, okay." There was capitulation. "We don't have eggs in stock."

Where had I heard that before?

"But you can buy eggs for the girls and we'll give you back the money."

"Two eggs per girl?" I asked.

"Yes, yes."

This was fine for us, because the eggs we bought were fresh from a farm. Who wanted cold-storage eggs?

We were happy. We had won.

The Board of Education was apparently happy, too, and just to pretend that they had won, they sent us seventy-four additional cartons of cornflakes.

"Okay," I said. "We'll compromise, even though most of the girls don't like cornflakes; we'll have both."

"Oh, you can't do that," I was told, "you asked for eggs. Just hold the cornflakes."

"You mean," I asked incredulously, "I can't open even one of the one hundred twenty-six cartons of cornflakes?"

"No."

When I put down the telephone, I laughed until the tears came.

With the Board of Education, confrontation brings hysteria. It's either that, or ulcers.

chapter twelve

Nonsense as a Method of Establishing Rapport

OR

Crazy Sometimes Works Best

Brenda in her floor-length black coat came prancing by my office. "You hear?" she asked. "There's gonna be snow."

"When?" I asked.

"Tonight, the weather man said three to six inches. I wish it'd snow hard enough so I wouldn't have to come to school tomorrow."

"Me, too," I said.

"You do?" she asked in surprise.

"Sure," I answered, "you think I'm not human?"

"Well, we have had snow days before," Mrs. Gray said. "The Superintendent closes schools when we have a bad storm."

"I was out West one summer," I said, "and I saw an Indian tribe do a rain dance."

"Did it rain?" asked Mrs. Gray.

"Poured," I answered. "Deluge. We couldn't get our car out of the mud."

"Yeah," yearned Brenda.

"Do you believe that, Brenda?" asked Mrs. Gray, "that a dance will bring rain?"

"Why not?" Brenda replied.

There was immediate spontaneous combustible cerebration. Mrs. Gray and I looked at each other. Why not?

"Let's," I said.

"Okay," Mrs. Gray agreed.

The sun was still shining, and we needed a quorum.

We rounded up Mr. Scarcella, Miss Grant, Mrs. Magnus, Mr. Friedland, and Mrs. Woodby, the teacher's aide. They were the only ones available at two o'clock.

"What's going on?" Brenda asked.

"Secrecy," I answered. "Can you keep your mouth shut?"

"Uh-huh," Branda agreed.

"Can you really do it, or shall I ask you to sign the agreement in blood?"

"I can really do it," Brenda promised.

"Not talk?"

"Not talk."

"To anyone?"

"To anyone."

"We're going to make a snow day," I declared. "We're going to dance a snow dance."

"You crazy?" she laughed.

"Magic," I answered solemnly.

"You will be the most powerful force of all," Mrs. Gray commandeered, "You, Brenda, will be our central focus. We'll dance in a circle around you."

We did. Holding hands, going clockwise, Mrs. Gray leading

the ritual, Mr. Friedland hopped, Miss Grant skipped, Mrs. Woodby pranced, and Mr. Scarcella yelled, "Ho, ho."

I collapsed with laughter.

Yvette, who had been banned from the rites, waited outside the door. She peered in.

"They're beatin the shit outa Brenda," she cried.

"They are not," Brenda yelled out and ran out laughing.

"What they doing, then?" she asked.

But Brenda had integrity. She wouldn't tell.

"Remember, Brenda," I said, privately to her, "if you tell on us, we'll all be fired."

"Yeah," Brenda agreed, "you must all be buggy in the head."

"Well, if the shoe fits—" I agreed.

"I wear size seven," she said.

Brenda did not go to work the next day.

"Why not?" I scolded.

"You said schools would be closed," she insisted.

"But they weren't," I agreed, "it didn't snow, after all, only a few flurries."

"I waited," Brenda cried, "I stayed at home, lookin outa the window and waited. You said—"

We paid her for a day's work. What else?

chapter thirteen

Mother, Beloved, You Are a Fighting Word

OR

The Search for Love

There is one word that can start a fight faster than any other word in the English language. Mother! Alone or coupled with another word, it is unmistakably a battle cry.

Even mature people, and certainly people who should know better, often react with irrational anger when the word is thrown at them. I once saw a prominent psychologist at Bellevue Psychiatric Hospital grab a child by the arm and yell, "Don't you dare call my mother names." I also heard an equally famous psychiatrist say to a child who was hurling obscenities with abandon, "Be quiet or I'll tell your mother on you."

Undoubtedly the origin of the word mother as an obscenity and a curse is related to the taboos of incest, but whatever its origin, its present communicative status is clear. Fight! Fight! Fight!

293

Girls may start an argument for any one of a hundred reasons, but the arguments generally don't come to blows until the first call of "your mother."

When girls fight about their mothers, they fight about themselves, about their right to be somebody, about their fears that they, in fact, are not "somebody."

Their fears become illogically verified when a girl points her forefinger at another. This gesture understood by everyone clearly states, "Your mother is dead." The words, spoken, are the most awful words a girl can hear. The curse is the worst curse of all. The fear that her mother will die and leave her is the primordial fear of every one of our girls. A mother's death brings with it a powerful mixture of confused emotions—sorrow at the loss of the love object, anger at "abandonment" by the mother, and depression in the wake of a loss of self-esteem. For to a longing child death becomes the ultimate of all rejection, a public announcement of parental rejection. In the face of such trauma, a girl's ego becomes tenuous and fragile. Who can love her now—a girl whose own mother has deserted her? To whom can she turn now?

She often has no one but us.

As a group, we provide support, an environment, a haven for the girl who has lost hers in reality, or emotionally, or who has never had one.

This does not mean we go about sanctimoniously dispensing saccharine and sentimental love. We definitely do not.

We set limits when they have to be set.

"I'm disappointed in you because you definitely know better," I told Aletta. "Sometimes you are so good, you're practically perfect, and then you stay in the park all morning instead of coming to school."

Aletta, of course, argued back at me, but later that day she came to my office and told me, "I'm comin early tomorrow."

Aletta wouldn't feel loved or secure if I didn't tell her when she was doing something wrong, and if I didn't tell it to her in such a way that she knows I like her but disapprove of what she has done.

Not setting limits is not caring, not loving. A mother who doesn't try to guide doesn't care. A mother who punishes one day and rewards the next day for the same behavior is so inconsistent that a child cannot be certain of her concern.

As head of the school, I find that the girls who are searching for a mother substitute direct the greatest amount of hate and the greatest amount of love toward me. If a girl has a rejecting mother, I must take all the abuse she would like to direct toward her, as well as receive all the love she has hoarded while searching for a parent to give it to. It is an awesome, beautiful burden; generally, first comes the hate (confrontation), then the love.

When Bertina came to us straight from the Training School, her hate was still profound.

She came slouching into my office and lethargically deposited her three bags of candy on top of some letters on my desk. It was an act of defiance.

"Well?" she asked.

"Well, what?" I answered.

"You wanta see me?"

"No," I answered, "I don't think so—why?"

"Aw, shit," she announced, "why did that teacher say you wanta see me?"

I knew I had missed my cue. Bertina was being difficult in class. The teacher needed help.

"As a matter of fact, I'm glad you're here," I said, "I did

want to speak to you. I wanted to ask you how things were going."

"Aw, shit—" she cried again.

"I guess that's the answer, then," I told her. "They can't be going all right, or you wouldn't be so angry."

"Think you so smart, don't ya?" She snarled.

"Not especially," I answered, "but I know you're angry all the time, and anyone who is angry all the time must be unhappy."

She didn't listen to what I had to say.

"No wonder someone wrote 'Fuck Dr. Rothman' on the wall."

"Oh—where?" I asked.

"Bathroom."

"Oh, well," I answered, "that's life, someone was mad at me today, I guess."

"Yeah," She surprised me. She hadn't answered with an obscenity. That meant she was feeling slightly better. Perhaps she had listened to what I had said and understood that I was trying to help her.

"How about rubbing it off?" I asked her.

"What?"

"The words on the wall."

"Nope."

"How about sharing some of your candy, then?" I asked. "I love chocolate."

She snorted, grabbed her bags even tighter, and left.

"I wouldn't give you nothin."

I let her go. I thought she went to a class, but I later learned that she had gone to the custodian and told him that she was delivering a message from me—that I wanted him to clean the bathroom wall.

I did not see Bertina for the rest of the day. When I was leaving my office at the end of the day, however, I noticed a wrapped package in my wastebasket. I opened it, and there, tightly secured, was Bertina's package of chocolate candy.

I understood. She was giving me her candy in the only way she knew how to give—ungraciously, a mite of acceptance mixed with a lot of hate. Obviously, she felt that she had already given me too much; first, by telling me what was written on the wall, and second, by delivering my supposed message to the custodian. It was clear to me, however, that she really didn't want ugly words about me written on a wall, nor could she just give me her candy outright. That would have been too much overt giving for her.

"The girls really love you," a visiting teacher seeking a job told me after she toured the school. "They told me you're their second mother."

A bombastic expletive, a favorite of the girls, burst unannounced in my head. It stayed there unexpressed, but oh, how I would have liked to try it out on her for effect and watch the expression on her face, because the girls simply do not talk that way. They simply do not express affection with words of affection. Mostly, they are unaware of how they feel. When they are aware of their feelings, they are often embarrassed. I didn't tell the visiting teacher that expressions of affection and love often come long after a girl has left. At the age of twenty-one, seven years after she had left. Astra, for instance, wrote,

Dear Dr. Rothman
I hope you are feeling fine.
Dr Rothman the day I was in Livingston
I wanted to say a lot of thing to you
But I guess I just couln't. You know

what Dr Rothman I guess you are right
what I am trying to say is well
all my life I wanted love from
my mother but I never got it
but when I in your office even
when you are not in you office
I feel like a new person.
Dr Rothman the girl in you school that
wanted to fight with me. I don't think
she know what she is doing. But I
hope some day she will. that day I
was going to say good-by to you.
I didn't know how. But when you
put you hand in my I wented to put
my armys around you and call you my
mom. Dr Rothman I guess I am saying
is if I had one wish in my life
with all my heart I would
wish that you were my mother
But I know I can never have that
wish. Dr Rothman I guess you were
right again. Because when I call you
on the phone I wented to say good-by
to you I was crying But then I said
to myself that big grils don't cry
well I was wrong. When I was geting on
the plane. all I did was looking at
your picture and I guess I was still
crying. yes Dr Rothman I guess I was
wrong about everything. But I know I not
wrong about you. Because you are one
person that I think you are a pretty
nice person to know. Dr Rothman you

picture is on my desk. and you are
in my heart. Dr Rothman please say hello
to mrs Landsman for me. Well I guess
I said all I wented to say to you in
person. But I guess I said it anyway
Well I guess I say good-by to you
for now and I see you again soon I hope

Love

Astra

Mrs. Gray, as assistant principal, receives her share of the love-hate dichotomy. She saw Silma in the lunchroom at breakfast and immediately knew that Silma was in deep emotional trouble. Silma was wearing a sheer red blouse through which could be seen an extremely decolleté white lace scalloped-edged brassiere. Her skirt was minuscule. It had been rolled up at the waist to make it even shorter than had been intended.

"You can't dress that way in school, Silma," Mrs. Gray told her, "you know it's inappropriate."

Silma responded explosively, "You callin me a whore?"

"I'm not calling you anything," Mrs. Gray explained, "I'm just saying you can't come to school dressed like that."

"Yeah?" Silma asked sarcastically. "You gonna tell my mother to buy me new clothes? My mother can't spend money on clothes just cause you don't like them."

"Oh, stop being silly, Silma," Mrs. Gray said abruptly. "You have beautiful clothes, you've worn them before, your mother doesn't have to buy you anything."

Then, because she knew Silma's mother well, she said, "I bet your mother didn't see you this morning before you left for school, or she wouldn't have let you leave the house dressed like that."

"Oh, no?" Silma's voice got loud again. "My mother don't care shit how I dress."

"That's not true," Mrs. Gray contradicted flatly. "Remember, I've talked to your mother many times, and I know she cares how you look, and she doesn't want you to come to school looking like that, I'm certain of that."

Silma's response surprised her, because it was the second time she asked the question.

"You callin me a whore?"

Before Mrs. Gray had a chance to respond, Silma went on.

"How you know I'm not? My mother thinks I am." She began to laugh.

"No, she doesn't," Mrs. Gray answered.

"Oh, no?" Silma laughed again, this time hysterically. "That's what you think—I know better." Her laughter suddenly froze, and she talked quietly almost to herself. Mrs. Gray had to strain to hear her.

"Maybe she's right. Maybe I'm no good. Maybe I don't deserve to live. Maybe I should be dead." She began to cry.

"Silma, come upstairs," Mrs. Gray urged, "and we'll talk in my office."

All of Silma's bravado left her. Silently, she went upstairs. Mrs. Gray carried Silma's breakfast tray upstairs, but Silma refused to eat.

"What's wrong, Silma?" Mrs. Gray tried to comfort her.

"Everything," sobbed Silma, "me and my mother—" her words were cut off by wild sobbing.

"Had a fight?" asked Mrs. Gray.

She shook her head violently, affirmatively.

"And can I help?" asked Mrs. Gray.

"Yes," she half screamed, half sobbed.

"How?"

"Tell my mother to love me, I want my mother to love me—" The sobbing wracked her body. She was one of the few girls ever to put her longing into words.

"I know your mother," Mrs. Gray tried to reassure her, "I think she does."

"She doesn't—send for her, you'll see, she doesn't, she won't even come for me, she told me when I came here she'd never come to school for me again, she's tired of me, she wants to put me upstate, she don't care where, just put me some place, so she don't have to see me—"

"No, she doesn't," Mrs. Gray answered. "If I ask her to come to school for a conference with you and me, I think she'll come."

"She won't," Silma contradicted.

"Yes, she will," Mrs. Gray stated. "I promise you she'll come."

It was a promise Mrs. Gray intended to keep despite all opposition from Silma's mother. But there was no opposition. Mrs. O. arranged to take time off from her job the following week. When she appeared in Mrs. Gray's office, she was exquisitely groomed in a white lace sheath. She was almost bride-like and delicately beautiful, but she was as hard and ungiving as Silma had said she was.

"Silma wants too much," she stated unemotionally. "I can't go on kissing and hugging her just to show her I love her. That's not me. She knows it, she knows I love her, and that should be enough."

Mrs. Gray felt her own anger rising but controlled it from coming through in her own voice or manner.

"Mrs. O., she's your daughter, and all she wants is for you to love her," Mrs. Gray explained.

"And she gets it," Mrs. O. stated bluntly, "Lord knows." For the first time, emotion crept into her voice; Mrs. Gray recognized it as irritation. "He certainly knows, she gets it."

"Does she?" murmured Mrs. Gray.

"Yes." Mrs. O. was finally exasperated. "But how can I be nice to her when she does everything wrong?"

Silma could no longer maintain her silence.

"I don't, she don't want me to have any friends, that's all, she don't want me to have my fun—"

"Friends?" Mrs. O. cried. "Did you tell Mrs. Gray when I give you permission to leave the house for one hour and you come home after four hours, do you tell her that?" She turned to Mrs. Gray. "And I don't know where she is. I go crazy calling up everybody to see where she is, and then she comes home and where she be but talking to her boyfriend for four hours? How can I trust her? I punish her, how can I be nice?"

"Is that true, Silma?" Mrs. Gray asked. "Do you go away for hours without letting your mother know where you are?"

"But I like him, and she won't let me see him," Silma explained sullenly.

"He's a bum!" Mrs. O. exploded. "He's not for you. He's a twenty-year-old bum. What does a twenty-year-old man want with a fourteen-year-old girl?"

"Silma," Mrs. Gray said, "your mother seems to worry herself sick about you."

"I know," Silma murmured.

"If she didn't love you, Silma, do you think she'd worry like this?" Mrs. Gray continued.

It took Silma a long time to answer. When she did, she meant it.

"No."

Mrs. O. began to cry. And she began to talk. For almost two

hours, she sipped coffee and talked, and her daughter listened. For the first time she saw her mother.

"Silma knows I love her. She's the only real person I love in my whole life. I want to show it to her, but I can't because when I'm soft with her, she does everything wrong, like going with this boy. And I'm afraid for her. She's like me. She's weak. When I had Silma, I was sixteen years old, and I thought I was in love. He was much older than me, he's an old man now, but I thought I was in love with him, and when I got pregnant, he said it wasn't his, but he offered to adopt Silma after she was born and he saw her in the street. Now why would he adopt her if she wasn't his? He didn't tell me that, oh no, he wouldn't have the nerve to tell me, but he sent a message with a friend my mother has that he would adopt her. Like hell I'd give her up, and he knows it. But then someone told Silma he was her father—she didn't know before—when she was about six, I guess. This friend of my mother's took Silma to the Apollo when he was playing. He's quite popular, you know, even though he's an old man now, he's a popular singer, and this friend told Silma, "There's your father on the stage.""

"What did you say, then," Mrs. Gray asked. "What did you tell Silma?"

"What could I say—yes, that's your father but he won't admit it, that's what I had to say, and she was only six, God, she was only six, and she goes to see him all the time and he buys her presents and he's nice to her and he tells her if she doesn't want to live with me, she can go live with him. Well, if he's not her father, why would he say things like that? Silma knows I won't let her go. He hasn't given her a name, so why should I let him give her anything else? No, my life isn't easy, and I'm trying to make it up to Silma, but I have to be strict with her, how else can she learn?"

"You don't want what happened to you to happen to her, is that it?" Mrs. Gray gently interrupted.

"Oh, yes," she sobbed, "I had no one to teach me. My parents were strict, especially my father. He wouldn't let me have my friends. I had to sneak out of the house to have friends. I don't want it to be that way for Silma, but I just can't trust her. And my mother doesn't help. She spoils her. She lets Silma go out and then lies to me to cover up for her. It's my mother's fault—all of it—even me—" She stopped for a second, and then the explosiveness of her anger surprised even her. It was as if she hadn't known, herself, how strongly she felt.

"I hate her! It's all my mother's fault. I don't want it to be like that with Silma and me. I want to live alone with her and be like a mother and daughter should, only I can't afford it, I need my mother to take care of Silma and stay at home while I work, but it's her fault, God, it's her fault."

Mrs. Gray gave her time to compose herself. "If it is," she said, "then you must do something about breaking away. You must leave your mother and take Silma with you."

Mrs. O. smiled at Mrs. Gray's suggestion. Both she and Mrs. Gray knew the truth, of course.

"No, of course it's not all my mother's fault." She smiled again. "She did the best she could. She was always afraid of my father, and she tried to make things nice for me by lying to him about when I went out. But it was no good. She should have stood up to him, and I shouldn't have been so strong-headed. I should have listened to my father a little, but I didn't. I listened to my mother complain about him but never stand up to him, and I listened because I wanted my mother to love me more than she loved him. Oh, how I wanted my mother to love me."

"Like Silma wants you to love her," Mrs. Gray said.

"I do, I do." Emotion overcame her again.

It was tragic. Silma and her mother were living the same pattern as Silma's mother and her mother before her. It was the same giving of love by the mother and the same unreceiving of love by the daughter. Something had happened in the communication, in the transit of love. If Mrs. Gray was to help Silma, the imperfection of the communicative process had to be explored. Mrs. O. had to learn to recognize her own mother's love, just as Silma had to learn to see the love Mrs. O. was offering her.

Mrs. O. began to weep again. So did Silma. But somewhere behind the tears of both, a new understanding was emerging.

Gloria was not unlike Silma. She had the same lesson to learn, only Gloria's lesson was harder because her mother, like an emotional sieve, barren and therefore insatiable, had so little love to give.

Gloria and her mother sat opposite me on the couch; Mrs. Landsman, on a side chair, sat between us.

Gloria had asked me to send for her mother.

"Honest, Dr. Rothman, she don't let me come to school every day," Gloria had complained.

"Why?" I asked.

She shrugged. "I don't know."

"Of course you know," I told her. "Why does she keep you at home?"

"To help," she said succinctly.

I pushed. "With what?"

"I don't know."

"Oh, come on, you know what you do when you stay home," I said, "so why does your mother keep you at home—to do what?"

"Nothin," she finally explained, "it's just that she don't tell me when it's time to get up."

But of course I knew there had to be more to it than that. Gloria, in her way, was asking for help.

I decided to start the interview with Gloria's version of her problem.

"Mrs. C.," I said, "Gloria simply has to come to school every day. She says you keep her at home."

"She's lying," Mrs. C. said sharply. She looked at Gloria. "I keep you home?" she asked. "Since when I keep you home? You're too lazy to get up, that's what the matter with you. If you had your way, you'd stay in bed all day."

"But you're her mother, Mrs. C.," I interjected. "If Gloria sleeps, don't you think you could awaken her to come to school?"

"She's made thirteen, she big enough to take care of herself now." She said it as if she were issuing a mandate.

Spontaneously, Mrs. Landsman and I looked at each other—it was almost as if we both heaved a sigh in unison. It was going to be a long, hard session.

"Mrs. C.," Mrs. Landsman said, "Gloria feels that you don't care about her, that you don't care enough about her to wake her up to come to school. You know, she's really like a little girl, she wants her mother to wake her up in the morning. That's all she wants."

"She just spoiled."

Spoiled! I despised the word. How is it possible to spoil a human being, to make rotten, to impurify with love and concern? Impossible! Contrary to popular belief, there is no such thing as too much love. Only too little. The way that rejecting parents find the word so available always astounds me.

Mrs. C. was enumerating her daughter's faults. "And she's jealous that I've got me a little happiness finally. She don't want me to be happy; it was fine when it was just Gloria and me, but now that I'm married, Gloria don't want me to have my happiness."

"Married, nothin," Gloria screamed. "You and him making noise all night, that married? Think I can't hear you laughin and gigglin and I can't sleep, and then I can't get up in the morning to come to school—it's your fault—"

Suddenly Mrs. C. jumped up and slapped her across her face.

"You like him better than you like me," she moaned.

Mrs. C.'s face changed in front of me. Her eyes narrowed, and she was flooded with bitterness; she seemed to forget entirely that Mrs. Landsman and I were still both there.

"Well, at least I can get me a man," she taunted. "Look at you—what can you get?"

Gloria could not bear it. She ran out of the room, and I caught a glimpse of Mrs. Landsman's face as she quickly followed her. She was as close to tears as Gloria.

I remained with Mrs. C., who was beginning to recover from her anger. She was now embarrassed.

"Children," she said, sitting down, "you can't do nothing right. She's just jealous, you know, because she didn't want me to get married again, but you know, Dr. Rothman, I have my own life to lead. I didn't have no mother to care for me. Gloria has, but she sure don't act like it."

We spent a long time talking about obligations to herself and obligations to Gloria. Part of the time, she cried. When we left my office, Gloria was at the bottom landing of the stairs, standing at the main entrance of the school. Mrs. Landsman was still with her.

"Mrs. C., she really does need you. Don't you think you might try to wake her in the morning?" I asked as we walked down the stairs together. "You don't have to give her breakfast, she can have that here with us, but wake her, kiss her, send her off to school so she'll feel you care. I know you do, but as you said, she's jealous now, and she needs just a little extra from you." Mrs. C. started to cry again.

"She does need clothes," she said almost inappropriately. "I know that."

Gloria watched her mother closely. The sight of her mother's weeping somehow soothed her. Instinctively, she reached out to her mother. Her mother held on to her arm.

"Dr. Rothman, could I take her with me to go shopping?" Mrs. C. asked.

"Would you like that?" I asked Gloria.

Her face lit up.

It was a happy second for both. They were close.

Neither Mrs. Landsman nor I could talk as we walked back to my office.

Mrs. Landsman wept inwardly for the child—I, for the mother. If we had reversed our positions, we would have wept just the same.

But we are not for weeping. We are for providing the love when no one can or will provide it and for uncovering the love that may be there somewhere, but hidden. We are for uncovering the person underneath the mother and for helping girls see that mothers have been people before they were mothers. A mother is a total constellation unto herself, as well as the love nucleus in the life of her daughter.

Girls who search for love search for it in many ways. When they seek it in pseudo-sexual relationships with other girls, they often arouse the anxieties of many adults, who label them homosexuals. At Livingston, we don't label and do not permit ourselves to react with anxiety when two girls are caught kissing or touching each other's breasts. We remember that homosexuality, like obscenity, is human contact, and it is the contact that is important, not the unacceptability of its expression. Moreover, we know that the majority of our girls do not and will not become homosexual in adult life. They are not homosexuals. They are merely reaching out to others, seeking acceptance, a relationship, a friend. They are following the normal course of adolescence, experimenting with sexual roles, playing a female role, assuming the male role. And because our girls are so honest and overt in their behavior, they do not inhibit their homosexuality any more than they inhibit other forms of behavior.

Adolescent pseudo-homosexuality is transitory. It is also safe. No one gets pregnant, and no one gets into a position of being used and then discarded by a man, the history of so many of the mothers of our girls.

"Maybe she needs more of that before she has a boyfriend," Priscilla's mother said to me. I had never heard a parent say such words before. I couldn't help it—I didn't want to be, but I was shocked.

Priscilla definitely did not need more of it. Like so many girls, Priscilla was struggling with her own feelings toward other girls. Partially she was attracted to them sexually. Partially, her own feelings were repugnant to her and morally unacceptable. She was going through the typical conflict of growing up, of assuming a sexual role. She wrote to Vera:

Dear Love—

Well knowing that you don't know who I am cause I didn't put no name so don't get mad and tell Dr. Rothman [or] Mrs Gray. No one, cause I want you to be mine but don't feel hurt or bad. I like you **as** mine, hope we make it. But remember no one but me and you or we both will get in trouble. Get it. But if you don't go with girls, just let me know by writing back. Hope you won't feel bad. If you know who wrote this then be cool with your shit or you will be a fool. Well, I am for real and hope you are for real with me cause I'm really digging on your love.

Write back.

Then, to make certain Vera wouldn't know who had sent it, she signed it with another girl's initials.

The letter was never sent, because she left it on my desk. She couldn't have told me more clearly that she wanted to talk to me.

When I returned the letter to her and asked why she had wanted me to see it, she replied with a question of her own.

"Who wants to go with girls?" she asked contemptuously.

"Do you?" I answered.

"With all them boys out there in the world," she asked, "what I want mess with them girls for?"

"I don't know," I answered, "why would you?"

"Not me, no sir, baby, not me," she declared, "I ain't no damn butch."

"Well, that's good, then," I answered. "So you can tear up that letter, can't you?"

"Yeah—"

But she left without tearing it up. I knew it wasn't resolved for her, nor likely to be, without intensive help from her counselor, Mrs. Langness.

The help was forthcoming, and Priscilla utilized it well. She found an identity in being attractive to boys. She was ready to be completely feminine. This time, she wrote her letter and sent it.

Dear Vera,

I don't mean no harm. But I am to young to be doing things like that. There are too many boys in this world. I am calling it quits. The reason I went with you was because I was scared. I am quitting you on my own. My friends are more important than trying to be a butch. So Vera if you are mad because of that I am sorry. We can still be friends. But not the kind you want.

From
Priscilla

Priscilla had made her adjustment. Vera was still struggling.

When Vera came to Livingston, her manner, her dress, her hair cut in mannish style, suggested masculinity. There was no doubt of the role she was advertising. She wanted everyone to know.

"I want to be a girl, I do," she once had said to me, "I want to go with boys, but, well . . . I don't know—"

"You don't know what?" I asked.

"Well, girls can't pregnant you," she blurted out.

Vera struggled with growing up sexually. She had no model on which to pattern herself. Her mother had deserted her when she was a baby, and her grandmother had raised her punitively. Vera was permitted no freedom, lest she turn out like her mother, an alcoholic and the mother of three children, each born out of wedlock, each with a different father. Her grandmother literally confined Vera to her house. She was not permitted to go out often. As a result, she rebelled with a vengeance. At the age of twelve she had listened to her grandmother and not gone out of the house except to go to school, but she had become pregnant by a man of fifty, a boarder in her grandmother's house. Her grandmother sent her to a neighbor for an abortion. At the age of thirteen, she was at

Livingston after an assault on a teacher and several incidents of drinking in school.

At Livingston she was a magnet. She was the boy in a school for girls. Partially, of course, she was attracted to homosexuality in reaction to the trauma of her pregnancy and abortion. Partially, she was curious and seeking friendship.

The turning point came after she had been with us for two years. She arrived at one o'clock in the afternoon.

I was the first one to meet her in the building.

"Are you just coming in now?" I asked.

"Yeah."

"Why?"

"Because I'm late."

I had to laugh. "I know you're late. But what I want to know is why you are late."

She walked away without answering. I intended to ask her teacher to find out the reason for her lateness and to ask her grandmother what time she had left her house. I didn't have to, for when I returned to my office, Vera was sitting there.

"Dr. Rothman?"

"Yes?"

"Can I talk to you?"

"Sure."

I went and sat next to her. Vera began to talk haltingly.

"You see, I met this girl in the shuttle, we was supposed to meet there and go to 149th, but then I wasn't so sure, I didn't wanta get in trouble, so we talked and she said she hadda go, but I didn't know, so by that time it was late and I didn't go to my job, it woulda been too late, so I came here, and that's all."

Her story really didn't make too much sense, and I knew I would have to piece it together.

I did, finally. One of Vera's friends had arranged a diurnal party starting at 10 o'clock in the morning for homosexual girls. It was organized well. The night before the planned party, girls drew lots to see with whom they were to be paired. Vera drew the name of a girl she had never met and who was not at the drawing of the lottery. She had met her for the first time at a prearranged spot on the 42nd Street shuttle. Her partner was a high-school girl cutting classes from another school and eager to go on to the party. Vera, however, was torn between her desire to go partying and her obligations to herself to go to her job. Her partner had no patience for Vera's conflict, and at noon, left her to go to the Bronx. Vera was too late to go to her kindergarten job in a nearby school so she came on to school. What achievement for her!

She was pleased with herself, yet somewhat depressed. From her point of view, she was a traitor to her friends.

"You're growing up," I said, "and beginning to think of yourself. You don't do things just for kicks anymore, or just because your friends are."

"I guess so," she said glumly.

"You're unhappy you didn't go," I said.

"I guess so," she agreed still glumly.

"You'd be more unhappy if you went," I went on.

"Yeah, I know."

"So?" I asked.

"So it's okay," she said.

"What do they do at these parties, Vera?" I asked. She looked up at me impishly and grinned.

"Huh?"

"What do you do?"

There was a glint in her eye. She was laughing at me.

"Dr. Rothman, don't you know?"

"No."

"Don't you read books?" she asked.

I laughed.

"Seriously," I said, "it's more than sex. Do you smoke pot?"
She became serious. "Yeah."

"Anything else?"

"No, no, I don't take hard stuff."

"Not you—" I answered.

"Oh well, ups sometimes."

"Pills?"

"Yeah."

"Why not snorting?" I asked. "No heroin?"

"Aw, no—think I'm nuts?" she asked. "If I wanna get high, I
drink."

"Well, why do you have to get high?" I asked. "Can't you
feel good just being Vera?"

"Don't run that nonsense at me," she said.

I didn't answer. There were minutes of silence.

"Yeah, that'd be jive," she finally said.

I am certain that one of the reasons Vera did not want to go
to the party was that she was really resisting drugs. She feared
getting caught up with it, and not going to the party was one
way of stopping herself. She would not be enticed by her
friends.

Many girls who are deeply struggling with their own sexual
identities are prone to look to drugs for their solutions. For
instance, I have never known a girl who as an adult became a
confirmed homosexual who did not become addicted to drugs.
This is not to say that all homosexuals become addicted. I am
saying that in my experience, adolescent girls who later use
drugs start out with strong homosexual tendencies. Drug use is
therefore related to a lack of identity. Women addicts are
certainly not all homosexual, although it is my own belief that

a very large percentage are basically homosexual in orientation, even those who prostitute to maintain the habit.

Most of our girls do not become addicted. They have seen the effects of drugs on members of their families and on their friends, they have lived closely with the horrors of it, and they do not want any part of the hard drugs. If they are looking for a high, they are inclined to drink liquor. Many of them smoke marijuana on weekends. Rarely, however, has a girl brought a drug to school. When she does, it is really a cry for help.

Ten years ago drugs were not a problem. Only the severely emotionally disturbed girls were drawn to them; they were a symptom of their illness, and could be treated within the context of the disease. Today drugs are a social disease, a contagious disease. It is part of our culture, and therefore the number of girls who drop out of school eventually to become addicted is increasing. It is of great concern to me, because as drugs are becoming more available, and more and more a part of youth culture, and therefore acceptable, more and more girls will find them harder to resist. The pressure of the group is strong. To be accepted by the group often becomes a prime motivation toward drug usage.

Yet, Vera had resisted. So do most of our girls, and it is an amazing fact—an absolutely amazing fact—that in a city where drugs can be purchased freely, most of our girls refuse. They have not given up, withdrawn, succumbed. They are aggressively fighting back. They are working at resolving their conflicts. They are finding their identities as human beings. They are finding that they are young women, and as their sexual conflicts become resolved, and their sexual identities become secured, they don't resort to drugs. The problem is, they very often become pregnant.

When this happens, the first spontaneous response of the

teachers is anger. We can almost put it into words. How dare she? After all the work we've put into her, how dare she? We feel betrayed. And then comes the realization that we have helped create the process whereby she has been able to reach out to another human being.

Vera had, and because Vera was beginning to see herself as feminine and attractive, she became feminine and attractive. She soon met a boy with whom she became deeply emotionally involved. He was eighteen years old and a car thief.

Weekends became torture for her. She knew it was wrong to steal cars, but she wanted to be with Archie, and being with Archie meant doing what he did. When I asked her if it wasn't hard to steal cars, she offered to give me a whole set of burglary keys that could start any car.

"That's how hard it is," she explained ruefully.

Archie was eventually arrested. Vera wasn't. She ran too fast to be caught by the police. She told me the story in a deep depression. Her grandmother did not know she was pregnant. Would I tell her?

"You won't punish her, now, Mrs. L.?" I asked. "You know a beating now could hurt Vera badly, don't you?"

"Don't worry," she said, "I won't hit her, not that she doesn't deserve it, it'd be one way of dropping that baby."

I didn't answer, because I knew she wouldn't hit her. My knowing that a girl is pregnant is often protection for her. I thought of Gail, whose mother had made her strip so that her clothes wouldn't be torn and then beat her with a leather strap. When that hadn't worked, she told Gail to jump from a rooftop and get rid of the baby or not go home. That's when Gail told me. I got her into a shelter that night.

Vera's grandmother was not likely to be that punitive, but there was no doubt about it, she did not want Vera to have the baby.

Mrs. Langness and I talked with her grandmother for hours. We tried to make her see that Vera needed that baby, she needed something entirely her own to love. Not receiving mothering, Vera wanted to give mothering. It was a reversal of a role. Her mother would exist in her child. It was an urgent need, but her grandmother would not hear of it.

Vera was absent three days. On the third day she called me.

"Dr. Rothman, my grandmother went ahead with her plan."

"Oh?"

"I'll be in school tomorrow."

"Are you all right, Vera?"

"Yeah, I'm okay, I guess."

I understood without her telling me. Vera's baby had been aborted.

I hoped that we could help.

I had hoped that Vera would have her baby, that being a mother would help her mature. I think she could have been helped to be a good mother. Now, it was unfinished business for her. With two pregnancies it was likely there would be a third, unless we could help Vera work out her feelings so that she wouldn't see having a baby as her only solution. If we could get her into nursing school, which is what she wanted, or could give her a job in a nursing setting, perhaps in a children's ward, her need to be mothered and to mother would be met, and then, perhaps, Vera could wait for motherhood.

It did not happen. Vera became pregnant a third time, and once more I had to break the news to her grandmother. This time Vera was permitted to have her baby.

Several days after she left to go to the special school where she would have her baby, I found her slang book, which is a notebook in which each page has a different question for a heading. Each girl answers each question and identifies herself by a code number. Vera's slang book was reflective of her emotional progress. The first page was headed "Are you a virgin?" The question on the second page was "Are you a butch?" The questions progressed. "Are you a faggot?" "Do you like being butch?" "Do you fuck good?" "Do you know only whores?" "Do you have a man?" "Does he fuck good?" "How long is his peter?" "Do you have any hair inside?" "How wide is your hole?" All of it led to the final question—"Do you need someone to love?"

Vera answered the final question herself.

"Hell, yes!" was written large.

Why do girls get pregnant? Not out of ignorance alone, although some do, of course. Vera certainly knew about contraceptives. So do most of the girls. They become pregnant out of their own deep need for a baby to love, a baby who is all their own. They become pregnant out of a need to be loved by a man, and often the pregnancy is a statement of the man's need to prove his virility. They become pregnant because they want adult status and independence from their parents. They want to live alone. And they become pregnant because they are angry at their mothers. Pregnancy is punishment and identification.

"See," said Pristine, "I'm like my mother, after all. Ain't this static for her?"

During the years, I have told over a hundred mothers that their daughters were pregnant. Girls generally tell their favorite teacher first before they tell me, but before they tell the teacher, they try to extract a promise of confidentiality.

Teachers, of course, cannot make such promises. The interesting thing is that girls do not really want them to.

"If I tell you somethin, would you keep it a secret?" Pearl asked Mrs. Greenthal.

"I can't promise I will," Mrs. Greenthal answered. "If it's

something that I must tell Mrs. Landsman or Dr. Rothman in order to help you, then I wouldn't be able to keep the secret, so if you're not certain you can trust me to use my judgment about whether or not I should tell them, then maybe you shouldn't tell me."

Pearl, of course, wanted to tell because she wanted and needed help. If Mrs. Greenthal had promised to keep the secret even before she knew what it was, she would not have been able to help. She would have been left holding a secret and having no resource with which to help Pearl. If she had broken the secret and told someone in order to help her, then she would have broken faith with Pearl.

Mrs. Greenthal told me, and I sent for Pearl. We discussed plans to send her to a school for pregnant girls. Pearl understood that when I was going to speak to her mother the plan would already be worked out, and both Pearl and her mother would have a direction in which to go. Things wouldn't seem so hopeless to her mother, and Pearl wouldn't feel so rejected, because she would have another school to go to. And after the birth of the baby, she could return to Livingston.

Most often girls want to continue coming to us during their pregnancies, but this is not a good idea. It arouses everyone's anxieties, including the staff's. What if there should be a fight in school and the girl were hurt? We could tolerate our own anxieties, of course, but we could not always deal with the anxieties of the girls. To some girls pregnancy is a condition to ridicule. Moreover, they often verbalize the idea that it is safer to go with girls than with boys. The pregnant girl herself often suffers. She is the misfit in school and is either ashamed and afraid to admit her pregnancy, sometimes telling the other girls that she was just "putting us on," and equally often coming to the office, openly demanding a sanitary napkin, in a pathetic attempt to deny the pregnancy. Or she may use her pregnancy as a means of defense. It is not uncommon for a girl to instigate gossip, to start fights, and then at the point of physical involvement, look to other girls for protection because she is pregnant.

I remembered Antoinette well. She was the first girl I had ever suspected of being pregnant. In fact, I was quite sure that she was pregnant, but it was a long time ago, and when I tried to talk about it to her, she looked at me incredulously and insisted that she was eating too much rice.

I didn't then have the nerve or the skill to confront her and thereby help her.

I started with a tentative, hesitant question.

"Aren't you putting on a little too much weight?"

She scoffed.

"Do you think I want to be as scrawny as you?"

She must have seen my consternation, because she really was quite solicitous of me. She didn't want to hurt my feelings, she assured me, but I just didn't know how much she loved that fried rice.

I hadn't helped, because Antoinette refused medical attention until she went to the hospital to give birth. Had she denied her condition to me alone or to herself, also? I really don't know, and I still don't. For my own learning, however, I wish I knew to whom the lie was directed.

Now I handle things differently. I must sometimes force girls to admit they are pregnant. How else can we get them the support they need, both medical and emotional?

Girls who are fearful of the reality of their pregnancy often become exceptionally and inexplicably aggressive. When a girl's behavior suddenly changes, when she becomes particularly obstreperous for no reasons that we can fathom, she is very often finding the only way she can to tell us about her fears.

The pregnancy rate is increasing at Livingston. Are we then failing? Yes, in a way I suppose we are. We have helped girls to the point of accepting themselves as attractive young ladies. We have helped girls who otherwise might have followed homosexual patterns to accept their feminine roles. We have taught them how to make effective social relationships with the opposite sex. Obviously, we have not gone far enough. We have not met all their needs, or they would not take on the burden of pregnancy at this stage in their lives. We have not given them the strength to see themselves as worthwhile human beings who can be accepted on their own terms without having to engage in sexual relations merely to please a man. The truth is that many of our girls endure, not enjoy, the sexual experience. They want to feel love, and they want to prove their own adulthood. In their search they are becoming increasingly younger. Thus, not only is pregnancy increasing among the girls, but it is increasing at the younger age levels of thirteen and fourteen!

The increasing focus on sex in our mass media, and teenage sex as a result of our youth culture, the defensiveness of the adults in our society and the aggressiveness of the youth, make it almost inevitable that many unstable young girls will become pregnant for a variety of unsound reasons, ranging from youthful rebellion to curiosity. The solution to this problem is not simple, by any means, although some people seem to think it is.

Some years ago, I got in touch with a well-known hospital clinic to set up a joint program of sex education, and, I hoped, pregnancy prevention.

The head of the birth-control clinic was a noted gynecologist. His answer was simple.

Give them some lectures, tell them about menstrual cycles, tell them about the pill—ergo, the end of pregnancy.

I knew he was wrong, but I was willing to try. We set up a program in which we selected six girls who, we thought, were high pregnancy risks; that is, they spoke about being pregnant, they had pregnancy fantasies, and they were desperately searching for a mother and a man to love them.

We carefully explained the project to the girls and their mothers, from whom we needed permission for the girls to participate. Mrs. Landsman explained to each girl and her parent that girls, escorted by a teacher, would go as a group once a week to the clinic, where they would be given a series of lectures on sex education. Everyone was enthusiastic. Many girls had questions about menstruation that they found difficult to understand. They were embarrassed; they tittered a great deal on the subway, but they were definitely interested. Then they faced the first lecturer, the noted gynecologist.

He had never met them before. Nevertheless, he did not hesitate to ask how many of them already had babies.

There was a gasp. They did not expect this question from a stranger. They also knew that their teacher knew that none of them had a baby. That, of course, was exactly the purpose of the program—to give them enough information so they would not become pregnant. The doctor seemed unaware of this.

Tina started it off, "I have twins," she said.

"Really?" he asked, much interested.

"Well, if that's what he wants," Isabel said later, "that's what he's gonna get."

"I had a baby," she said primly. "It died."

"That's too bad," he commiserated properly.

Joanne said, "Me, too, mines died, too, it was a girl."

He was sorry all over again.

"I got a boy," said Josephine.

"How old are you?" he asked.

"Thirteen," she answered.

He was really pleased.

The teacher didn't say a word. She couldn't betray the girls. Besides, she felt he deserved it.

They giggled and laughed during his questioning.

"They were so responsive," he told me later, "what do you mean they were putting me on?"

"That's what they were doing," I assured him, "putting you on. Consciously, they were putting you on, of course. Actually, you were arousing a great deal of anxiety."

He aroused even more anxiety when he introduced a speaker from a well-known commercial pharmaceutical firm. With colored charts of circles and lines and dates of a calendar she explained the menstrual cycle.

"That's ministration?" asked Isabel, pointing to the chart. "How come it's got green on it, not red?"

"Because it's not blood, stupid," Tina explained.

The lecturer hastily gave them sample sanitary napkins and explained why the product of her firm was better than any other product.

The lesson was ended.

On the subway ride back to school, the girls started to examine their samples. They took the napkins out of the envelopes.

"Hey, mister," Tina shouted, "wanta bring it home to your wife?"

The teacher was glad it was a one-station ride. She tried to silence them in a hurry, but of course they didn't listen. They were too stimulated and—too insulted.

I met with the hospital staff, and I objected strongly to our girls being given a sales pitch by a drug company. If menstruation was to be discussed, why not by a doctor who could explain it in a way the girls could understand? Why were they given a sample? Anyone who works with adolescent girls, never mind disturbed and aggressive girls, would know this was an asinine thing to do. But I was outraged at more than their stupidity. I was furious at their bigotry.

Would the doctor, I wondered, have asked a group of white girls from suburbia whether they already had babies? I doubt it. But our girls were black. He did not hesitate. I withdrew from the project. I would not have the girls subjected to such indignity.

I also learned that sex education belonged in the schools, with teachers and counselors the girls respected and who respected them. Just dispensing information was not the answer. Answers had to be personalized as sex experience are personalized. Discussions have to be held in private interview, with feelings exposed and explored. Sex education as a so-called lecture course—impossible! Especially when it is done by outsiders.

Over and over again, I learn that every service must be given by the school at the school. I should love, for instance, to start a nursery school at Livingston for girls who already have babies. The girls simply won't send their young children to nurseries in their own neighborhoods when they get to that age. Instead, their mothers care for the babies, and the girl returns to school. In effect, both infant and girl become siblings, and the grandparent who has raised the girl ineffectively in the first place continues to raise the baby in the same ineffective manner.

We might break that cycle if we had our own nursery, if we could teach our girls how to be mothering mothers, if we could teach them facts of child development, if we could teach them how to care for their children the way they would like to. I am trying to interest the Board of Education in setting up such a program. To date—no sale!

Having the baby is not the end. Girls must learn how to enjoy their babies. The nursery would be the beginning of enjoyment. Actually, we like it when girls bring their babies to school.

Showing off their babies is tremendously important. Twice a year, at Christmas and in June, we have Baby's Day. Every girl brings her favorite baby; no questions are asked. Girls bring their own babies and the babies of friends. Some girls bring every baby on the block. Girls without babies bring brothers and sisters. The faculty members also bring their children, even their grown children and their husbands and wives, because it's a happy, sharing experience—a sharing of our families and friends. We had no restrictions until thirteen-year-old Princetta came along. She wanted to bring her baby, only he turned out to be a sixteen-year-old boy. We said no to that. What insights we get as we watch Vera tenderly feeding Mr. Phipp's little girl, with love, concern, compassion, or as we watch Iona ditch her four little sisters and one little brother, as she runs around, laughing and smiling with everyone, occasionally giving each child a resounding smack for crying, but never once giving them something to eat or paying them the slightest attention.

We look at the beautiful little children, and we look at their mothers.

Some of the mothers will have matured emotionally because of their children. Many will not. Our next step is to help them mature.

We need that nursery school!

chapter fourteen

What Could Be ...
and Should Be

What happens to the girls who come our way? Where do they go when they leave?

When the school was organized, the Board of Education decided what should happen. They decided that girls should return to the regular school system. That was the stated goal. "To return girls to the mainstream of education."

For the first few years, I accepted that goal, and when we didn't return girls to the "mainstream," I felt we were failing. Then I learned it wasn't our failure that we weren't returning girls to the regular schools, it was our success. If the mainstream is polluted, should we send girls back?

I refused to accept this goal as a condition of existence of the school. Most of our girls are severely damaged, socially, emotionally, sometimes culturally, and we're not going to cure them by having them here one or two years and then throwing them back into the regular school community. We don't cure anybody. We don't cure society's ills, and we would have to if we were to cure the child. I don't know any psychological therapy that does cure, but we do help girls learn alternate ways of behavior, and we do give them the insight and the strength to continue to live under the stresses they do.

The Board of Education seems to forget the fact that mature people, motivated for therapy and change, are treated by psychiatrists for long periods of time, years, in fact, and no one demands of the psychiatrist that the patient be cured within a specified period, nor that the patient once released be asked to cope with his problems without support. That's a ridiculous demand, yet that is what the Board of Education asks of us when they expect us to change our girls' behavior and then return them to the morass of the big system in which their problems developed in the first place. So, by all standards of the Board, we are a school that fails. We don't send girls back.

Our girls need a hot-house culture. They need to be nurtured for years to come. Inner growth and self-insight don't prepare anyone for assassination. Return to regular schools would be just that. We have reached the point where remaining at school and going from our school directly to college or specialized training is the answer. Not until the city high schools become more like us do I feel we should entrust our girls to them.

And for those girls for whom we are terminal education, and these are the majority, what happens to them? Some get married and become housewives, the largest percentage get jobs and do well, married or unmarried, and almost all keep in touch.

Egedir came in, laughing, bubbling, exuberant, to tell us she was earning a hundred and thirty dollars a week as a typist. She looked at the girls with disdain. "Was I like that?" she gasped.

She was. And worse.

Minnie came for a transcript of her record. She was working

with a brokerage firm in Wall Street. She couldn't wait to leave. The girls reminded her of what she had been. She wants to forget. I don't think she will be back.

Marion is married and divorced and the mother of two children, on whom she lavishes a love she did not receive when she was a child.

Edna is a civil service employee and engaged to be married.

Arcenia graduated from an evening high school with an academic diploma. She is now a fashion model.

Delores is still floundering. On her last visit she told us to send her records to a community college where she had been accepted on scholarship. When we sent the records on, we found that they had never heard of her. Poor Delores was trying so hard to be important for that one hour she visited. Perhaps her lie is her way of telling us she needs help now. She knows her lie will reveal this, and that we will reach out to her once more.

And Berenice? What happened to her? She was sent to the Training School as a child in need of supervision because she kept running away from home. Who wouldn't have?

She had tried. She really had. And the teachers had tried, but what Berenice needed we did not have—a residential school that could offer her sanctuary. And in the end we really failed with Berenice because we were not able to find sanity in the world for her.

Sanity? Where is it?

Inez came in with her three-year-old daughter, Patty. Patty was sucking her thumb.

I embraced her.

"How are you, Inez?"

"All right."

"How is Maria?"

"All right."

She was very subdued, not like the Inez of before, loud, angry, pretty.

Her two front teeth were gone. Her hand was immobilized in a clear plastic cast. Her fingers were taped.

"What happened to your hand?"

"Nothin."

She was descended upon by girls who didn't know her but who love to see children. For a while she became part of the crowd of girls outside my office.

Theodora's parents were in my office, so for a half-hour I forgot about Inez.

Then she was there again. I was getting ready to leave the building for a meeting.

We walked down the street together. Patty, although she didn't know me, clung to my hand.

"How have you been, Inez?" I asked.

Her eyes clouded up. "You know my mother died."

We stopped in mid-street. I looked at her closely and saw the hurt.

"I know," I said, "I went to the funeral chapel."

"You did?" she seemed shocked.

"It was the last day of school in June, remember? I went on Saturday, but no one from the family was there."

"You saw her?" here eyes clouded again.

"Yes, and I signed the book of callers. Didn't you see my name there?"

"My brother got the book. He wouldn't give it to me."

"Oh." I felt awful. It might have helped her, knowing I was there.

"Well, I was there, and I called you several times. Didn't your brother tell you?"

"No."

We started walking again.

"Maria is on drugs," she said suddenly.

"Oh, no," I stopped walking again. There was Maria in front of me, smiling and happy. She was being married to the father of her son. There was Mrs. C., exuberant, loudly moving from guest to guest in the recreation room of the housing project in which they lived—and Inez, she was there—ungracious and sullen, seemingly annoyed that Mrs. Murrain and I, with our husbands, had come to her sister's wedding.

Inez's paralyzed hand brought me back to King Street.

"After my mother died—" she shoved her hand at me— "that's how I got this, it's paralyzed, I go for treatment on Thursday, Maria cut me with a knife."

"Cut you with a knife? Why?"

"Cause we had a fight—after my mother died."

She began to cry silently.

"You're still grieving, aren't you, Inez?"

She nodded.

"Can I come back to school?"

"Who will take care of Patty?" I asked.

"Somebody."

"Who?"

"Somebody."

"I think maybe you can," I answered.

There was a smile.

"But it's hard to talk in the street. Can you come tomorrow morning to see me and we'll talk about it?"

"Yeah."

"And bring Patty."

"Yeah."

"And do you think Maria needs help, too?"

"Yeah—"

"Can you help her?" I asked.

"That's how come she cut me," she answered, "she wouldn't listen."

"Well, do you think I can help her?" I asked. "Would she listen to me?"

"Yeah—you wouldn't know her, she looks so bad."

"Where does she get the money for the drugs?" I asked. "Where's her husband, what does he say?"

"He workin for the post office. He takes care of the kids."

"And the money, how does she get it?"

"Welfare."

"How much of a habit does she have?" I asked.

"It's bad."

"Welfare money can't be enough," I answered.

"She got friends."

We walked some more.

"Can you tell Maria to come and see me, Inez?" I asked. "Will she come?"

"Yeah."

We parted at the corner. I was late for a Board of Estimate hearing at which I was scheduled to present a proposal. I would much rather have stayed with Inez. She needed me then, not the next day.

She never made it back the next day, which was Thursday, nor on Friday. On Saturday morning I called her house, but Inez did not live there any more. I did not know to whom I spoke, but Inez had moved away.

"Does she come around?" I asked.

"Sometime."

"Can you get a message to her?"

"Maybe."

"Will you try?" I asked.

"Depends."

I identified myself.

"Yeah, I'll tell her."

I had to be satisfied. I know she will call—when, I don't know, but she will call.

I cannot get Inez and Maria out of my mind. I cannot forget their mother. Society had betrayed her. Mrs. C. had not died. She had just given up, and yet once she had been a beautiful eighteen-year-old dancer, winning the Harvest Ball National Contest. Is this where her dream had ended—with Inez crippled and Maria a junkie?

Beyond Livingston, what?

So far, nothing, for Delores and Inez and Maria.

What could be?

•A Livingston Residence for Inez and her baby, a place where Inez could live and come to school to learn. A place where the Berenices and Joans and Amandas and Virginias could live during the periods of special crises in their lives when they cannot face returning home, or when they have no homes.

•A Livingston nursery for Patty, and for all babies and all the girls, a place where the girls can learn mothering, where the babies can receive the attention babies need.

•A Livingston School for drug-addicted girls, like Maria, a school for them, where the treatment comes through the school, and where the treatment is therefore mandated, because schooling is mandated. As it is now, education is compulsory, but treatment is not. It's wrong.

And for the girls on the waiting list, so they need not wait so long—and for all the children, disturbed or otherwise, who are being short-changed by a school system that is failing them —more Livingston Schools.